The Decline of British Economic Power Since 1870

The Decline of
British Economic Power
Since 1870

M. W. KIRBY, BA, PhD
Lecturer in Economic History, University of Stirling

London
GEORGE ALLEN & UNWIN
Boston   Sydney

First published in 1981

GEORGE ALLEN & UNWIN LTD
40 Museum Street, London WC1A 1LU

© George Allen & Unwin (Publishers) Ltd, 1981

British Library Cataloguing in Publication Data

Kirby, M W
    The decline of British Economic power since 1870.
    1.   Great Britain – Economic conditions – 19th
    century
    2.   Great Britain – Economic conditions – 20th
    century
    I.   Title
    330.941'082   HC255   80-41781

    ISBN 0-04-942169-7

Set in 10 on 11 point Times by Altonprint
and printed in Great Britain
by Billing and Sons Ltd., Guildford, London and Worcester

Contents

To Edith and Ray Kirby

Preface

I have written this book because I believe that the roots of Britain's economic predicament in the final quarter of the twentieth century are to be found in the equivalent years of the last century. Thus, any attempt to explain the current problems of the British economy by reference to the period since 1939 or, worse still, from the early 1960s, is necessarily incomplete in so far as it lacks historical perspective. This is particularly dangerous when economic policy prescriptions are being formulated which appear to pay little or no regard to the deep-seated nature of the problems to be tackled. Hence, this is not a textbook in the conventional sense: its coverage is incomplete and the treatment of some issues is cursory to say the least. It is rather an interpretative essay, written from the standpoint of an economic historian, which attempts to incorporate the findings of the latest research on the reasons for Britain's economic decline in the last 100 years. As such, I hope the book will have a wide appeal, not just to students of economics and recent political and economic history, but also to the general reader who wishes both to understand the nature of the so-called 'British disease' and to assess the respective merits of the solutions currently being advocated for reversing the process of industrial decline.

I have incurred a number of debts in the writing of this book, not least to my colleague Professor R. H. Campbell. He has been unstinting in his encouragement and has given liberally of his advice. I am also indebted to Dr N. L. Tranter and Dr R. B. McKean, to the former for his stringent criticisms on certain chapters and to the latter for giving me an invaluable overall perspective on the period of Britain's decline. Naturally, I am solely responsible for any errors of fact or interpretation. My thanks are also due to Dr W. H. Janeway for permission to quote from his Ph D thesis on the second Labour government and to Miss M. E. A. Hendry for transforming a manuscript bordering on the illegible into a first-class typescript. Finally, I wish to pay tribute to my wife's forbearance during the last two years: she has coped admirably with the frustrations of an author who finds the process of writing agonisingly difficult.

M. W. KIRBY
Stirling, November 1979

List of Tables

1

The British Economy 1870–1913: the Descent from Hegemony

In 1913 Britain stood at the centre of the international economy, the world's greatest trading nation providing, through the City of London, sophisticated financial and commercial services which underpinned the structure of world trade. The current account of the balance of payments was heavily in surplus and the exchange stability of the pound sterling unquestioned. The economy, moreover, was currently experiencing a phase of cyclical expansion, capped by an impressive export boom. In short, Britain's economic position on the eve of the First World War appeared to be one of great strength. Yet it is salutary to remember that well before the turn of the century many of those doubts and uncertainties with which a later British public was to become so familiar were already present among the business and investing classes of late Victorian society. The rise of tariff protection in overseas markets after 1870 and the increasing encroachments of foreign sources of supply, both for agricultural and manufactured products, in the domestic market itself, had conspired to undermine the confident optimism of the mid-Victorian era when the supremacy of British industry had gone unchallenged and the future of domestic agriculture seemed assured.[1] The period between 1873 and 1896 was one of falling prices and profits, the years of the 'Great Depression' in agriculture, trade and industry when, increasingly, the dogma of free trade began to be questioned and the security of Britain's international economic position reassessed. The 'Fair Trade' movement of the early 1880s and the 'Made in Germany' campaign of the following decade were among the early manifestations of a developing xenophobia in British society,[2] a defensive and nationalistic reaction to the challenge of foreign economic rivalry which reached its zenith in political terms in the early years of the twentieth century in the movement for closer commercial integration of the empire in order to isolate Britain from an increasingly hostile world.

As if to confirm the validity of this developing pessimism in late

Victorian Britain the available statistical indices point to a deterioration in the country's economic performance in the half century
before 1914. One of the most outstanding features in the structure of
the balance of payments, for example, is the growing merchandise
trade deficit. In terms of both volume and value, imports were growing
more rapidly than exports, a situation which rendered the country
increasingly dependent for the maintenance of living standards
upon the receipt of invisible income derived from international
business services and interest and dividends from overseas investments (see Table 1, p. 138). The volume of exports continued to grow
after 1870 but at a declining rate, both in relation to what had been
achieved earlier in the century and in comparison with Britain's
principal overseas competitors, Germany and the USA (see Tables 3
and 4, pp. 140-1). What was particularly disturbing was the
deceleration in the rate of growth of manufactured exports (measured
in constant prices) from 3·3 per cent per annum between 1853 and
1873, to 1·6 per cent per annum between 1873 and 1899. Thereafter,
the growth rate revived (2·7 per cent per annum 1899–1913) but this
was due to a combination of unprecedentedly high capital exports and
an adverse movement in the terms of trade. For an industrial economy
which had come to depend for its prosperity upon a buoyant and
expanding export trade this was a serious situation and it was
inevitably reflected in the country's steadily declining share of the
world market for manufactured goods (see Table 2, p. 139). This
falling off in export performance was accompanied by an indifferent
record in terms of the growth of gross domestic product (total
output)[3] and of industrial production (see Table 3, p. 140). Whilst it is
important to note that there was no sustained deceleration in their
rates of growth after 1870 and that there is a slight downward bias in
the industrial growth figures for the later part of the period, once
again the comparison with overseas competitors and the earlier
achievement is unfavourable (see Tables 3 and 4, pp. 140-1). As for
measures of the efficiency of the British economy the relevant
statistical indices are especially disappointing. After two decades
of stability in the 1860s and 1870s the growth rate of industrial
productivity (calculated by dividing the number of operatives into
the index of industrial production) registered a sharp fall in the
1880s with a further reduction in the following decade (see Table 3,
p. 140). From 1890 to the outbreak of the First World War,
industrial productivity grew extremely slowly at an average annual
rate of 0·25 per cent as compared with 1·87 per cent from the mid-
1860s to 1880. As in the case of industrial production, the later
figures should be revised upwards to take account of higher growth
sectors in the economy enjoying a more rapid rise in productivity, but
this would only slightly modify the general picture of decelerating

productivity growth. It is noteworthy that the lag in efficiency was particularly marked in such key exporting industries as cotton textiles, coalmining, iron and steel, and possibly general engineering.[4]

Measures of efficiency based upon the productivity of labour are only a partial indicator of the efficiency of a country's productive processes. A more all-embracing concept applicable to the economy as a whole is that of total factor productivity, a measure specifically designed to compare changes in total output with average changes in inputs of labour and capital. Total factor productivity is usually referred to as 'the residual' in so far as it measures the contribution to the growth of output of improvements in the *productivity* of resources after allowing for the growth of the labour supply and capital accumulation. In other words, it provides some indication of the extent to which total output is affected by changes in the quality and structure of the factors of production and also the ability of an economy to utilise its resources in the most productive manner. As a statistical measure, therefore, total factor productivity could be determined by a wide range of influences, from the organisation of productive processes and managerial and entrepreneurial standards, to the allocation of resources and the extent to which the economy is subject to restrictive labour and business practices. According to the latest estimates of the rate of growth of British total factor productivity, after a period of stability between 1873 and 1890 it thereafter declined with a particularly poor performance in the years 1900–07.[5] It should be stressed that the residual is a very crude statistical measure of efficiency subject to errors arising from data deficiencies,[6] but despite this qualification it does seem that the rate of growth of efficiency of the British economy was slowing down towards the end of the nineteenth century, possibly reflecting a low rate of structural change in favour of higher productivity sectors and a general lag in technical progress.[7]

The distinctive nature of Britain's industrial structure was in fact one of the most outstanding features of the pre-1914 economy. In 1907 the old-established staple trades of textiles, coalmining, iron and steel and general engineering accounted for approximately 50 per cent of net industrial output and employed 25 per cent of the working population.[8] Most were heavily dependent upon an increasingly narrow range of export markets located mainly within the British Empire, South America and Asia, and coalmining, textiles and iron and steel alone contributed over 70 per cent of the country's export earnings.[9] It is this 'bias' towards the staple industries which has led some economic historians to conclude that the economy was 'over-committed' with too high a proportion of its resources located in industrial sectors which were technologically static and possessed a

low or negative growth potential.[10] The market and commodity composition of exports helped to retard the development of such technologically sophisticated industries as electrical engineering, scientific instruments and apparatus, road vehicles and advanced chemical products. These industries were the 'wave of the future' and their slow development before 1914 rendered Britain highly vulnerable to changes in the international economy. This is not to suggest that the pre-1914 economy was completely resistant to structural transformation since there were, in fact, quite marked changes in the distribution of the occupied labour force. Agriculture suffered the greatest proportional losses with mining and the tertiary sector (transport and public and professional services) registering the greatest gains. The latter, however, were noted for their relatively low levels of productivity with the result that intersectoral shifts in the structure of the labour force contributed little to the growth of the economy.[11]

Britain's faltering growth performance has led many economic historians to conclude that the period after 1870 was marked by economic failure. The economy though not in absolute decline, was experiencing a rate of retardation which went beyond what could normally be expected at that stage of Britain's economic development.[12] This was especially applicable to the years after 1900 when the economy was 'probably growing more slowly than at any time since the beginning of modern economic growth in the late eighteenth century'.[13]

Failure implies responsibility and one impressive aspect of the debate on the country's growth performance has been the enthusiasm with which its participants have sought to cast the blame for retardation. Even those who would deny the validity of a thesis of general failure have been unable to resist the temptation to identify those elements in late Victorian and Edwardian Britain which allegedly served the economy ill. For some the faults lay with the entire private enterprise system which subordinated national to purely private interests,[14] while for others of a more selective frame of mind the responsibility lay with particular groups and institutions within society, such as the education system, the capital market, trade unions and entrepreneurs.

A factor of major importance in underpinning the charge of failure is the unsatisfactory nature of those arguments based upon the 'inevitability' of retardation in a mature industrial economy. In the latter context, several observers have referred to a 'climacteric' in Britain's economic development in the latter half of the nineteenth century. In the years after 1870 economic growth was checked by a combination of the exhaustion of available technological opportunities (either in the application of steam power and iron to industrial processes by 1870,[15] or in the rise of a mass-production steel industry

after that date)[16] together with an exogenously determined fall in the rate of growth of exports.[17] Hence, subsequent retardation was largely the product of an accident of timing: the technological lull before the exploitation of the dramatic innovations of the twentieth century in electrical power, for example, and advanced chemical processes, coincided with the spread of industrialisation overseas reducing the stimulus to invest in innovation.

Although the climacteric thesis has much to commend it, it can only be of limited value as an explanation of retardation. Both versions of the argument are highly dependent upon the unreal assumptions that innovation and the rate of export growth are the prime movers in the process of economic development. It is conceivable that in the early stages of industrialisation a key role in the growth of productivity can be fulfilled by a small number of 'leading sectors' with a high rate of innovation, but in a relatively mature economy it is far more likely that productivity growth is dependent upon technological advances, often of a small-scale nature and continually applied throughout industry as a whole. In relation to exports the climacteric thesis is on stronger ground. Industrialisation overseas inevitably meant a reduction in the British share of world markets. As Lord Kaldor has pointed out, in commenting on the general process of industrialisation after 1850:

> The *successful* latecomers to industrialisation were able to attain much faster rates of growth both of 'outside' sales and of total production, than Britain achieved in the heyday of her industrial supremacy, and for that reason were able to overtake her, one after the other, in a relatively short space of time. This is because, given the size and the rate of growth of the world market at any one time (including in that notion any particular country's 'own' or 'protected' market), the *successful* challenger which is able to increase its share in the world market is bound to have a faster rate of growth than that of the market as a whole and *a fortiori*, of the country whose share in the world market is reduced in consequence.[18]

Kaldor is clearly referring to the process of import substitution and successful exporting to third markets undertaken by the German economy after 1880 and the USA after 1890. Within the framework of Verdoorn's law[19] they were able to take advantage of 'increasing returns' or the economies of large-scale production, whereas Britain, confronted by more slowly growing markets both at home and abroad, was bound to be increasingly handicapped in overseas markets by lower industrial investment and lagging labour productivity. Nevertheless, despite the validity of this kind of argument it remains true that the rate of growth of a country's exports can be determined also by *domestic* factors, in the nature of demand in the home market, for example, which may restrict the potential for scale economies or, more to the point in the present context, by the reaction of industrialists in late-nineteenth-century Britain to the challenge of overseas industrialisation. Thus an analysis of retardation based upon its inevitability according to the notion of the 'climacteric' cannot by itself provide an answer to the question as to why the pre-1914 economy remained overwhelmingly committed to the staple industries to the detriment of higher growth sectors. Nor does it provide an adequate explanation for the reason why, of all the possible responses to foreign competition, British industrialists chose the weakest and most conservative course of action, entering new but markedly less prosperous markets while remaining heavily reliant upon existing product ranges and techniques of production.[20]

One popular and deceptively simple explanation which has been advanced in answer to these questions is based upon Britain's 'early start' in the process of industrialisation. After decades of expansion the staple industries were confronted by an 'interrelated' or 'complementary' capital stock. To the extent that technical advances in one sector entailed radical changes in dependent stages of production, modernisation was rendered both difficult and costly.[21] Unhindered by the deadweight from the past and with a greater awareness of the benefits to be derived from advanced technical education and research, the German and American economies were industrialising on the basis of more sophisticated technology and forms of industrial organisation. By 1913 they were relatively diversified, encompassing most of the traditional staple industries and also the new growth sectors of international trade – the technologically advanced industries whose products, as noted above, were of comparatively limited importance in Britain's exports of manufactures.[22]

Like the 'climacteric', the 'early start' thesis is not without an element of plausibility, especially when applied to individual industries (the railways being the classic examples of interrelatedness), but it remains unsatisfactory as an objective explanation of industrial retardation as a whole. In the first instance, it is only logical to presume that the pioneering industrial country in any subsequent phase of development should be able to maintain its leading competitive position simply because it possesses the considerable advantages of accumulated technical expertise and the requisite financial resources to apply that expertise.[23] In other words, it would be wrong to presume that the difficulties of writing off past capital and the problem of interrelatedness were significantly greater in Britain than elsewhere.[24] Other economies may have been more diversified by 1914 but they also possessed their ageing industrial sectors, many of them utilising early British technology, and they arguably suffered in much the same way as those in Britain are alleged to have done.

A far more critical explanation of Britain's relative economic decline has centred on the collective failings of industrialists. In general terms it has been claimed that there was an unhealthy aversion to meeting foreign competition where it was most severe. Rather than improve the efficiency of their businesses and develop new lines of production British entrepreneurs remained obstinately committed to the staple trades, content to limit their commercial activities to 'safe' imperial markets and other areas in underdeveloped parts of the world which had yet to be penetrated by foreign competition. In short, entrepreneurs failed to respond energetically to the challenge of overseas industrialisation and sought the line of least resistance. More specifically, in an era of rapidly developing technology and in marked contrast to their German counterparts, they adopted a dismissive, almost cavalier attitude towards technical education and research with the result that by 1914 Britain had lost technical superiority in almost every staple industry.[25] It is true that the most recent research has revealed a considerable degree of interest on the part of firms producing high-grade steels in utilising the services of highly competent industrial consultants in the generation before 1914,[26] but in the absence of more such case studies the general picture remains of a widespread lack of interest in applied science and technology. In the staple trades few production engineers and scientists were employed and of those that were, most enjoyed low status in the hierarchy of firms with poor conditions of service and limited promotion prospects.[27] To a certain extent the shortage of trained manpower can be attributed to the inadequacies of the country's education system: the established English universities and public schools were suffused with the influence of the classics and other non-vocational disciplines,[28] while the emergence of an organised technical and secondary-education sector – vital for the production of an intermediate class of shopfloor foremen and supervisors – was delayed until well after 1890.[29] Add to this bureaucratic inefficiencies together with financial parsimony and the picture emerges of a society which accorded low social prestige and priority in economic terms to applied science and technology. Yet it is equally valid to maintain that these inadequacies were a partial reflection of the limited outlook of industrialists themselves. Practical experience in the workshop was raised to the level of a mystique and 'college-trained' men were looked upon with disdain.[30] The 'rule-of-thumb' methods and 'practical tinkering' of the pioneering phase of the Industrial Revolution were the curse of large sectors of British industry and they went hand-in-hand with increasingly outmoded forms of industrial organisation, based upon the small-scale family firm or partnership. Legal obstacles to the growth of firms had been removed in the 1850s but by 1914 British industrial organisation remained 'partly ossified at a relatively immature level of development'.[31] One major consequence of this was the loss of economies of scale, both technical and commercial. Possibly the most outstanding area of neglect in the latter category was in overseas marketing. Unlike their German and American competitors, British firms were generally too small to offer attractive and competitive credit facilities: few commercial travellers were employed and, as many a consular report lamented, techniques of salesmanship were crude and amateurish.[32] Heavy reliance was placed upon the traditional merchanting system in overseas marketing: separate selling and productive organisations created a barrier of communication between manufacturer and customer, a major disadvantage in promoting the sale of advanced technical products rather than relatively simple consumer goods.[33] Thus the fragmented structure of British industry arguably precluded the establishment of the direct selling and overseas distributive organisations which were such an important factor in aiding the expansion of German and American manufactured exports after 1880. By encouraging the sale of 'traditional goods in traditional markets' the merchanting system intensified industrial overcommitment 'and indirectly reduced or at least gave little encouragement to technical change'.[34] A further manifestation of entrepreneurial weakness was to be found in the slow adoption of American methods of manpower utilisation. Payment by results and mass-production technology made little progress in British industry before 1914 with the result that labour was both inefficiently organised and underutilised.[35] It is true that ignorance and prejudice in the trade union movement, in conjunction with restrictive labour practices, were partly to blame for the lack of interest in the principles of 'Taylorism'.[36] American employers, on the other hand, confronted by extremely weak labour organisations, rarely encountered opposition to piece rates and the mechanisation of industrial processes before 1914.[37] As several critics have argued, however, British employers themselves must share the responsibility for the hostility of labour towards 'scientific management'. In times of financial stringency far too many firms were eager to reduce wages as an alternative to organisational reforms which would have been of long-term benefit. The result of this was to intensify trade union suspicions of proposals to rationalise production methods and to contribute directly towards mutual feelings of mistrust and antagonism between management and workers in the entire field of labour relations.[38]

The British entrepreneurial class of the late nineteenth century has thus been the subject of a considerable volume of criticism which has placed it at the centre of the debate on the reasons for Britain's relative economic decline. The mere cataloguing of alleged deficiencies in business performance can, however, be of little use in explaining why entrepreneurs acted as they did. In this respect there are two competing hypotheses. The first is essentially a variant of the 'early start' thesis, but whereas the latter lays stress on the purely technological barriers to innovation, the former attaches greater weight to social and psychological impediments in the way of a more vigorous entrepreneurial response. In its simplest form the argument is that by the final quarter of the nineteenth century entrepreneurs were succumbing to the symptoms of 'third-generation decline' – a growing antipathy towards the conduct of their businesses which manifested itself in an increasing proclivity to squander the hard-won wealth of their forebears in ostentatious and extravagant living. These attitudes were reflected in a substantial element of complacency in the running of British industry.[39] This kind of generalised reasoning is, however, open to serious question. It has been pointed out that in the late nineteenth century few British firms were in the third generation of control and of those that were it is possible to find as many examples of efficiently run and successful enterprises as of those that failed.[40] One important study of the mechanical engineering sector has stressed that the great majority of firms reached the third generation of control only after 1914 and the same source has further emphasised that the relative ease of entry into many engineering trades before that date subjected the industry as a whole to 'constant rejuvenation'. In those areas where there were demonstrable technical or commercial shortcomings – in the manufacture of agricultural machinery and medium-range machine tools, for example – it has been argued convincingly that objective market factors – in particular the lack of a sufficiently large home market and the varied nature of export demand – were as much to blame as entrepreneurial weakness.[41] It is also worth noting that Britain did manage to retain an impressive international lead down to 1914 in a number of industries, ranging from the armaments sector of heavy industry and shipbuilding, to advanced textile machinery and heavy machine tools.[42] Studies of the production and marketing records of industries such as these have gone a considerable way towards undermining the blanket hypothesis of entrepreneurial failure.

Further examples of vigorous entrepreneurship are to be found in the tertiary sector of the economy after 1870, in distribution with the rise of the multiple chain store, and in the provision of international services in the spheres of banking, shipping and insurance.[43] Nor should the rapidly expanding consumer industries, such as the manufacture of pharmaceuticals, soap and confectionery, be neglected. It may well be the case, as one writer has commented, that 'a major indigenous electrical engineering industry would have proved a greater long-term asset to the economy than a large, efficient jam-making or chocolate industry' but, as the same source has also admitted, the generalised condemnation of entrepreneurial standards is invalidated to the extent that it fails 'to relate managerial effectiveness to its precise business context'.[44]

More recent studies of entrepreneurship, often with the aid of quantitative economic analysis, have utilised the concept of 'rationality' in the choice of techniques and forms of industrial organisation in order to avoid the dangers inherent in hindsight judgements. This alternative approach to the study of Britain's economic performance and of the country's entrepreneurs in particular, is grounded in the belief that an analysis based upon the assumption of 'failure' is grossly misleading since objectivity demands that patterns of business behaviour should be related to the contemporary economic environment facing entrepreneurs.[45] Two examples, drawn from the traditional staple industries – cotton textiles and coalmining – will suffice to illustrate the nature of the argument.

The cotton textile industry had been the most important growth sector in the early stages of the Industrial Revolution. By 1830 it accounted for 50·7 per cent of the value of total British exports and the figure was still as high as 24·1 per cent in 1913. Whilst few historians would deny that the pre-1914 industry was remarkably successful in exploiting new sources of demand in the face of mounting indigenous competition in its traditional overseas markets,[46] in common with other British industries it has been severely censured for its technical stagnation. The conventional criticism, based upon a comparison with the American industry, is that there was a failure to replace the outmoded mule with the more efficient, capital-intensive ring spindle. Criticisms have also been levelled at the weaving section to the effect that its record in the installation of fully automatic looms *vis-à-vis* its principal foreign rivals was abysmal. Both of these criticisms appear to carry greater weight because the new technology was readily available to the industry from Britain's own textile machinery makers who developed a thriving export trade in the latest equipment before 1914. But in their apparent resistance to technological innovation it may well be that cotton entrepreneurs were acting in an entirely rational manner. The impressive study carried out by Sandberg has shown that ring spinning techniques were introduced in the USA because the cheapness of the unskilled labour employed more than compensated for the higher cost of the raw material necessary for this particular process. Similarly, with the automatic loom, the high capital cost of installation was outweighed by savings in labour costs.[47] These conditions did not apply in the British industry mainly because there was a readily available supply of highly skilled operatives who could be employed with advantage in manufacturing processes which were comparatively labour intensive.[48] This is not to suggest that the industry remained technologically stagnant. In the spinning section, for example, substantial gains in productivity were achieved throughout the nineteenth century by means of continuous technical modifications, mostly of a minor character, but cumulatively significant. Sandberg, moreover, has contended that in the period between 1907 and 1913, of the additions to spindle capacity relating to the coarser yarn counts, a significant proportion, perhaps the major element, was composed of ring spindles, an important conclusion in view of his calculation that ring spinning *was* cost effective for the lower yarn counts produced by the British industry.[49]

The second illustration of the alternative approach to assessing standards of entrepreneurship is of particular significance. Coal, as Lloyd George was to proclaim in the midst of the First World War, was 'Paramount Lord of Industry' – a vital producers' good which occupied a critically important position at the heart of the British industrial economy. Between 1885 and 1900 the total value of output rose from 3 per cent of national income to 7 per cent[50] (although it fell back to 4 per cent in 1905), whilst in volume terms it grew impressively from 147 million tons in 1880 to 287 million tons in 1913. It is worth emphasising that much of the expansion was in overseas markets: as in cotton textiles the last prewar year was one of record exports with one-third of total output being marketed overseas. Unlike the cotton industry coalmining did not depend on an imported raw material and with its dominant position in British shipping it made a major contribution to the country's balance of payments.[51] At one time, the statistics of expansion were sufficient by themselves as an indicator of the industry's successful performance in the years before 1914, but more recently it has been argued that they masked deep-seated problems which were to play a considerable role in the industry's troubled interwar history. Unenthusiastic towards technical innovation and large-scale business enterprise, the colliery entrepreneur failed to solve the dual problems of falling labour productivity and rising costs of production.[52]

The fall in labour productivity, which set in during the 1880s, was a direct consequence of the ageing of many of the industry's productive units.[53] In 1914, nearly two-thirds of all the coal produced came from collieries which had been projected before 1875. The fact that they had been sunk in an earlier period of mining technology militated against efficient production and, as resort was had to thinner and less productive seams in the period of rapid market expansion after 1880, output was increased principally by the recruitment of more labour to the industry. At first sight it appears incontrovertible that the introduction of machine mining on an extensive scale (as in the USA) would have helped to mitigate the effects of declining productivity but it is necessary to take account of geological and other natural conditions which rendered mechanisation on the basis of the available equipment impracticable in many of the coalfields. There is, too, the problem of related costs – the fact that it was difficult to justify the installation of coal cutters without incurring additional and proportionately much greater expenditure in the provision of a power supply and face conveyors. But if a neglect of technical innovation is not necessarily a sign of entrepreneurial weakness it must be set against the loss of economies of scale resulting from an equivalent lack of interest in business combination. With only limited recourse to the capital market before 1914 almost one-half of the annual output of coal was still being mined by private companies as late as 1925. The typical colliery undertaking was small scale, privately owned and often supplying only local markets. Several explanations can in fact be advanced for the industry's lack of progress towards greater integration – the rich diversity in geological conditions, the mineral royalties system, the divergence of interest between inland supplying and exporting districts, the lack of a 'national' conception of the industry on the part of the great majority of colliery owners together with their individualism and fundamental optimism engendered by the secular expansion of markets. But the two factors which alone go far to explain both the small scale of the industry and the lack of technical change are the wage-payment mechanism and the availability of labour. From the 1870s onwards wages in the industry were regulated by selling-price sliding scales. A base year for prices was chosen and thereafter wage rates were calculated in direct relation to the movement of prices. The importance of the sliding scale was that in periods of trade recession and falling prices it enabled colliery owners to safeguard their financial position through 'automatic' wage reductions, a crucial advantage in an industry where labour costs amounted to 70 per cent of total costs of production. Furthermore, since sliding scales were negotiated on a coalfield basis between the district owners' and miners' associations they encouraged the competitive reduction of prices so that trade recession was invariably accompanied by an intensification of interdistrict competition. This degree of cost flexibility, perpetuated under the conciliation board system which began to replace sliding scales from the end of the 1880s onwards, acted as a major disincentive to integration in the coalmining industry. It also helped to reduce the attractiveness of machine mining. In this it was augmented by the ready availability of labour stemming from the depressed agricultural counties augmented in the longer term by the high rate of natural population increase in the coalfields themselves. Between 1889 and 1913 productive capacity in coalmining increased by 60 per cent while in the same period numbers employed underground increased by more than 90 per cent and those on the surface by 185 per cent. It is noteworthy that in years of peak demand for coal, recruitment to the industry increased dramatically indicating that there was no shortage of labour 'at wage rates corresponding to prices which the consumer was already offering for coal'.[54]

Studies such as these of individual industries serve to reinforce the view that there can be no easy assumption that standards of entrepreneurship were declining before 1914. Admittedly, the staple industries were to encounter extreme market difficulties after the First World War but it is no argument to claim that nineteenth-century entrepreneurs should have been expected to anticipate the First World War, its dislocative economic effects, and the severity and duration of the interwar depression. As one writer has pointed out, 'It seems wrong to condemn businessmen's decisions by reference to hindsight arguments or because they base their decisions on benefits to the individual firm rather than the economy as a whole'[55]. 'A capitalistic environment may produce a rate of innovation well below the social optimum' but the individual entrepreneur cannot be expected to estimate external economies.[56] A more capital-intensive and structurally integrated coalmining industry would undoubtedly have benefited the pre-1914 economy and, in the longer term, enabled the industry to meet the economic difficulties of the interwar period more successfully than it did, but it seems reasonable to conclude that declining labour productivity and resistance to structural change were the inevitable consequences of the distinctive economic environment in which colliery owners operated – abundant supplies of labour with a marked degree of cost flexibility against a background of secular market expansion.[57] Similarly, in cotton textiles, the surplus productive capacity of the interwar period cannot stand as a condemnation of the investment decisions of the prewar years. 'What reason could there be for not investing in cotton mills in 1905 when profits expected and realised up to the war were comparable with any elsewhere?'[58] Why should textile manufacturers have abandoned the mule spindle when there was a readily available supply of relatively cheap and highly skilled labour with a long tradition of urbanised industrial employment? The true irony of the market situation confronting the industry after 1920 was that even if there had been substantial investment in new technology, overseas markets, especially in the Far East, would still have been lost with an equivalent waste of real resources.

The argument that entrepreneurs may have been acting rationally in the conduct of their businesses does not, of course, dispose of the hindsight view that a more rapid transfer of resources to higher-growth sectors should have been achieved before 1914. What it does accomplish is to focus attention upon the economic factors which permitted the British economy to retain a comparative advantage in international trade in those industries heavily reliant upon traditional skills and labour-intensive techniques of production. In this context there are two key factors which must be considered, first, the extensive investment in overseas assets undertaken in late Victorian and Edwardian Britain and secondly, the complexity of the country's position in an evolving international economy. Few economic historians would disagree with the view that together they constitute two of the most distinctive elements in the pattern of British economic history in the years between 1870 and 1914.

The international movement of factors of production was of critical importance in the development of the world economy in the second half of the nineteenth century. Between 1850 and 1914 more than 40 million people emigrated from Europe to areas of expanding settlement located mainly in the temperate zones of the world – principally to North America and to a lesser extent Australia, New Zealand and South Africa. This vast movement of population, to which the UK contributed substantially, was accompanied by an international flow of capital of equal proportions. Britain was by far the largest lender to the areas of settlement. From a figure of £260 million in 1854 the cumulative total of British overseas assets had grown to £4,107 million by 1914,[59] most of it in the form of passive portfolio investment for the financing of railway construction and other social overhead capital projects, mainly in the form of dock and harbour facilities. The net total of overseas investment on an annual basis had averaged slightly below 2 per cent of the gross national product in the years 1811–50, but thereafter the rate began to climb steadily until it stabilised at an annual level of 5·2 per cent of gross national product between 1870 and 1913. No country, before or since, has invested as high a proportion of its resources abroad over such a sustained period. By the end of the century, the London capital market 'had become primarily an instrument of external finance'[60] and in 1913, by no means an exceptional year, over 80 per cent of the capital issues in the City of London were for investment overseas. On the eve of the First World War, Britain owned 43 per cent of the world's stock of overseas assets and to place this figure in its historical perspective, it is probable that the real value of this British overseas investment exceeded the total American capital invested abroad today.[61]

In seeking the causes of Britain's industrial retardation some historians have attributed a special role to the export of capital. In its most extreme form the argument is that the institutions of the City, many with Continental émigré origins, were ignorant of the conditions and needs of British industry and their bias towards large foreign issues produced a scarcity of capital resources in the domestic economy. Low domestic investment retarded the growth of productivity rendering industry uncompetitive and was thus an important cause of the country's declining share of world trade in manufactured goods.[62]

This highly critical interpretation of the behaviour of the capital market is difficult to reconcile with the view that since Britain's financial institutions were the most sophisticated in the world by the late nineteenth century, the channelling of such an enormous proportion of investment funds overseas could hardly have been the result of an irrational rejection of the benefits to be derived from higher domestic investment. This view presupposes, of course, that the rate of return on foreign investments was higher than that on domestic investment. Whilst economic historians are divided in their opinions as to whether this was the case, it does seem to explain why overseas investment was so substantial during the years of the 'Great Depression', from 1873 to 1896. The question remains, however, as to why domestic investment failed to revive to any appreciable extent after 1900 when the recovery of industrial profits was well under way. One possible explanation of this is that the lack of confidence engendered by the depression led to a fall in replacement investment with the result that economic revival failed to produce an acceptable level of profits for industrial investors. After 1900, therefore, overseas investment still remained an attractive proposition and its growing volume might well have contributed to the poor growth performance of the Edwardian economy.[63] A difficulty with this argument is that it tends to ignore the methods by which industry in general raised finance in Britain before 1914. The typical firm, as in coalmining, was small scale, organised in the form of a partnership or private limited company, and securing its financial requirements through bank loans and trade credit or, more usually, through the ploughing back of profits. Many industrial sectors, moreover, remained labour intensive and therefore did not require large-scale capital funding.[64] The argument probably has greater validity in relation to the financing of more risky ventures in the newer industries. It is true that one study of the motor industry before 1914 has demonstrated convincingly that the growth of some of the larger, if ultimately unsuccessful, firms was not held up by capital shortage,[65] but this ignores the requirements of the 'less spectacular, sounder, and probably smaller firms which were the potential sources of growth'.[66] Here the problem was not so much the availability of finance, but the relatively unfavourable terms upon which it could be borrowed. British overseas investors preferred to hold high-grade foreign bonds and securities to domestic equities and it is certainly conceivable that this raised the costs of borrowing for some of the more risky home investments.

It is also difficult to refute the claim that overseas lending served to encourage structural rigidities in the economy by tying industry to a restricted range of export markets. One of the major consequences of foreign investment was that it stimulated the development of international trade in primary products. Britain was the first to benefit from this trade and, from the 1860s onwards, aided by a steady reduction in the costs of ocean-going transport, it began to develop a close trading relationship with the primary producing countries of the world, exchanging staple manufactures for foodstuffs and raw materials. Beneficial though this trade may have been before 1914, its long-term effect was to retard the development of more advanced industrial sectors in the British economy. This can be illustrated particularly well by reference to the engineering industry which became increasingly dependent in the later nineteenth century upon export markets in the less industrialised countries. The result was that by 1913 Britain possessed an incompletely developed engineering sector: the most advanced machinery (notably in the critical area of machine tools) had to be imported from abroad, mainly from the USA and Germany, and this raised the costs of those firms which utilised engineering goods in their production processes.[67]

Overseas investment thus retarded industrial growth by reinforcing the overcommitment of the economy to the old-established industries. This does not mean that investors were acting irrationally in the generations before 1914. The great attraction of foreign investments lay in their security, combined with high or moderate yields: the staple industries gave every appearance of continuing profitability. Higher domestic investment in the newer industries would therefore have required investors 'to make real sacrifices in terms of current income'. It is also worth re-emphasising the role played by overseas investment in underpinning the domestic standard of living. Reference has already been made to the growth of international trade in primary products and the central role of British lending in this process. Investment in international transportation improvements after 1870 led to a favourable movement in the terms of trade which remained unchecked until the early years of the present century: the cost of imported foodstuffs fell and this contributed directly towards a rise in the level of real incomes for the vast majority of the population.[68] The price that was paid for this – the sacrifice of domestic agriculture and the strategic dangers inherent in the country's growing dependence upon external supplies of foodstuffs – was a high one, but, as it has also been argued, the close economic relationship between Britain and her principal suppliers meant that overseas investment was in a sense tantamount to investing in the primary sector of the British economy itself.[69] Clearly, the export of capital carried with it both costs and benefits and to take the discussion further it is necessary to consider the nature of Britain's involvement in the wider international economy.

The role fulfilled by overseas lending in stabilising the pattern of international settlements was one of the most impressive features of Britain's external economic relations in the years before 1890.[70] The manner in which this was accomplished can be illustrated by assuming the existence of economic recession in one of the country's principal trading partners – the USA. In these circumstances British exports to the American market would contract leading to a fall in foreign income which would, in turn, result in a reduction in British demand for primary products and a further decline in British exports. To the extent that recession reduced the attractiveness of lending to the USA, British investors would redirect their attentions to the domestic economy, to the housebuilding sector for example, and the established staple industries, or, alternatively, seek other profitable outlets abroad in the primary producing countries. In the period before 1890 the empire countries (excluding Canada) were central to this process. Since the great bulk of their exports were directed towards the metropolitan market a redirection of British overseas investment in their favour could outweigh the effects of a reduced demand for primary products, enabling the empire countries to meet their external debt obligations and to continue to import Britain's staple manufactures. The working of this mechanism was dependent upon Britain's dominant position in the world economy and it was a source of international economic stability at a time when the world was divided into several independent areas of multilateral settlement. Since these were linked only through the UK, a redirection of the flow of British lending could prevent the transmission of trade recession from one area to another.[71]

From about 1890 onwards, the pattern of international trade began to change markedly in the direction of a truly integrated international economy with multilateral settlement of trading accounts. In the industrialising countries of Continental Europe, the USA and later Japan, demand for foodstuffs and raw materials was growing rapidly. Increased quantities began to be imported from abroad, much of it from the British Empire. Although the industrialising countries increased their sales of manufactures to the primary producers – mainly at the expense of British goods – the balances of their merchandise trade moved into deficit, most notably with India and Australia, and to a lesser extent with Ceylon, Malaya, and British West Africa. The deficits of the European countries, however, were financed by their own trading surpluses on visible account with Britain, and invisible account with the USA, while the latter counterbalanced its European and Indian deficits by means of surpluses with Britain and Canada. Britain thus enjoyed merchandise trade deficits with the USA and Continental Europe and also with a number of its imperial territories – Canada, New Zealand, South Africa, East Africa, Ceylon and Malaya. These were offset by impressive surpluses with West Africa, Australia and, in particular, India.[72]

The British economy was thus at the centre of this new network of multilateral settlement which developed after 1890. These years coincided with the 'high summer' of the international gold standard, a period which witnessed the final triumph of gold as the basic means of settling international indebtedness.[73] For an individual country adherence to the gold standard required the fulfilment of three conditions: first, a commitment to a fixed rate of exchange for its currency; secondly, to the free convertibility of the domestic currency into gold and all other currencies; and thirdly, to the linking of the domestic money supply to the movement of gold in and out of the country. The prevailing theory of the operation of the gold standard was based upon the 'price-specie-flow' mechanism as set forth in classical economic analysis. In the event of sustained balance-of-payments deficit a country would experience an outflow of gold which, in reducing the volume of currency in circulation, would result in a fall in the level of internal prices, a movement which would eventually produce external equilibrium. Towards the end of the nineteenth century, the theory was modified to take account of central-bank monetary policies. In the case of the Bank of England it was argued that a decline in the ratio of reserves to liabilities (as gold flowed out of the country) would lead the Bank to raise its discount rate (Bank Rate) in order to increase interest rates generally and to produce a restriction of credit. This action would tend to reinforce the effects of the price-specie-flow mechanism and would thus provide an additional impetus towards external equilibrium.[74]

This theory of 'automatic' balance-of-payments adjustment under the gold standard was to play an important role in the formulation of monetary policy in Britain in the years immediately following the First World War. Within orthodox financial circles there was an unquestioning belief that the expansion of the international economy after 1870 had been dependent upon stable monetary relations and that this was a direct consequence of the adherence of international bankers and national monetary authorities to the 'rules' laid down under the gold standard (see below, pp. 40-1). It is now accepted that this was an oversimplified view and that in reality the gold standard mechanism was far more complex than that set out in the classical analysis. It is in fact more accurate to describe its operation as conforming to a sterling rather than a gold standard. As one authority has observed, 'sterling operated as an international currency on equal terms with gold'.[75] It was the principal medium of international exchange with gold only being transferred between countries as a balancing item. Given this role, it was vital that sterling should not only be in liberal supply but that it should also be a currency of unshakeable strength. Before 1914 these conditions were fulfilled as a result of the structure of Britain's balance of payments. Theoretically, the fact that the balance on current account was in continual surplus could have given rise to a serious adjustment problem elsewhere in the international economy. This did not occur, however, because of the sustained flow of investment funds from the British economy and also because the country continued to adhere to a policy of free trade. One factor which the classical theory of the gold standard failed to take into account was the international movement of capital. In the British case, the annual net ouflow of funds abroad more or less matched the current account surplus. Britain, therefore, unlike, say, the USA, did not amass large gold reserves with the result that the borrowing countries were relieved of the adjustment problem inherent in the operation of the classical theory.

Free trade fulfilled a dual function. In the first instance, open access to the British domestic market meant that borrowing countries could service their international debts by exporting to Britain. Secondly, free trade played a key role in the developing network of worldwide multilateral settlement after 1890. It enabled the USA and industrial Europe to finance their purchases of primary products by exporting manufactures to Britain. In the same way that British overseas investment provided international liquidity for many primary producing countries, the visible trade deficit fulfilled a similar function on a truly international basis. One close observer of Britain's overseas trade has pointed out that industrial competitors could obtain their supplies of primary products by exporting to Britain thus effectively reducing the competitive pressure in foreign markets. Britain's ongoing commitment to free trade therefore played an important role in restraining international economic rivalries. Without access to the British market 'both Industrial Europe and the United States would have been forced either greatly to adapt their internal economies and seek new sources of supply – for example, develop and extend their own colonies and active spheres of influence – or intensify world competition in manufactured goods. Probably the growth of world trade would have slackened and international friction would have increased.'[76] Thus, a unique set of circumstances – the widespread availability of sterling and its great strength as an international currency combined with the favourable structure of the balance of payments to place Britain at the centre of the international economy. No wonder then that J. M. Keynes in a brilliant polemic written in the aftermath of the First World War, characterised the years between 1870 and 1914 as 'an extraordinary episode in the economic progress of man', an age of commercial stability based upon an economic 'Pax Britannica'.[77]

The pre-1914 international economy was not, however, inherently stable. Keynes for one was well aware that its mechanism was finely balanced (see below, p. 24) and there were certainly emerging sources of strain and weakness which in retrospect had profound implications in the long term for Britain's own economic stability. The growth of international demand for primary products, for example, meant that British overseas investment could potentially no longer fulfil its former stabilising function. In the event of simultaneous recession in several of the major industrial countries the volume of British lending, though still substantial, was insufficient to halt the transmission of the depression to the primary producing countries and therefore unable to prevent a decline in British exports. Secondly, the USA was emerging as an influential force in the international economy after 1890. With rising exports of manufactured goods and virtual self-sufficiency in the supply of basic foodstuffs, the USA moved into balance-of-payments surplus with Canada, Australia and Argentina, 'countries which had required only minor multilateral settlement of their accounts in the 1880s'. Furthermore, America's own exports of foodstuffs began to decline after 1900 with the result that Britain, obliged to seek alternative supplies, began to develop trade deficits with Argentina and Canada. The deficit with the USA was thereby reduced, but since Britain continued to import large quantities of manufactures, a balance-of-payments adjustment was required.[78]

The evolving pattern of international trade meant that by 1913 Britain was dependent for the stability of its entire payments position upon its growing trading surplus with India. It has been estimated that in that year alone India financed more than two-thirds of Britain's total deficits.[79] The balance-of-payments situation *vis-à-vis* industrial Europe, China and Japan was improving (in the European case because of rising coal exports), but this was largely offset by the mounting deficits with Canada and Argentina, with the addition of Australia and Brazil in the final years before 1914. The importance of India to Britain lay in the fact that the former enjoyed trading surpluses with those areas where Britain was most heavily in deficit. A significant proportion of Indian exports was admitted duty free to a number of important European markets and up to 50 per cent to the USA. This meant that as long as the Indian market remained open to British manufacturers, Indian exports, in an increasingly protectionist world, would indirectly overcome foreign tariff barriers for the British economy.[80]

Britain's international economic position in 1913 was thus a vulnerable one. In the domestic market foreign manufactures continued to make the inroads that had begun well before 1900. The merchandise trade deficit with the USA alone, amounting to £82 million, heralded the emergence of a 'dollar problem' in the network of international payments which was to be a source of weakness for Britain in later years. The growing economic dependence on India was one consequence of this before 1914. Even here there were elements of weakness, for British exports to the Indian market were dominated by low-grade cotton piece goods. Already, before 1914, there was a developing indigenous industry and Japanese exports were beginning to penetrate the subcontinent. This raises once more the whole question of overcommitment in the structure of British industry. In 1913 Britain's exports of traditional manufactures were concentrated in the primary producing countries of the world. As long as their levels of economic activity continued to rise and the prices of their products remained high the impact of foreign industrial competition would be blunted. But in the event of a serious downturn in their economies resulting from recession in the industrialised countries, Britain would inevitably encounter immediate and serious problems of structural maladjustment.

One major solution was advanced before 1914 for overcoming the problem of foreign competition. This was the campaign for tariff protection, first espoused by the 'Fair Trade' movement in the early 1880s and later combined most spectacularly with the concept of Imperial Preference by Joseph Chamberlain in his tariff reform campaign in the years after 1903. Whilst Chamberlain's motives were politically complex,[81] in economic terms the campaign had as its ultimate rationale the historic community of interest within the British Empire, based upon the exchange of manufactures for primary products. In return for tariff preferences on their exports of foodstuffs and raw materials to the metropolitan market, Canada, Australia and New Zealand would offer their own preferences on British manufactures. Export markets for British industry would thus be guaranteed within the empire, and the empire as a self-contained commercial unit would be able to use its external tariff as 'a retaliatory battering ram' to enter protected markets elsewhere in the international economy, in industrial Europe and the USA.[82] From the purely economic perspective there were two flaws in this conception of an 'imperial Zollverein'. For one thing it conflicted with the 'cosmopolitan capitalism' of the City of London and the market interests of a number of key exporting industries. Whilst tariff protection and preferences were supported strongly by industrialists in the metal-working trades of the West Midlands, they could have little appeal for Britain's cotton manufacturers, colliery owners and shipbuilders, many of whom were confronted by rapidly expanding export markets in the decade before 1914 – the very years which, ironically, coincided with the mounting of Chamberlain's campaign. Neither could they have any attraction for the British financial community, dependent as it was upon the invisible earnings derived from the country's deep involvement in overseas commerce and investment.[83] Indeed, there were those in Britain, principally the followers of the arch theorist of Liberal-Imperialism, Halford J. Mackinder, who were quite prepared to contemplate a diminution in the role of industry in the economy. In Mackinder's word's, in view of the inevitable tendency 'towards the dispersion and equalisation of industrial and commercial activity throughout the world' the greater the financial advantages that would accrue to Britain in its position as 'the controlling centre'. In a famous series of addresses to the Institute of Bankers in December 1899 Mackinder concluded 'that the financial importance of the City of London may continue to increase, while the industry, at any rate, of Britain, becomes *relatively* less'.[84]

The Chamberlain programme was in fact based upon an increasingly outdated view of the true role of the British Empire in the international economy. It has already been noted that in the period after 1890 the empire countries, together with other primary producers, had been drawn more and more into a worldwide trading network. Imperial preference may have been an attractive policy to New Zealand and Canada – countries which continued to direct the great bulk of their foodstuffs to the UK market – but it could be of little interest to those imperial territories with increasingly complex trading links outside the empire. Ironically, this applied with great force to India and most of all, to Britain itself. In 1913 the empire was very far from being a self-sufficient economic community. Britain obtained only one-fifth of its net imports from the empire and this proportion had remained remarkably stable from 1880 onwards despite a dramatic territorial expansion in imperial possessions.[85] Neither had there been any appreciable change in the direction of British capital exports towards the 'formal' empire.[86] What the tariff reformers failed to perceive, therefore, was that 'the sale of Empire products throughout the world made possible the smooth flow of Britain's trade and far more important for international goodwill the smooth flow of the trade of most other nations'. In short, the empire made its contribution to British prosperity as 'an open dynamic system integrated into the main current of the international economy'. In terms of its pre-1914 evolution it could never have served as a defensive mechanism against foreign competition.[87]

All of this is not to deny that the British economy was confronted by emerging problems of structural maladjustment. A critical weakness in the protectionist case as it was advanced before 1914 (a general rather than a selective tariff on imports) was that it could not solve the fundamental problem of overcommitment in a specialised trading economy. Indeed, by acting to fossilise the industrial structure protectionism would have made the problem far more difficult to overcome. There is in fact little evidence to suggest that in the circumstances of the *pre-1914* international economy the necessary adjustment to new patterns of trade would either have been impossible to achieve or protracted. In the years after 1870 the contribution made by the staple export industries was slowly declining as a proportion of overseas earnings and national income. The rise of the service sector, both domestic and international, the growth of new consumer industries – soap, footwear, bicycles and food processing – all of these developments were indicative of the adjustment process which was under way in the pre-1914 economy.[88] But the transition to a more diversified economic structure of the kind described was wholly dependent for its smoothness and ultimate success upon a stable but expanding international economy, well insulated from the shock of war and other random disturbances, both political and economic. Unfortunately, these conditions, vital to the economic well being of Britain, did not survive the First World War. By destabilising the international economy and by intensifying the pressure of foreign competition the war and the peace settlement which followed, accelerated the need for structural change and, at the same time, placed major impediments, both psychological and material, in the way of this process. It is in this context that the tariff reformers came nearest to an accurate assessment of Britain's international position on the eve of the First World War, that in the words of Chamberlain himself 'a great Empire' whose economic base was founded on 'jam and pickles' and interest from foreign loans was not only at the mercy of every cyclical disruption in the world economic order but also highly vulnerable to the growing political and military challenge posed by competing countries possessing the indigenous strength of efficiently organised and strategically important 'productive' industries.[89] In the final analysis, the pursuit of economic rationality within the framework of an international division of labour, however attractive to contemporary (and latter-day) economic theorists and the cosmopolitan capitalists of the 'City', was not necessarily in accord with the preservation of the wider national interests of an imperial power of the first rank.[90]

2

The British Economy in the 1920s: Growth and Stagnation

In June 1919 J. M. Keynes resigned as senior representative of the British Treasury at the Paris Peace Conference. Six months later he published a vitriolic denunciation of the Versailles Treaty and so initiated a controversy which divides historians to this day. *The Economic Consequences of the Peace*[1] was a brilliant work of high polemics – 'one of the finest pamphlets in the field of political economy [if not] ... in the English language'[2] – but coming from the pen of one who had so recently been intimately involved in the negotiations on the economic clauses of the treaty it was widely assumed by contemporaries to represent 'a factual economic analysis that could be trusted even if other aspects of the book might be less reliable'.[3] Keynes's purpose in publishing such a work was to undermine the moral and economic bases of the treaty. In the former case he argued explicitly that the terms meted out to the defeated powers were inconsistent with undertakings given at the time of the Armistice, and implicitly that they were an affront to that spirit of magnanimity in victory which he believed to be an essential hallmark of European and British civilisation.[4] On the economic follies perpetrated by the peacemakers Keynes was equally unmerciful in his strictures. The statesmen assembled in Paris had failed to comprehend the fragility of the international financial and trading mechanism that had been destroyed by the war. The commonly accepted view that the pre-1914 international economy was inherently stable was an illusion: 'Very few of us realise with conviction the intensely unusual, unstable, complicated, unreliable, temporary nature of the economic organisation by which Western Europe has lived for the last half century. We assume some of the most peculiar and temporary of our late advantages as natural, permanent and to be depended on, and we lay our plans accordingly.'[5] Deficient in foodstuffs and raw materials, industrialised Europe had achieved a sustained improvement in living standards by expanding its manufactured exports to the primary producing regions of the world and the mechanism of exchange had been provided by a mutilateral trading system which had permitted the flow of merchandise and finance with minimal disruption. Now, as a consequence of the war, this organisation had been destroyed, the stream of supplies disrupted and a substantial part of the European population deprived of its means of livelihood. The international gold standard had been abandoned, currencies destabilised and banking and credit systems either suspended or seriously distorted by the exigencies of war. What was required of the peacemakers, therefore, was the negotiation of a treaty which would avert the threat of starvation and revolution in Europe by restoring international economic stability as soon as possible. At the very least they should refrain from adding to the dislocation directly attributable to the war. Instead, they indulged in the lunacy of attempting to reconstruct the economy of Europe on the prostration of its central pillar – Germany.

In retrospect Keynes was guilty of exaggeration and excessive pessimism in his predictions. He underestimated the resilience of economies in the face of seriously adverse circumstances and presented an incorrect analysis of the movement in the terms of trade between Europe and the primary producing countries.[6] His arguments were also politically naïve in the circumstances of 1919. The creation of a Free Trade Union under the auspices of the League of Nations would have mitigated some of the worst economic effects of the fragmentary territorial settlements imposed on the defeated powers, but this was to ignore the desire for fiscal autonomy on the part of successor states, endowed with inadequate financial and industrial resources, and with a new-found national consciousness to assert.[7] The cancellation of all inter-allied war debts and the floating of a substantial international loan would have contributed greatly to the political and economic rehabilitation of Europe, but this was to expect too much of the USA, the principal war creditor, an argument which also applied to a French government, obsessed by the problem of military security, in relation to the scaling down of the reparations clauses of the treaty.[8]

Yet in purely economic terms, Keynes was surely correct in his analysis: he alone appeared to appreciate the extent to which the old economic order had been destroyed by the war. The revival of a smoothly functioning European economy with a restored Germany at its centre would be extremely difficult to achieve and Keynes's political naïveté cannot be divorced from his deep awareness of this fact. It was also entirely appropriate that a citizen of the UK should write such a book for, of all the former belligerents, Britain had most to lose by the failure of international reconstruction. The prewar economy had been deeply penetrated by foreign trade – more so than

any other industrial country. Large sectors of industry were highly
geared to export markets and a set of specialised commercial
institutions had developed which were greatly dependent upon
overseas trade. Britain therefore had a vested interest in the revival of
the European economy and that of Germany in particular. Multilateral trade, from which the country had benefited so much before
1914, could not be resumed in the face of widespread and occasionally
catastrophic currency depreciations, disrupted trading links and an
extreme scarcity of international credit. By themselves, however,
these things were insufficient to ensure Britain's economic recovery
after the war and although the problems confronting his own country
were not Keynes's primary concern there is sufficient evidence in *The
Economic Consequences of the Peace* to indicate that he was aware
that the country was on the brink of an era of social and industrial
disruption: 'The most serious problems for [Britain] have been
brought to a head by the war, but are in their origins more
fundamental. The forces of the nineteenth century have run their
course and are exhausted. The economic motives and ideals of that
generation no longer satisfy us: we must find a new way and must
suffer again the *malaise* and finally the pangs of a new industrial
birth.'[9] It would, indeed, be a tribute to Keynes's powers of perception
if this passage was referring to the very real problem of structural
maladjustment confronting Britain at the end of the war as a result of
secular changes in the international economy, some of which had
been intensified and accelerated after 1914.

The final quarter of the nineteenth century had witnessed the rise of
the USA as a major industrial competitor, a country whose economic
structure in 1913 already reflected many of the new growth opportunities of the twentieth century. Now, as a result of the war, the USA had
received a dual boost to its already considerable industrial production
– in providing for the needs of its allies and in increasing manufactured
exports to countries formerly dependent upon European and British
suppliers. The First World War thus accelerated America's industrial
lead: by 1920 the level of industrial production was 20 per cent above
the prewar level and with minimal distortion in the economic structure
the USA entered the postwar world in an extremely favourable
competitive position. Japan was also a principal beneficiary of the
war. With only marginal involvement in the conflict, industrialisation
had proceeded unhindered at a time when Europe's traditional trading
links had been severed. This was reflected in a significant expansion
in Japanese exports to Asian and Far Eastern markets, mainly to
India, China and the Netherlands East Indies. To the extent that
enhanced Japanese export penetration represented a permanent shift
in Eastern market shares this could only have serious consequences
for the postwar revival of British trade, especially in the various

branches of the cotton textile industry where much of Japan's industrial development was concentrated.[10]

Intensified competition from the USA and Japan were not the only sources of potential difficulty for British exporters after the war. Numerous less developed countries had also received a stimulus to industrial growth following the disruption in the flow of traditional European exports. The most impressive advances were to be found in the White Dominions, notably in Canada. By 1918 Canadian manufacturing output had surpassed that of the agricultural sector, accounting for 44 per cent of the total product of the economy: the number of motor vehicles in use had risen from 51,000 in 1913 to 276,000, and the shipbuilding and aircraft industries were well established. In Australia developments were not as rapid, but even here 'over 400 products were manufactured for the first time and some new export trades created' during the course of the war. Elsewhere in the world advances in industrialisation were far less impressive in the sense that they did not lead on to modern economic growth, but the war was noted for its stimulus to the manufacture of cotton textiles in India, China and Latin America.[11]

Enhanced export competition, the rise of indigenous industries and economic nationalism – all of these phenomena by themselves posed a considerable threat to the British economy. Together with the ongoing process of technological change, symbolised by the new application of electrical power and the internal combustion engine, they were the collective manifestation of an emerging crisis of structural transformation affecting most, if not all, of the European economies. According to Svennilson the resumption of economic growth after 1918 required 'a complete transformation of the economic structure [of Europe], including a development of new industries in order to squeeze out resources, including labour, that could be used more effectively in new fields'.[12] There are grounds for believing that the task would be accomplished with the greatest difficulty in Britain, a country whose inherited industrial structure 'conformed so little to the pattern of international specialisation that was becoming the optimum'.[13] Before the war, Britain's export trade had been dominated by the old-established staple industries, most of them increasingly dependent upon sales to agrarian-based countries with relatively low per capita incomes. Two-thirds of the country's manufacturing exports had belonged to commodity groups which were to have a declining share of world trade in the interwar period. The cotton textile industry was the outstanding example in this respect – highly susceptible to foreign and indigenous competition and also to the damaging impact of technological change. In conjunction with the coalmining industry it had dominated British exports in 1913: it had fulfilled an important role in underpinning the balance of payments and had been the key element in

Britain's favourable trading relationship with India. The need for structural adjustment had certainly been present in the pre-1914 economy, but not in an acute form. For Britain, it was one of the principal economic misfortunes of the war that it intensified the problem of industrial overcommitment and at the same time destroyed the old international economy – 'the chief established instrument for guiding and easing adjustment to general economic changes'.[14] The restoration of Britain's economic health was thus partly dependent upon the re-establishment of a stable and expanding international economy, free from the devastating effects of currency mismanagement and trade restrictions. Unfortunately, the outlook in this respect was bleak in the extreme. In the last chapter it was noted that the gold standard system of the pre-1914 era had coincided more in reality with a sterling standard centred on the City of London. Britain had dominated the working of the international economy and although the system was betraying increasing signs of strain before 1914 it had worked well, largely because of the favourable structure of Britain's balance of payments and the related facts that sterling, at one and the same time, was a currency of unimpeachable strength and in liberal supply. The war, however, helped to undermine London's ability to fulfil its former international role. The wartime sale of overseas assets (approximately 10 per cent of the total), the disappearance of London's short-term creditor position, together with the incurring of substantial war debts to the USA[15] – all of these factors were conspiring to reduce the volume of invisible income from abroad. Combined with a weakened trading performance on visible account, this meant that Britain was unlikely to be in a position to earn the necessary overall payments surplus to invest abroad as she had done on an extensive scale before 1914 (see Table 5, p. 142). It was highly unlikely, moreover, that other countries would be in a position, or indeed willing, to assume responsiblity for London's former stabilising role. Berlin, a rising commercial centre before the war, was likely to be crippled for some time by financial disorders and reparation payments, while Paris possessed neither Britain's international trading links nor the necessary financial resources to shoulder the burden alone. In many ways the natural successor to London was New York, a financial centre that was bound to assume greater prominence in view of America's transformed international financial position into one of substantial net credit – exclusive of intergovernmental debts.[16] This was a direct consequence of the war when loans had been floated in the USA on behalf of its allies and when substantial foreign holdings of American securities had been liquidated. But while New York had the requisite financial resources it possessed little tradition of foreign lending and even less in terms of central-banking experience. Its institutions were arguably lacking in the necessary expertise and were in no position to provide a full range of commercial services. It was by no means certain, therefore, that the USA could be relied upon to act as a controlling and stabilising influence in the international economy.[17] A further potential source of strain was to be found in the deteriorating position of the primary producing countries. One recent authority has pointed out that they, too, were confronted by a structural transform- ation problem as a result of the long-run tendency for their terms of trade to decline as the rate of population growth in Europe slackened after the mid-1880s. During the war, primary production, with the aid of technological innovation, had expanded dramatically, particularly for wheat and sugar in the face of falling European production. If and when the latter revived the primary producing countries which, collectively had accepted 70 per cent of Britain's manufactured exports in 1913, would be confronted by the problems of oversupply and falling incomes to the further detriment of Britain's staple export trades.[18]

In this harsh and uncertain postwar environment the overriding task for Britain was clear: capital and labour had to be transferred as rapidly as possible to those sectors of the economy with the greatest long-term growth potential both in the domestic and the export market: the overcommitment of resources to the staple industries had to be reduced. To the extent that this did not take place the inevitable by-products would be large-scale unemployment and undercapacity utilisation with all that that implied in terms of human misery and economic waste. The remaining part of this chapter provides an assessment of Britain's economic performance in the decade of the 1920s in the light of these factors.

The consensus among economic historians is that the statistical growth record of the economy in the 1920s was at least as good, if not superior, to that of the late nineteenth century. The economy, in other words, reverted to its 'normal' rate of growth following an abysmal performance in the decade-and-a-half before the war.[19] Between 1920 and 1929 industrial production (including building) grew at the rate of 2·8 per cent per annum and industrial productivity at the remarkably high rate of 3·8 per cent per annum.[20] Using the more all-embracing measure of gross domestic product and the conventional bench-mark years of 1924 and 1929 the rate of growth of output was 2·3 per cent per annum. This serves to reinforce the impression of an improved growth record on the several years preceding the war. As to the sources of growth it would appear that the key element was enhanced total factor productivity: with the growth rate of total factor inputs fairly constant in the 1920s (1924–9) and directly comparable with the level achieved in the period 1899–1913 (1·3 per cent per annum) the residual contributed approximately 1 per cent to the annual growth of output.[21] Once again, this compares favourably with the prewar achievement.

It is in their interpretation of this record of growth that historians are divided. There are two principal views. First, there are those who have argued that the 1920s 'formed a watershed between the old industrial regime of the pre-1914 era and the new industrial economy of the post-1945 period'.[22] The first interwar decade witnessed the creation of a 'viable [industrial] base ... which ensured that steady growth would take place in the future': they were, in short, years of 'fairly rapid economic progress'.[23] The justification for this view is derived from an examination of the qualitative and structural changes that were taking place in the economy at this time. In this context there were three major factors that differentiated the 1920s from the prewar decades. In the first instance, there was a shift in the pattern of investment in favour of new, high-growth sectors. Fully one-third of the total gross capital formation for the years 1920–30 (£251 million out of £750 million) was accounted for by five rapidly growing 'new' industries – rayon, electrical engineering, motor vehicles, chemicals and paper and printing.[24] These industries had not accounted for anything like this proportion of investment before 1914. Secondly, improvements in business organisation began to make real headway in Britain for the first time: amalgamations and the elimination of redundant capacity were the key elements here.[25] Finally, by focusing attention on the concepts of gross and replacement investment the optimistic case lays considerable stress upon the introduction of new techniques in industry. An excellent illustration of all three of these trends is to be found in the experience of the motor vehicle industry. Between 1922 and 1929 the number of producers fell by more than one-half and by the latter date 'all the larger firms [three firms accounted for 75 per cent of total output] without exception were reaping the benefits of mass production, mass markets and new manufacturing techniques': the price of cars fell by 33 per cent between 1923 and 1929 and taking the years 1924–9 output grew at the impressive rate of 5·6 per cent per annum.[26] All of this is not to suggest that the older staple industries were unaffected by these favourable trends. In terms of productivity growth coalmining, shipbuilding and mechanical engineering were three of the best performers, outstripping the electrical engineering and chemical industries. In coalmining there were few improvements in industrial organisation but mechanisation underground proceeded fairly rapidly after the war and contributed significantly to the 18 per cent rise in productivity between 1924 and 1930. Similarly, in the iron and steel industry the labour productivity of blast furnaces increased by almost 25 per cent between 1923 and 1930, a result of the introduction of larger blast furnaces and other associated technical improvements.[27]

In seeking the causes of this improved industrial performance considerable stress has been laid upon the favourable legacy of the war, in particular the stimulus it gave to technological progress in existing industries – in shipbuilding, general engineering and steel production – and the fact that a number of products, such as motor vehicles, aircraft, advanced machine tools, chemicals, magnetos and ball bearings, were manufactured extensively in Britain for the first time.[28] The war was also noted for its impact upon methods of industrial production – the impetus under the pressure of unprecedented war requirements towards greater standardisation and assembly-line techniques. The Ministry of Munitions had a key role to play in this in the engineering industry, notably in relation to machine tools where a trade association – the Associated British Machine Tool Makers – was established in 1916–17 to give effect to the government's rationalisation plans.[29] Scientific and industrial research also benefited from the war and its importance received official recognition with the foundation of the state-sponsored Department of Scientific and Industrial Research in 1916, an organisation which not only financed research directly in universities and colleges, but also encouraged industrialists to establish their own research associations. As Pollard has concluded, 'The discovery of applied science by British industry may be said to have dated from those years, though it was still in an embryonic stage.'[30] Finally, the wartime allocation and rationing schemes encouraged the process of amalgamation in industry – in steelmaking, shipping and among the railway companies. Government-sponsored inquiries were openly critical of the old nineteenth-century competitive system. As a Board of Trade Committee on the shipping and shipbuilding industries commented in 1918: 'Whilst individualism has been of inestimable advantage in the past, there is reason to fear that individualism by itself may fail to meet the competition in the future in Shipbuilding and Marine Engineering, as it has failed in other industries. We are convinced that the future of the nation depends to a large extent upon increased co-operation in its great industries ...'[31] Even the coalmining industry, the supposed bastion of die-hard individualism, responded to the mood of the times, when, in 1919, the employers' Mining Association issued for private circulation to its members a pamphlet setting out proposals for district cartel arrangements with national co-ordination bearing a very close resemblance to the marketing clauses of the Coal Mines Act of 1930. It is possible that if the industry had avoided a politically charged, industrial-relations crisis at the end of the war then colliery owners might have been willing to reorganise on the basis of private initiative.[32]

Thus the war was by no means detrimental to Britain's economic progress. In the reversion to a peacetime economy, a process which was largely completed by 1921, not all of the progressive developments fostered by the war were lost. 'Perhaps for the first time businessmen were brought face to face with the grim reality that they had to adopt more scientific methods of production and reorganise their plant and equipment on more efficient lines, and generally pay much greater attention to securing economies in the use of factors of production.'[33] Hence any account of Britain's economic development in the 1920s which emphasises the deleterious economic effects of the war to the detriment of its more favourable legacy is presenting a one-sided picture.

The alternative interpretation of the 1920s stresses the fact that although the rate of economic growth reverted to the average levels attained during the late nineteenth century, it did so against a background of unprecedentedly high levels of unemployment. For the greater part of the decade the economy was in the 'Doldrums', becalmed in a sea of unemployment[34] which rarely fell below one million for any length of time – roughly 10 per cent of the insured labour force (see Table 6, p. 143). If it is true that 'any sensible comparison of growth rates has to involve some attempt to relate what was actually achieved in different periods to what was potentially achievable', then the existence of the 'intractable million' of unemployed throughout the decade is indicative of a considerable growth potential foregone.[35] It can, of course, be argued that the employment problem was centred on a very restricted range of labour-intensive industries which were experiencing critical difficulties in their export markets, such as shipbuilding, coalmining and cotton textiles. In view of the structural changes taking place in the international economy alluded to earlier, their contracting levels of employment were of positive long-term advantage to the growth of the economy.[36] Apart from its contribution to the rising productivity of the staple industries the 'intractable million' thus represented the regrettable but necessary 'shake out' of labour as part of the process of structural adaptation. As far as it goes, this analysis is correct: the old staple industries were overmanned and their growth prospects, based upon an expansion of exports on the prewar pattern, were negligible or non-existent. Nevertheless, the fact remains that unemployment was sustained at such a high level for so long and a necessary concomitant of the process of structural adaptation is that unemployed resources are actually *transferred* into higher growth sectors. The key issue for British economic history in the 1920s, therefore, is not to downgrade or deny the progress that was made in reorientating the economic structure away from excessive dependence upon a narrow range of exporting industries, but to analyse the reasons for the slowness of this process. Such an analysis will involve not only a consideration of entrepreneurial standards and attitudes in the old-established industries, but also a critical review of government policy in relation to both the domestic and external sectors of the economy.

Any assessment of the structural problems confronting British industry in the 1920s must begin with the impact of the war and its immediate aftermath. In certain industries capacity had been expanded after 1914 to meet wartime requirements. Reference has already been made to the stimulus given by the war to sectors such as motor vehicles, aircraft and advanced machine tools, industries which 'had the best selling prospects of all types of goods and for which Britain was not unfitted to supply ... in quantity in view of the growing importance of the engineering sector in the economy.'[37] But the war also resulted in the growth of productive capacity in the shipbuilding, iron and steel, and general engineering industries, and this war-induced expansion was further intensified during the boom conditions of 1919–20. The boom, which began in April 1919, lasted for approximately one year. Its direct causes were to be found in the backlog of demand for civilian goods, the need to reconvert industrial equipment and replace that which was worn out, and the renewal, at least on a temporary basis, of former overseas trading contacts. It was facilitated in large measure, however, by government financial policy. At the end of March 1919 Britain formally abandoned the gold standard (the sterling–dollar exchange had been pegged at \$4·76½ to the pound since January 1916). The prime policy consideration was that the British price level, as a result of wartime inflation, had risen far more rapidly than that in the USA. Although an official committee under the chairmanship of a former Governor of the Bank of England, Lord Cunliffe had earlier recommended that Britain should return to a full gold standard at the prewar dollar parity (\$4·86 to the pound) as soon as possible,[38] a view which was confirmed in its final report published in December 1919,[39]. Lloyd George's coalition Cabinet understandably rejected a policy which would have necessitated an immediate and severe deflation of prices – and hence wages – at a time when military demobilisation was taking place against a background of politically motivated unrest in a number of key industries.[40] It was only from the middle of 1919 onwards that the Treasury and the Bank of England began to receive ministerial support in controlling the boom. Fear of inflation and the parlous state of government finances were the prime considerations[41] but it was not until 6 November that Bank Rate was raised from 5 to 6 per cent. In the middle of December, the Chancellor of the Exchequer, Austen Chamberlain, announced to the House of Commons his acceptance of the recommendations contained in the final report of the Cunliffe Committee for the 'cessation of government borrowing ... economy in public expenditure ... and note issue limitation'.[42] This statement served to underline the commitment of the financial authorities to return to the gold standard at the prewar dollar parity, a policy which received final confirmation in the middle of April 1920, when Bank Rate was raised to 7 per cent.

It has been pointed out that this second raising of Bank Rate

> came just at the right time to ensure that the (over-) optimistic
> expectations of businessmen (who had apparently believed that
> the prosperity generated by the restocking boom would last
> forever) which were falling fast ... were replaced in the shortest
> possible time by deep pessimism which was later reflected in a
> drastic downturn in investment. This pessimism was all the
> stronger (and well founded) given that the authorities had left no
> room for doubt that dear money once imposed would be
> consistently maintained ...[43]

Indeed, Bank Rate remained at the penal level of 7 per cent for almost
a year, but was only one of several factors which had a severe
deflationary impact upon industry and the economy generally at that
time. These included a restrictive budget in April 1920, Treasury
controls on government expenditure, the cancellation of orders for
goods and, finally, the collapse of export markets towards the end of
the year, a factor which played a major role in precipitating a highly
damaging sixteen-week coal lockout in the spring and early summer of
1921 (see below, p. 35).

The importance of the postwar boom for the economy is that it had
seriously adverse consequences for Britain's industrial structure.[44]
The boom was, in fact, artificial, characterised by speculation in
property and commodities. It was also an era of company flotations –
a financial orgy in the buying and selling of industrial concerns at
vastly inflated prices, often on the basis of borrowed money, much of
it derived from a highly liquid banking system. According to Pigou
between £500 million and £550 million of credit was made available
by the banks 'for industrial and other purposes' during the course of
the boom.[45] Some of the worst excesses were to be found in the cotton
textile industry: in the latter half of 1919 the buying and selling of
mills was almost a daily event and by the end of April 1920, 109 mills
with an original share capital of £4·5 million had been sold for £31·7
million.[46] The shipbuilding and iron and steel industries were
similarly affected. In the former case thirty companies were floated in
one month alone, with a combined capital of £4 million, while in the
latter, the nine largest firms increased their capital from £20 million to
£67 million during the course of the boom.[47] Thus, the wartime profits
of these industries 'were dissipated in a frivolous manner and they
were left with a heavy burden of debt as a result of increased interest
liabilities, the issue of bonus shares and the watering of capital'.[48]
Large sections of British industry were to be plagued by the disastrous
financial legacy of the boom throughout the ensuing decade. It was
particularly unfortunate that the most extreme forms of speculation
took place in those industries which were soon to encounter serious

market difficulties. The response of the Federation of Master Cotton Spinners' Associations to a request from trade union representatives for its views on the likely effects of the extensive transfer of mills on the future prospects of the industry provides an excellent illustration of the commercial outlook of businessmen at this time. It was pointed out that the adoption of a forty-eight-hour week in the industry and a similar reduction in working hours in overseas industries had effectively reduced world capacity for the manufacture of cotton textiles. Buoyant demand conditions would be sustained by the continuing growth of world population and the present diminution in the supply of cotton goods.[49] In retrospect such optimism was extraordinary as it was absurd. The only valid defence of the federation is that its members could not realistically have been expected to foresee the severity and duration of the interwar depression in their export markets. For the cotton industry, the last prewar year, 1913, had been one of record exports: it had been subject to periodic slump before the war yet the overall trend of output had been one of marked expansion. From the viewing point of 1919 was there any reason to believe that the prewar pattern would fail to re-emerge? In short, the years of secular expansion before 1914 had implanted standards of what was normal and correct in the minds of businessmen and they were carried over into the 1920s when they played a crucial role in retarding structural adjustment in the economy. The experience in the coal-mining industry which followed the collapse of its export markets in December 1920 provides a further illustration of this important point.[50] Up to that time the industry had been under state control with colliery owners in receipt of a guaranteed profit. Confronted by rapidly falling prices the government advanced the official date set for decontrol from August 1921 to March in order to avoid the payment of a subsidy to the industry from the Exchequer. Decontrol meant an end to national wage bargaining and a concomitant reduction in wages. The miners, still smarting in the aftermath of the Sankey Commission, when the government had rejected the majority recommendation in favour of nationalising the mines, opposed the owners' terms and remained locked out for sixteen weeks. For the owners the issues at stake were clear cut and unambiguous. The war had been an exceptional occurrence which had given rise to exceptional measures. Once it had ended the industry would, sooner or later, have to revert to normal trading and commercial standards. Trade recession in 1921, although universal in its severity, was to be met by tried and tested methods: wage reductions on a district basis were to be followed by their natural corollary – interdistrict competition until such time as the market improved, as it was almost bound to do, if the prewar experience was to be trusted (see below, pp. 44-5, for further consideration of this point).

Employers were not alone, however, in their desire for wage reductions. Opinion within the Bank of England and the Treasury was also committed in this direction as an immediate solution to the problem of mounting unemployment in the staple export trades. The Treasury, heavily influenced by the views of the Governor of the Bank, Montagu Norman, issued the following notes of guidance to Lloyd George for use at the Gairloch conference on unemployment in September 1921:

1.   The fundamental causes of unemployment are of a world-wide character, namely (a) impoverishment and dislocation of the means of production consequent directly or indirectly upon the war (b) the impediments in the way of new enterprise caused by political and economic instability ...
2.   The most immediate influence in Great Britain is the relatively high cost of production caused mainly by the higher rates of wages.
3.   There is no short cut for avoiding the necessary process of adjusting our costs to those of our competitors ...
4.   It is inevitable that during the process of readjustment a proportion of unemployed must be supported by dole or relief.[51]

The results of the Gairloch discussions were revealed to the House of Commons by the Prime Minister on 19 October. After announcing that extra financial resources would be made available for assisting the emigration of ex-servicemen to the Dominions, for an existing export credit scheme and for unemployment relief works, Lloyd George predictably concluded that the major contribution to the alleviation of unemployment was to be found in wage reductions: only then would British industry be able to compete effectively in overseas markets.[52]

But if wage reductions were the most desirable economic objective in the short term, the restoration of the gold standard at the prewar dollar parity was regarded as a *sine qua non* of Britain's economic health in the longer term. The interim report of the Cunliffe Committee had concluded that 'Unless the machinery which long experience has shown to be the only effective remedy for an adverse balance of trade and an undue growth of credit is once more brought into play, there will be a grave danger of a progressive credit expansion which will result in a foreign drain of gold menacing the convertibility of our note issue and so jeopardising the international trade position of this country.'[53] In this sense the return to gold was a means of guaranteeing the restoration of financial stability, a vitally important consideration in the aftermath of a war which had left Britain with a vastly increased national debt and inflated cost and price levels to match.

One of the most impressive features of the Bank of England's activities during the course of the 1920s was the cultivation of links with overseas financial authorities. As the historian of the Bank has commented, this departure from the conventional insularity of international bankers arose initially because the Bank, under Norman's leadership, had 'a missionary zeal for the economic and financial reconstruction of Europe, both as a direct stimulus to the revival of international trade and as part of a wider ambition to see the monetary systems of Europe bound together in an international gold standard' centred on London.[54] International financial conferences at Brussels in 1920 and Genoa in 1922 and the financial rehabilitation of Central and Eastern Europe, in which Norman played a major role, 'were always set in the context of a restoration of the international gold standard'.[55]

The Genoa conference was an important landmark in the development of international economic relationships in the 1920s in that it revealed a fundamental division in objectives between the British and American financial authorities.[56] The former attended the conference in order to persuade the assembled delegates of the need to establish a gold exchange system whereby member countries would deposit their gold and foreign exchange reserves in a 'reserve currency' centre (either New York or London) which would issue 'IOUs' in the form of interest-bearing bills. The reserve currency centre would then link the exchange system to gold by maintaining its own reserves in that metal. For the British authorities the attractions of these proposals were obvious. Under a gold exchange system it was likely that the major proportion of international reserves would accrue not to New York but to London, the pre-eminent financial centre, and in so doing would strengthen Britain's balance-of-payments position. This would, in turn, encourage a movement in the sterling exchange towards the prewar dollar parity ($4·86 to the pound), a movement which would bolster Britain's international economic prestige. A major prerequisite for Britain's successful return to the gold standard was the equation of British and American prices. Since the latter had not risen to the same extent as those in Britain during the war and succeeding boom the adoption of a gold exchange system would limit the need for a potentially damaging deflation of domestic costs. A further attraction of the system lay in the fact that it would discourage a fall in world prices by preventing a 'competitive scramble for gold reserves'. Worldwide deflation and depression were to be avoided if the level of British exports was to stand any chance of sustained recovery. London would be the controlling centre of the system and this would 'enable it to direct the flow of American capital in ways beneficial to world stability in general and Britain in particular'.[57] According to the Treasury the British proposals were essentially 'a plan by which gold will be economised if there is a scarcity, or an excess divided among the [central] Banks if there is a surplus'.

The British plan was accepted by the delegates at Genoa but found little favour in the USA. For the latter a gold exchange system possessed few attractions. With massive and rising gold reserves, together with a strong balance-of-payments position, America did not require 'the undependable crutch of large foreign balances' and the threat of a decline in the world price level was of minimal importance. America's interests lay in the direction of a worldwide gold standard which would permit the expansion of American trade and finance. The emergence of reserve currencies would encourage the formation of economic blocs which could curtail the opportunities for business expansion.[58]

At first the USA adopted a passive stance on the Genoa proposals. In 1923 the Federal Reserve Bank of New York supported Norman in his plans to restore financial stability to the Austrian and Hungarian economies on the basis of a sterling-linked gold exchange standard.[59] The basic difference in approach emerged only in the aftermath of the stabilisation of the German economy. In April 1921 the Reparations Commission had set a figure 132 billion gold marks (approximately $33 billion) as the gross sum to be extracted from Germany under the penal clauses of the Versailles Treaty. Although this sum and the schedule of payments were reluctantly accepted by the Weimar government the settlement soon encountered overwhelming operational difficulties both in terms of the cash instalments and payments in kind. By the middle of 1922 the German economy was subject to intense inflationary pressure and the government began to seek an accommodation with the ex-allies for a moratorium on reparations payments. Deeply suspicious of Germany's motives the French and Belgian governments embarked upon a military occupation of the Ruhr industrial area in January 1923 with the object of forcing Germany's compliance with the reparations settlement. The Weimar government responded with a policy of passive resistance, financed by resort to the printing press. The resulting hyperinflation of the currency, deliberately induced in order to discredit the reparations settlement, was ended in September 1923 when the government instituted a major reform of the currency based upon a new unit of account, the rentenmark, valued at one billion old marks.[60] Whilst the issue of the rentenmark was a success it was not until 1924, when the currency was converted to a gold monetary standard based on a new Reichsmark, that Germany's financial stabilisation was secured. This was facilitated in large measure by a new plan for the payment of reparations (a scaling down of the instalments and an extension to the period of repayment), formulated by a committee composed of 'non-political experts' chaired by an American, General Charles C.

Dawes. The Dawes Plan, as it came to be called, was accepted by the Reparations Commission in April 1924 and was implemented in the early autumn, backed up by a highly successful international loan of 800 million gold marks floated by the German government in London and New York. Utterly convinced of the necessity for restoring the German economy the Bank of England was heavily implicated not only in the negotiations on the Dawes Plan and international loan, but also in the reconstruction of the Reichsbank. For the Gallophobic Norman this had presented unprecedented opportunities for involvement in international politics and financial diplomacy, epitomised by his intimate and friendly working relationship with the gifted Reichsbank President, Hjalmar Schacht.[61]

The British finanicial authorities could be forgiven for regarding Germany's economic rehabilitation and the military evacuation of the Ruhr industrial basin in April 1924 as marking the real beginnings of international economic stability. The Dawes Plan appeared to have solved the vexed and disruptive question of reparations and there were justifiable hopes that the problems of European monetary inflation were well on the way to being overcome. There were, however, two factors of considerable significance in all of this. First of all, the German currency had been linked to gold and the dollar rather than sterling and this had dealt a major blow to British hopes for the establishment of a gold exchange system centred on London. For the USA the threat of an Anglo-German sterling bloc had been averted and by the spring of 1925 only minor states, such as Austria and Hungary had stabilised their currencies in terms of sterling. Secondly, towards the end of 1924 a new danger began to emerge – the fact that several British Dominions were about to break the tie with sterling and link up with the gold dollar.[62] In these circumstances the Bank of England and Treasury began to discuss in earnest the timing of Britain's own return to the gold standard.

Britain returned to gold at the prewar sterling–dollar parity in April 1925, a full eight months before the expiry of the Gold and Silver (Export Embargo) Act. The overall rationale of the desirability of return has been indicated above (see p. 36) and the detailed story has been chronicled expertly from the standpoint of the Treasury and the Bank of England by Moggridge, with Sayers, Howson and Costigliola contributing valuable additional information in their respective studies of the Bank of England, domestic monetary management and Anglo-American financial relationships.[63] The adoption of the prewar parity is conventionally interpreted as arising from moral and political judgements involving considerations of financial probity and rectitude and also Britain's international economic prestige.[64] As every student of modern British economic history is aware the pound was henceforth overvalued by approximately 10 per cent in relation to the dollar, with the result that the financial authorities were obliged to devote considerable attention to the structure of American interest rates and prices. In the deliberations which led to the decision to return, the emergence of the USA as a rival financial power was a key consideration, not least for the Chancellor of the Exchequer, Winston Churchill. Acutely aware of the persistent and unfavourable differential between British and American costs, the Chancellor pressed Norman and the Treasury on the possibility of maintaining a 'managed' or paper currency, without the 'discipline' of gold. In the meantime British gold reserves would be shipped to the USA to stimulate inflation, thereby avoiding the necessity for domestic deflation which would have harmful effects on British industry. But Churchill's proposal, which was designed to pass the burden of adjustment consequent upon Britain's return to the gold standard on to the USA, received little support in the Bank and the Treasury. Norman emphasised that to perpetuate a managed currency would lead to Britain's economic isolation to America's advantage while Sir Otto Niemeyer, the Treasury Controller of Finance, rejected the gold transfer plan as unworkable and stressed that Britain's readoption of the gold standard would stimulate world trade and, in the long term, aid the recovery of British exports.[65] Finally, there was the danger of imperial economic disintegration at a time when the physical resources and markets of the empire were of increasing importance in view of Britain's weakened international economic position. In Janurary 1925, following the visit of an American–Dutch financial commission, the South African government had announced its decision to adopt the gold standard whatever the intentions of the British authorities. The Australian government was also prepared to act unilaterally and Canada had done so already. These events proved decisive for Churchill and were instrumental in securing his acquiescence to the views of Norman and Niemeyer. If Britain failed to return to the gold standard the Dominions would be drawn irrevocably into the American economic orbit with their currencies linked to gold on the basis of the dollar. In short, as Costigliola has concluded, the return to gold in 1925 'signified Britain's bid to reinforce imperial ties, regain its former status as focus of the world economy, and strengthen its position relative to the United States'.[66]

   With the benefit of hindsight it is clear that the guiding principles of economic policy in the postwar years were based upon a particular view of the workings of the old international economy and Britain's favourable position within it. The rallying cries of 'back to 1914' and the 'return to normalcy' were symptomatic of an unshaken faith in the prewar order. What was lacking in official financial circles throughout the 1920s was an awareness of the fact that London's earlier role as a financial centre and arbiter of the international gold standard had depended not upon its own intrinsic strength combined with an 'automatic' adjustment mechanism, but very largely upon Britain's temporary economic predominance among the major trading nations, together with the distinctive structure of the balance of payments.[67] But, as noted already, the war had irrevocably weakened Britain's international position. The sale of overseas assets, the default of debtors, Britain's own war debts, and the rise of an American merchant marine – all of these factors were tending to reduce the favourable balance of invisible trade. In 1924, for example, the value of the invisible surplus in terms of 1913 import prices was £250 million – £89 million below that of 1913 and, taking the same years, the visible trade deficit was £180 million above that of 1913. As Moggridge has emphasised, multilateral settlement of trading accounts, one of the most impressive features of the pre-1914 economic world, was becoming progressively more difficult for Britain during the 1920s.[68] In the last chapter it was noted that Britain's trading surplus with Asia, Australia, Africa and, in particular, India, had helped to cover deficits in Europe and America. The deterioration in Britain's trading position between 1913 and 1924 was dramatic. While there was a marked improvement in the position in relation to central and south-eastern Europe this was more apparent than real: it was merely a reflection of the temporary disruption of long-established trading contacts with German exporters. Particularly noteworthy were the Asian and North American figures. The former conceal a decline in the vital surplus with India from £23·3 million to £12·8 million, a result of the mounting difficulties confronting the Lancashire cotton industry vis-à-vis Indian and Japanese competition. In many ways, however, the most serious area of deterioration was with the 'dollar area' where the trade deficit rose by £156·4 million. In the light of Britain's war-debt position, the wartime sale of dollar securities and the rise of New York as a centre of international finance 'The British pattern of multilateral international settlements and the British balance of payments were more involved in the American economy and its successful management than previously, given Britain's need to finance her large bilateral deficit by earning sufficient surpluses in third countries.'[69]

That Britain was confronted by an adjustment problem was clearly recognised in the discussions which preceded the return to gold. Niemeyer, the leading advocate of the prewar parity, spoke of the 'discomforts' of return, a clear reference to the likely difficulties in maintaining the sterling–dollar parity. Reginald McKenna, Chairman of the Midland Bank and former Liberal Chancellor of the Exchequer, expressed the view that 'restoration will be hell', while Norman believed that adherence to the gold standard would require a high Bank Rate.[70] In general terms, however, the weight of official opinion held to the view that the adjustment problem would either be alleviated by a rise in overseas and in particular American prices, or overcome without undue difficulty by a modest deflation of domestic costs and prices, an argument reinforced by experience in the postwar depression when average weekly money wage rates had fallen by 38 per cent and the cost of living by 50 per cent in the two-year period from January 1921 to December 1922.

The major dissentient voice in the discussions which preceded the return to gold was that of Keynes. Having failed to secure acceptance for his 'managed' currency proposals he had pressed for a delay in the decision to return – until full parity had been achieved and maintained without undue strain.[71] Now that Churchill had rejected these arguments, Keynes, convinced that sterling was seriously overvalued at the old parity, launched a scathing attack on the Treasury in the person of the Chancellor. Arguing that the return to gold necessitated a 10 per cent reduction in costs in Britain's exporting industries, Keynes claimed that the adoption of the prewar parity was justifiable only on condition that *all* wages and prices were reduced by an equivalent amount. *The Economic Consequences of Mr Churchill,*[72] like his earlier attack on the Versailles Treaty, was a superb polemic with a passionate denunciation of the government's financial policy enhanced by his portrayal of the miners as the first victims of a soulless 'economic Juggernaut', representing 'in the flesh the "fundamental adjustments" engineered by the Treasury and the Bank of England to satisfy the impatience of the City fathers'.[73] This reference to coalmining was highly apposite – a leading exporting industry which, at the time of the return to gold, was already encountering severe financial difficulties in response to the progressive collapse of its overseas markets. It is true that labour costs had been substantially reduced in 1921, but only after a lengthy and bitterly fought dispute. This experience was ignored by the authorities in 1924–5 as was the fact that the general deflation of the economy after 1921 had been assisted by cost-of-living-related wage agreements in a number of industries.[74] These agreements had subsequently met with increasing trade union resistance. Even in coalmining, despite the defeat of 1921, the structure of district wage rates was governed by a national agreement rendering it extremely difficult to reduce wages in particular coalfields without provoking considerable labour unrest.[75] It is well known that the General Strike and miners' lockout of 1926 were fought unsuccessfully over this precise issue of wage reductions in the industry's hard-pressed exporting districts.[76]

It is tempting to conclude that the coalmining industry's exporting problems were the primary result of an overvalued currency, but although the return to gold cannot have helped the industry's international competitiveness, the claim that this was directly responsible for the coal crisis ignores the fact that the onset of the industry's financial difficulties pre-dated the return and were intimately linked with the resumption of German coal production on a large scale following the military withdrawal from the Ruhr in April 1924. In this light it is, perhaps, ironic that the gold standard discussion took place without any reference to the structure of costs and prices in the German economy, Britain's principal European industrial competitor.[77]

The real significance of the events of 1926 is that they mark a watershed of sorts in Britain's postwar economic history. Whilst the consensus among historians of labour is that 'the General Strike merits historical study less for what it changed in the labour movement than for what it revealed of the unchanging',[78] it is arguable that for many employers it was a traumatic occurrence, the first openly decisive challenge to the restoration of prewar normalcy. The strike itself and succeeding miners' lockout demonstrated the excessively high cost in social and political terms of the imposition of wage reductions alone as a solution to the economic difficulties confronting exporting industries.[79] The trade union movement suffered a resounding defeat in 1926, yet despite the continuation of trade recession employers in general refrained from mounting an attack on wage levels. Given the rigid commitment of the authorities to the existing exchange rate for the pound, the General Strike was one of several factors which served to encourage the search for a less painful means of achieving cost reductions. It is against this background that the 'rationalisation' movement in British industry in the later 1920s should be considered.[80] It was Sir Alfred Mond (later Lord Melchett), progressive colliery owner and co-founder of the great chemical combine ICI, who played a leading role in popularising the case for a fundamental reorganisation of British industry after 1926.[81] According to Mond, rationalisation was applicable to a wide spectrum of industrial activities, new and old, from electrical engineering and motor vehicles, to cotton textiles and coalmining. In so far as it was relevant to the problems of the staple industries, rationalisation was seen to be a panacea for the loss of competitive efficiency endemic in the existence of surplus productive capacity. Horizontal amalgamations were a direct means of overcoming the slowness of market forces in securing the elimination of marginal concerns: only then could production be concentrated in the most efficient firms and effective overseas selling organisations established. There were, however, numerous obstacles in the way of this process. In coalmining, for example, colliery owners resisted amalgamations after 1926 and instead favoured the formation of marketing schemes in order to stabilise the general level of coal prices. The values of nineteenth-century individualism were certainly under attack, but a response to adverse trading conditions which centred on cartelisation was hardly calculated to increase competitive efficiency. Convinced of the merits of large-scale organisation in coalmining, Baldwin's Conservative government steadfastly refused to countenance any coercive measures which might undermine the private-enterprise system.[82] In the spinning section of the cotton industry, on the other hand, where the necessary coercive power *was* forthcoming, primarily from the Bank of England, the experience of the late 1920s was not such as to inspire confidence in the merits of industrial reorganisation in structurally fragmented industries. The role of the Bank of England in bringing about the formation of the Lancashire Cotton Corporation in 1929 was more in the nature of emergency relief for certain banks than for the reconstruction of the spinning section of the industry. At the time of the corporation's formation the opinion was expressed that it was merely a financiers' combination 'thrown together in order to enable the banks to liquidate their questionable holdings'. Support for such a view stems from the fact that of the first twenty-nine companies absorbed, most were recapitalised concerns dating from the postwar boom, heavily indebted to the banks and consistently unable to pay dividends. It should be emphasised, too, that the corporation encountered overwhelming difficulties in the co-ordination of production between its constituent mills.[83] In the absence of a 'parent firm' to provide an organisational core and with serious managerial deficiencies, this particular form of rationalisation, based upon the multi-plant merger, was a spectacular manifestation of the human and organisation constraints on company growth.[84]

Further barriers to rationalisation included interpersonal relations between leading industrialists and the so-called 'wait-and-see' attitude engendered by conceptions of the nature of demand in the prewar period, together with the financial strength of those firms in the staple industries which had accumulated large reserves before the war and in the succeeding boom. In the case of personal relations, the classic illustration is provided by the failure of the numerous attempts to rationalise the structure of the Scottish steel industry in the 1920s and early 1930s.[85] Whilst a limited number of mergers took place, more ambitious schemes foundered on the personal animosities between the industrialists involved, the extreme complexity of the problems of company valuation, the reluctance of the stronger firms to be dragged down by the weak, and finally the existence of vested interests in the form of the joint-stock banks. It has to be said also that in the absence of government subsidisation, businessmen in the iron and steel, shipbuilding and engineering industries were not unaware of the social costs of closure in heavily localised industries, and the commerical dangers inherent in the dispersal of closely knit and highly skilled labour forces.[86] This leads on to the perceptions of industrialists as to the future course of demand, perceptions which, as noted above, were heavily influenced by experience before 1914. As in the case of the Scottish steel industry there is a well-documented case study which illustrates this issue in a graphic manner. This concerns the North British Locomotive Company, founded in 1903 as a result of the merger of three of Scotland's leading locomotive builders.[87] The amalgamated firm was not particularly profitable even before 1914 at a time when markets were generally buoyant, but it survived the entire interwar period in market conditions of extreme difficulty only to be forced into liquidation in the 1950s. Most of the company's contracts in the 1920s were substantially unprofitable; in the first half of the 1930s the situation worsened to the extent that contracts became extremely difficult to obtain while losses on those negotiated were on occasion 'appalling'. How then did the company avoid the need for product diversification and the ever-present danger of liquidation? The answer is basically twofold: first, the eternal (but diminishing) optimism of the directors that trade recovery was 'round the corner', and secondly, because this particular firm, unlike many of those in the iron and steel and cotton industries (see above, pp. 34-5), emerged from the postwar boom in a much strengthened financial position so that it was able to meet trade collapse by drawing on accumulated reserves. It is a point worth noting at this stage that the continuing commitment of industrialists to the staple trades was arguably justified by events in the later 1930s when industrial recovery finally got under way on the basis of a combination of domestic consumer demand and, in the case of shipbuilding in particular, the resumption of Admiralty orders on a regular basis. The recovery in demand fully justified the 'wait-and-see' policy adopted for much of the preceding fifteen years.[88] As the historian of the North British Locomotive Company has pointed out in criticism of the view that structural readjustment should have been more rapid:

> To expect an increase in demand after 1920, and to base policy, ... on such an expectation, may have been short-sighted, ... but to have done otherwise required a rapid change in outlook by those reared in the tradition of the production of steam locomotives before 1914, and one which seemed less necessary by the later 1930s in any case .... To suggest the Company should have acted otherwise would be to suggest it should have escaped from the limitations of its time and place and have acquired the wisdom of hindsight granted only to latter-day historians.[89]

There is a danger, however, that in citing particular examples of the kind indicated above the barriers to rationalisation will be overstressed. Hannah's study of the growth of corporate enterprise in Britain has demonstrated that the 1920s witnessed an unprecedented merger movement in a wide spectrum of industries, both in the old staples and in newer sectors such as electrical products and motor vehicles.[90] The motives for amalgamations were as numerous as the industries affected. The legacy of the war (see above, p. 31), critical comparisons with overseas competitors in Germany and the USA,[91] the impact of direct large-scale foreign investment in Britain,[92] the weight of semi-official opinion, as evidenced, for example, by the reports of the Balfour Committee on Trade and Industry[93] – all of these factors encouraged the growth of merger activity in the middle and later 1920s. Hannah's analysis does lend some support to the view that the improved growth performance of the economy at that time was due to enhanced total factor productivity arising in part from improvements in industrial organisation. But it is also possible that in removing former limitations on supply, the increasing scale of operations and associated cost reductions in the newer industrial sectors aided economic growth by helping to counteract the overall deficiency of demand in the economy of which the recession in the staple industries was a major cause.

In so far as it is possible to identify a consensus view among contemporaries as to the benefits of rationalisation, it would appear that it was regarded, first and foremost, as a solution to the difficulties confronting the staple industries: the lowering of costs through the achievement of economies of scale would lead to the recovery of lost export markets. The initial impact of amalgamations would be to increase the numbers out of work, but the immediate effects of this would be mitigated by the unemployment insurance scheme and in the medium and longer term by the dual possibilities of increased employment opportunities in the expanding sectors of the economy and in the revived staple trades.[94] All of this was splendid in theory but in practice the issues were less clear cut. In the first instance, as Hannah has conceded, the transfer of redundant resources from declining to expanding sectors was unlikely to be particularly rapid in a period of widespread unemployment. Skilled labour, and entrepreneurial and capital resources too, as in locomotive building and shipbuilding for example, tended to be 'industry specific' with the result that where the transfer of resources did occur, it tended to be 'more a convenience than a necessity'.[95] Secondly, as far as the staple industries were concerned, rationalisation, like other cost-cutting measures, such as wage reductions and increased working hours, was unlikely to have more than a minimal impact upon overseas sales. Because of changes in the international economy, Britain's comparative advantage in industries such as shipbuilding, heavy engineering and cotton textiles was declining, a problem compounded after 1925 by the overvaluation of sterling.

The declining fortunes of the staple industries were inevitably reflected in the balance of payments. The position has been well summarised by Moggridge:

> As a result of her disappointing post-1924 export performance and the rising level of imports (mainly foodstuffs and raw materials), Britain became increasingly dependent on her invisible earnings to cover her growing trade deficit and allow new net foreign investment. Until 1929, the rise in invisible earnings more than offset the deterioration on trade account – £74 million as against £46 million. However, the improved position depended almost completely on rising overseas investment income and on war debt and reparations payments which transformed the Government account. Shipping earnings, on the other hand, fell as freight rates declined and as Britain's share of the available traffic fell slightly. Short interest and commissions remained almost stagnant. Given that a large proportion of overseas investment income came from cyclically sensitive equities and given that the whole edifice of war debts and reparations was rarely without uncertainties the payments position had its precarious elements ...[96]

For the 1920s as a whole, the current account surplus averaged £114 million per annum (see Table 5, p. 142), a seemingly impressive figure, but one which represented a 46 per cent decline in monetary terms, and considerably more in real terms when compared with the average annual surplus of £206 million for the years 1911–13.[97] This deterioration in the balance of payments had important implications for London's role as a financial centre. In the years 1924–8 the volume of new foreign long-term overseas issues exceeded the current account surplus by more than £300 million. This had never occurred before 1914 and had been prevented before 1925 by informal controls exercised by the authorities over the export of capital.[98] Following the return to gold the unofficial embargo on capital exports was lifted and the resources for long-term lending, where they were not covered by the current account, 'were derived mainly from foreign short-term funds attracted to London by relatively high interest rates and by the security and liquidity of the Treasury Bill'.[99] The dangers inherent in this situation need hardly be exaggerated in view of the fact that a considerable proportion of this 'excessive' overseas lending was obtained from volatile and unstable sources. This was especially true in the case of French foreign investment in the period after 1924, since much of it was in the form of a flight of capital from the franc in favour of more stable foreign currencies, notably, the US dollar and sterling.[100] 'Hot money' flows of this kind between rival financial centres were potentially dangerous since their rapid withdrawal could be a major source of strain in the receiving country, unless its reserve position, like that of the USA, was one of fundamental strength.[101]

But this hardly applied in the case of Britain.[102] Before 1914, with a substantial current account surplus and secure short-term creditor position, London had underpinned the international financial system on the basis of an extremely low level of gold and currency reserves. But because of the war, Britain had become a short-term debtor and the relative weakness on trading account throughout the 1920s prevented the accumulation of a sufficiently high level of gold and currency reserves.[103]

London's vulnerability was further exacerbated by the conditions under which a number of countries stabilised their currencies in relation to gold after 1925. Rather than adopt a full gold standard on the prewar model they were obliged, partly because of a maldistribution of world gold reserves in favour of the USA, to adopt a gold exchange standard under which they augmented their official reserves by accumulating foreign exchange, mainly in the form of dollar holdings in New York and of sterling in London. Like private 'hot money' flows these official foreign currency holdings were liable to withdrawal at short notice in times of crisis. The implications of this for London and New York were clear: they had to hold stocks of gold in excess of their own financial and trading needs. In the case of the latter this presented no difficulties, but for London the acquisition of these new short-term liabilities, which in itself required the maintenance of international confidence in sterling, was a major source of strain in the later 1920s.[104] Britain had, of course, been an ardent advocate of a gold exchange system since the Genoa conference in 1922, but in the circumstances of the later 1920s the country's liquid short-term funds were simply inadequate to meet the claims which might arise. One answer to this difficulty would have been to place a strict ban on capital exports, but such a policy would have been inconsistent with London's claim to be a centre of international finance.[105] More and more, Britain's external viability was coming to depend upon a combination of 'moral suasion' on the part of the authorities to discourage excessive overseas lending whether to the empire or elsewhere in the world, and the maintenance of high interest rates in order to attract and retain foreign short-term funds, a task made doubly difficult owing to the existence of more than one international financial centre. In short, the postwar decentralisation of the international monetary system, with the rise of New York and Paris, rendered the business of international clearing more complex and less efficient and also served to encourage the transfer of short-term funds in response to changes in interest rates and fluctuating foreign confidence in currencies.[106]

Yet another weakness in the international financial system after 1925 was the adoption of offsetting monetary policies by central-bank authorities. 'Few countries were prepared to sacrifice the stability of

their domestic economies completely for external equilibrium.'[107]
Thus, for much of the decade the Federal Reserve Bank of New York
took measures to offset the domestic impact of gold inflows in order to
avoid the dangers of inflation. In France, too, following the liquidation
of foreign exchange holdings and the growth of a large balance-of-
payments surplus after 1928, the resulting gold inflows were partly
neutralised in order to avoid inflation and to retain the competitive
advantage bestowed by an undervalued currency.[108] Even in Britain,
the Bank of England attempted to insulate the domestic economy
from the impact of gold flows. Indeed, 'As compared with the
traditional automacities to which it was supposed to have returned,
the Bank went to quite extraordinary lengths ... Ricardian critics
with a simple creed could have complained that the Bank was not
playing the gold standard game according to the rules.'[109] The
technical achievement of the Bank after 1925, in minimising the
effects of London's financial weakness on domestic trade and
employment was very real but the evidence indicates that political
considerations played an important role. The Treasury, afraid that a
higher Bank Rate would exacerbate the unemployment problem, was
in no way inhibited in expressing strong disapproval at any proposed
increase in the rate. 'As a result Bank Rate tended to be frozen [at a
level of 4½–5 per cent] and to be relatively useless as a short-term
policy instrument.'[110] The Bank was thus obliged to adopt 'short-term
palliatives' to compensate for this limitation on its freedom of
manoeuvre. 'Moral suasion' to counter capital exports was just one of
several expedients adopted after 1926. These included the resumption of active gold market and foreign exchange operations, and co-
operation with foreign banking authorities to relieve the pressure on
London.[111] All of this was in marked contrast to the prewar experience.
With more than one million workers unemployed on average in every
year throughout the 1920s the commitment of the authorities to the
defence of the existing exchange rate presented an acute conflict
between considerations of domestic and external equilibrium. With
monetary policy as an instrument of economic adjustment virtually
neutralised, and in view of the Baldwin government's pledge to refrain
from introducing a measure of general tariff protection after the 1924
general election, this left fiscal measures as the only remaining policy
instrument for dealing with unemployment. But here again there were
strong constraints on the government's freedom of action.

Responsibility for fiscal policy lay with the Treasury, an institution
obsessed with the desire to avoid inflation and endowed with a
considerable determination to reduce the vastly increased national
debt inherited from the war. In view of the primacy attached to debt
retirement, the Treasury reverted as soon as possible after 1919 to the
prewar norm of strict economy in government expenditure. While

substantial relief was obtained from a considerable reduction in defence expenditure,[112] this was offset to a significant extent by the rising costs of the social services as conventionally defined, including unemployment benefit. For many contemporary observers the growth of the latter was especially disturbing in so far as it constituted 'a dangerously open-ended commitment on the part of the state, especially during conditions of financial stringency'.[113] The same considerations applied to contra-cyclical public works for the relief of unemployment. The Unemployment Grants Committee, a co-ordinating authority for the implementation of such works by local authorities, had been formed during the postwar depression. Although its establishment immediately preceded the launching of the campaign for public expenditure cuts following the recommendations of the Geddes Committee in 1922, the relief-work policy remained largely intact mainly because much of the expense had to be borne by the local authorities themselves, and also because the belief was widespread that the depression in the exporting industries was a temporary phenomenon.[114] In the later 1920s, however, with the emergence of the 'hard core' of one million unemployed, the Treasury became increasingly hostile to public works and, as indicated already, government policy for the relief of unemployment became oriented more towards the achievement of cost reductions, first of all by means of wage cuts and secondly by rationalisation, reinforced after 1927 by a scheme of assisted labour mobility under the auspices of the Industrial Transference Board.[115]

The debate on fiscal policy in the late 1920s centred on this very issue of state-sponsored public works projects. The Liberal 'Yellow Book', *Britain's Industrial Future*,[116] published in 1928, advocated the establishment of a National Investment Board to oversee a national reconstruction programme involving large-scale public expenditure on housing, roads, electricity, telephones and agriculture. These proposals were derived from the embryonic views of Keynes and the relevant sections of the book subsequently appeared with suitable embellishments, in the form of Lloyd George's general election manifesto in the spring of 1929. The manifesto, bearing the ambitious title *We Can Conquer Unemployment,* called forth the full weight of financial orthodoxy in the form of a White Paper prepared by the Treasury at Baldwin's request.[117] The economic basis of the 'Treasury View' was grounded in the belief that there was a finite level of savings in the economy. Hence the borrowing requirements for a state-financed public works programme would push up interest rates and least inevitably to a reduction in private investment: inflation might be stimulated and the balance of payments adversely affected. Thus the Liberal programme would accentuate the difficulties currently affecting the exporting industries. It was completey at variance with the real need of the economy – the revival of the export trade through cost reductions and rationalisation.[118] Although this extreme formulation of 'neo-classical' employment policy was soon modified to take account of Keynes's criticisms – notably in the evidence of Sir Richard Hopkins, Niemeyer's successor as Controller of Finance at the Treasury, before the Macmillan Committee on Finance and Industry in 1931[119] – the orthodox Treasury view of fiscal policy in relation to unemployment relief remained practically intact for the greater part of the 1930s.

In view of its restrictive orthodoxy, it is tempting to erect a scathing denunciation of the interwar Treasury, with Keynes and his followers cast in the role of enlightened heroes and the Treasury knights as intellectually bankrupt villains. There are, however, several reasons why such a view should not be pressed. As well as being conspicuously lacking in political influence *vis-à-vis* the Conservative and Labour Parties, Keynes's ideas were in a continuous process of evolution and, until the publication of his *General Theory* in 1936,[120] they lacked the detailed theoretical framework necessary to convert academic and ultimately Treasury opinion.[121] Secondly, it should be borne in mind that it is impossible in the circumstances of the 1920s, if not the interwar period as a whole, to consider fiscal policy solely from the standpoint of economic objectivity. Sir Warren Fisher, Permanent Secretary at the Treasury, was especially concerned to emphasise the political and administrative constraints in the way of an ambitious public works programme. Thus, Lloyd George's 1929 programme was condemned as necessitating 'the substitution of autocracy for Parliamentary Government'. Even if 'a Mussolini regime' with a considerable bureaucracy at its disposal 'could be proved to be desirable for the "war" against unemployment ... the Country would [not] stand for it'.[122] Furthermore, in view of the accepted parameters of Britain's economic position in the late 1920s Treasury orthodoxy arguably provided the most appropriate set of policy responses:

> Given the weakness of the British balance of payments, a fixed and over-valued exchange rate, and the monetary climate which these two conditions required, the Treasury View contained an element of truth. It was the familiar vicious circle of policy-making in the twenties: external pressures dictated a policy of monetary caution, which in turn restricted freedom to use active fiscal measures for fear of adding to external difficulties.[123]

It remains to be said that the 'vicious circle' was broken not by the protracted impact of an international economic crisis of unprecedented magnitude, but by the financial consequences of a further world war.

It is possible to argue that the financial policies pursued by the authorities both before and after the return to gold were not seriously inimical to the health of the economy. Aldcroft, for example, has questioned the deflationary impact of monetary policy in the 1920s. As compared with the period before 1914, interest rates in the 1920s were comparatively stable and this may have compensated to some extent for the increased cost of borrowing. Certainly, if the trend of new industrial issues is considered, there was an upward movement during the course of the decade, culminating in a boom in 1928–9. Bankers' advances, moreover, were rising steadily from 1922 and by the end of the decade were substantially in excess of the levels reached in 1919–20. It is true that gilt-edged securities, with an average yield of 4·5 per cent, provided an attractive alternative to industrial investment, but it should also be borne in mind that the return to gold, in stabilising the currency, may well have increased business confidence.[124]

Aldcroft's thesis has not gone unchallenged. More recently it has been claimed that the restrictiveness of monetary policy severely hampered industrial investment. Whilst conceding that the volume of new issues expanded up to 1928, Howson, for example, has pointed out that 'the 1928 new issue boom was dominated by speculative securities of the quick-return and high-yield type'. Purely financial issues for investment trusts and holding companies were popular while many of the new industrial ventures in such areas as films, gramophones and radio and photographic equipment, soon collapsed. Thus to the extent that the new issue boom was a response to the return to gold 'it was hardly an unmixed blessing for the UK economy'.[125] It is also necessary to take account of the financial consequences of the postwar boom. Rather than enforce the liquidation of firms which were incapable of repaying debts incurred in the boom, the banks permitted industrial overdrafts to reach unprecedented heights: overdrafts were frozen for much of the decade and this arguably slowed down structural transformation by rendering capital scarce for 'the new industrial leaders'. Thirdly, there was the problem posed by the 'Macmillan Gap' – the barrier encountered by small firms in gaining access to adequate external funding, a task made doubly difficult in an era of high interest rates. It can, of course, be countered that the major proportion of industrial finance was traditionally derived from internal sources so that the cost of borrowing was an unimportant consideration in investment decisions. But this is to ignore the fact that 'the easier the terms on which a firm expects to be able to borrow whenever it needs to, the more it can use its internal funds on investment'.[126] In circumstances of economic depression, therefore, with limited or non-existent profits and low internal liquidity, many firms were hampered in acquiring new physical assets by the limitations set by monetary policy.

These views dovetail neatly together with the argument that a lower parity for the pound 'would have provided a better basis on which to solve those problems which centred around the transition of the industrial structure from the nineteenth to the twentieth century'. The enhanced competitiveness of British industry and of the international service sector would have eased the pressure on the balance of payments and in so doing 'would probably have strengthened the real forces underlying Britain's long-term growth'.[127]

In assessing the merits of these opposing views, it should be emphasised that there are strengths and weaknesses on both sides. In general terms, Howson's analysis is perceptive and convincing. Its great merit lies in the fact that it lays stress upon the positive relationship between technical and structural change on the one hand, and the level of aggregate demand in the economy on the other. The importance of the latter is ignored by Aldcroft in his assumptions that the stock of resources is limited and that technical progress is exogenous to the economic system. As Howson concludes, 'Technical progress and structural factors are not independent of aggregate demand and with one million unemployed there could have been more expansion in the new industries even if the old were not declining, if aggregate demand had been growing sufficiently to create profit expectations favourable to investment in the new industries (primarily domestic-based)'.[128] Closely allied to Howson's thesis is Moggridge's claim that a lower parity for the pound, in boosting British exports, would have had significant and favourable repercussions upon Britain's external economic position.[129] In this he is supported by Pressnell who has argued that a devaluation of the entire sterling system against the US dollar in particular would have increased its overall earnings to Britain's ultimate benefit. It is important to remember that Britain's dollar earnings 'came less from direct trade with the USA than indirectly through surpluses with those outer sterling countries which had surpluses with the USA'.[130] Whilst conceding the possibility of raised tariff barriers in the USA and Britain's low import elasticity of demand, Pressnell is concerned to stress that an 'imperial devaluation' of the pound would have raised the competitiveness of sterling countries in third markets and also within sterling markets themselves. These are cogent remarks but the important general point remains that as far as Britain itself was concerned it is highly unlikely that a 10 per cent devaluation of the pound would have had more than a minimal impact upon the level of exports in view of the much lower unit wage costs abroad and the very low price elasticity of demand for many British exports in the late 1920s. In short, Moggridge seriously underestimates the competitive weakness of British industry in overseas markets. It has already been noted that the financial difficulties of the coalmining industry predated the return to gold (see above, pp. 42-3), but this was only one aspect of Britain's exporting difficulties. These dated from the 1870s and, but for the emigration of 6 million Britons between 1870 and 1914, a substantial unemployment problem would have emerged in the prewar economy.[131]

Given Britain's international economic position in the 1920s there was simply no way in which the economy could avoid the effects of deflationary pressure arising from the depression in the staple industries. As it was, overvaluation of the pound did at least serve to keep down the cost of imports, a significant advantage in view of Britain's inelasticity of demand for many imported foodstuffs and raw materials. But where Moggridge's case is particularly weak is in his suggestion that the adjustment problem presented by overvaluation – its adverse consequences for both the level of domestic economic activity and the external account – had serious international consequences. Whilst accepting that a more buoyant British economy would have had favourable repercussions elsewhere, it is difficult to accept that this would have had anything other than a marginal impact upon the operation of a restored international economy which was inherently unstable.

Dominating the international economy of the late 1920s was the USA, the world's greatest manufacturing and exporting nation, its principal investor and creditor, and major importer of primary foodstuffs and raw materials. The key position of the USA meant that the level of its domestic economic activity and the economic policies pursued by its political and financial authorities were of paramount importance to the numerous countries whose fortunes were closely linked with it, either as suppliers and customers, or debtors. In the same way that Britain had underpinned the pre-1914 multilateral trading system, this role was now thrust on the USA, a country endowed with immense financial resources but, as events were to prove, singularly lacking in the necessary knowledge and expertise which would enable it to meet its considerable international economic responsibilities. Many of America's suppliers of primary products enjoyed trading deficits with European countries which, in turn, were in deficit to the USA. Thus the pattern of multilateral settlement after 1925 rested on three fundamental props, first, the continuing outflow of investment funds from the USA to Europe and elsewhere, secondly, the continuing willingness of the USA to import primary products, and finally, a European balance-of-payments surplus with the primary producing countries payable in gold and dollars to enable Europe to meet its trading deficit with the USA.[132] These conditions were largely fulfilled between 1924 and 1929. American foreign investment increased dramatically after the stabilisation of the mark and was directed principally towards

Germany and the primary producing countries both in Europe and on the periphery. The effect of this international investment, to which Britain also contributed, was to produce the economic boom of the late 1920s, characterised by rising industrial and primary production on a worldwide basis. In the four years from 1925 to 1929, the former rose by more than 20 per cent and the latter by more than 10 per cent, an impressive performance by historical standards.[133] However, the prosperity engendered by the boom was more apparent than real: it was built upon insecure foundations and this was to have major consequences for the British economy.

In the case of Germany, it was American foreign lending, augmented by British and Dutch investment, which provided the resources for economic reconstruction and, perhaps most important of all, for that country's annual payments on reparations account to the European ex-allies. The dangers inherent in this situation were twofold. First, a considerable proportion of American lending was on a short-term basis, much of it directed towards the German banking system which permitted the use of these funds for long-term capital projects, some of which were of a non-productive nature. Secondly, since the European ex-allies used reparations receipts to meet their own war-debt obligations to the USA, a circular flow of funds, completely unrelated to normal trading transactions, was brought into being and, in conjunction with 'hot money' flows, vastly complicated the business of international clearing.[134] The situation could, of course, have been considerably eased had the US government not persisted in its refusal to accept that there was a link between the payment of reparations and war debts. Germany, in fact, borrowed abroad three times as much as was necessary to meet its reparations obligations: the country's ability to meet the annual interest charges on these debts and to sustain the liquidity of the banking system was possible only as long as the flow of American lending continued. In relation to Germany, therefore, Britain's vulnerability lay in the fact that any curtailment of American overseas lending could provoke 'a scramble for liquidity' in Central Europe. Banking assets would be frozen and the crisis might well spread to Britain with serious financial consequences in view of the country's short-term debtor position and limited gold and currency reserves.

The primary producing countries were also in a potentially weak position in the later 1920s. Fundamentally, their difficulties stemmed from the growing overproduction of a limited number of important foodstuffs and raw materials – wheat, sugar, rubber and coffee. Primary production had increased dramatically during the war and succeeding boom (see above, p. 29) and it was further stimulated after 1924 by international investment, principally from the USA to Central and Eastern Europe, Canada and Latin America, and by

Britain to Australasia, Asia and Africa. On a strictly commercial basis there can be little doubt that much of this foreign investment was of questionable value in view of the postwar revival in European production and in the light of the secular decline in Europe's population growth, together with changing dietary habits associated with a rising standard of living. In the years after 1926 this was reflected in a marked deterioration in the terms of trade of the primary producing countries.[135] For the UK the implications of all this were, again, extremely serious at a time when the proportion of British exports to Latin America, the empire, and those areas in Asia as yet unaffected by foreign and indigenous competition, was rising. The changing direction of Britain's export trade in the 1920s rendered the country 'particularly exposed to an international slump as the import capacities of her growing overseas markets depended heavily on export earnings from primary products and new overseas investment, both of which were strongly cyclical'.[136] Once again the stability of Britain's international economic position was dependent on the USA. As long as the level of American foreign investment and the volume of its primary product imports were sustained, the weaknesses in that position would be concealed.

3

The British Economy in the 1930s: Recovery on the Dole

In the summer of 1928 the world economic system was subjected to a major destabilising shock emanating from the USA. The mounting speculative boom in the domestic economy and the efforts of the Federal Reserve Board in attempting to restrain it by raising interest rates, resulted in a severe cutback in the volume of American foreign lending to the primary producers on the periphery of the international economy and also to Europe.[1] Dependent upon a sustained inflow of foreign capital to maintain external equilibrium the debtor countries were forced to draw on their limited reserves of gold or foreign exchange in order to close the widening gap in their payments balances.[2] As a solution to temporary difficulties this was an acceptable reaction but the burden of adjustment to externally generated deflationary pressure was rendered impossibly onerous by a second blow to international equilibrium. Once again it stemmed from the USA and took the form of a downturn in the level of domestic economic activity in the summer of 1929. The collapse of the American boom was to initiate the most severe economic depression in modern history and to destroy the delicate mechanism of an international economy already subject to destabilising forces.[3]

The position of the USA as a major importer of primary raw materials has already been noted (see above, p. 54). With the onset of recession, America's imports of primary products were severely curtailed and this, added to the decline in European import demand consequent upon the earlier reduction in American foreign lending, exacerbated the problems confronting primary producing countries on the periphery. With deteriorating trade balances and mounting external debt obligations many of these countries released stocks of commodities on to an already glutted world market in a vain attempt to maintain their foreign income.[4] This merely served to accentuate the decline in prices with the result that they were soon subjected to intense deflationary pressure through the medium of the international gold exchange standard. This was followed by currency devaluations, in some cases outright default on debts, and eventually the abandonment of the gold standard in Australasia and Latin America in the final months of 1929 and early in 1930.

For the UK the consequences of these events were extremely serious. Falling world commodity prices and the decline in the volume of international trade led to a reduction in Britain's visible exports and an even more precipitate decline in the favourable balance of invisible trade. Although the effect of this on the balance of payments was mitigated to some extent by a considerable improvement in the terms of trade, a net deficit on current account was recorded in 1931, only the third occasion on which this had occurred since the end of the war.[5]

The deterioration in the trading position was accompanied by a marked rise in the rate of insured unemployment, from 9·7 per cent in 1929 to 22·0 per cent in 1931. As might be expected, in view of the collapse in demand on the part of many of Britain's primary producing customers, the worst affected industries were the staple export trades. In cotton textiles, for example, the unemployment percentage rose from 14·5 in 1929 to 31·1 in 1932 and, taking the same period, in the woollen and worsted industry from 15·6 to 26·6, in coalmining from 18·2 to 41·2, in shipbuilding from 23·2 to 59·5 and in iron and steel from 19·9 to 48·5.[6] Not until the rearmament boom of the late 1930s were these industries to regain any semblance of prosperity.

The progressive breakdown of the international economy coincided with the period of office of Ramsay MacDonald's second Labour government, in theory committed to the implementation of radical policies for the achievement of 'socialism', but in practice severely circumscribed not only by its minority status, but also by MacDonald's belief in 'gradualism' and the Treasury's continuing adherence to economic orthodoxy.[7] In one major respect, however, the new government was relatively profligate. In January 1930 the benefits payable under the unemployment insurance scheme were increased and the rules of access liberalised. At the average level of unemployment ruling in the 1920s the increased expenditure could probably have been met from an insurance fund that was actuarially sound, but as unemployment rose to unprecedented heights after 1929 the government, in attempting to balance the fund, resorted to borrowing from the Exchequer. In 1930 the deficit in the fund amounted to £75 million; in 1931 it was expected to rise to £100 million, a development which the Treasury under the ultra-orthodox Philip Snowden, viewed with the utmost alarm.[8] As has so often been emphasised, Britain in comparison with other industrialised countries possessed an extremely generous and comprehensive insurance scheme and the subsidisation of the fund by the Exchequer was regarded in orthodox financial circles as a dangerously open-ended commitment which might, in extreme circumstances, lead to national insolvency. In his evidence before the Royal Commission on Unemployment Insurance in January 1931, Sir Richard Hopkins, presumably with Snowden's approval, emphasised that 'continued state borrowing on the present vast scale without adequate provision for repayment by the Fund would quickly call in question the stability of the British financial system'. He concluded that there could be 'no question' of writing off the existing debt: it had to be repaid.[9]

By the standards of the interwar period as a whole, the Labour government did not pursue excessively restrictive financial policies.[10] Despite the key position occupied by Snowden, Britain alone of the major countries affected by depression refused to follow the deflationary path. 'Her relatively generous social services were not only maintained but somewhat increased in scope: despite the shrinking of the tax base, government expenditure continued to rise; no serious attempt was made to balance the budget'[11] before 1931. Ironically, the pressure for retrenchment, when it came, stemmed from a Liberal Party which had moved steadily away from the principles of Lloyd George's expansionary election programme in 1929. Following on the proceedings of the Royal Commission on Unemployment Insurance the Liberals were successful in forcing the government to appoint a Committee on National Expenditure under Sir George May, the former Secretary of the Prudential Assurance Company, to suggest ways of reducing public expenditure on current account. The May Committee which was to report in August 1931[12] produced 'one of the most influential and misguided official reports in recent economic history',[13] a document which contained a classic statement of the orthodox economic position and which was to play a considerable role in the downfall of the Labour government (see below, p. 62).

As for the international economy during Labour's period of office, attempts to revive it were bedevilled not only by its inherent instability but also by the antagonisms and misunderstandings that existed between the major financial powers. In the late summer of 1929, at the international conference at The Hague to consider the report of the Young Committee on the scaling down of German reparations payments, Snowden had severely antagonised the French delegation with his belligerent stance in seeking to increase Britain's financial share.[14] In the autumn of 1930 a further breach in Anglo-French relations was precipitated by the attempts of the German government to secure the total cancellation of reparations. This was clearly repugnant to French interests, but was by no means incompatible with the long-standing British view that the restoration of international economic equilibrium could only benefit from the liquidation of all inter-allied war debts, a development which might be facilitated by the policy of the German government. As Skidelsky has cogently remarked, in the final months before the demise of the Labour government Britain was pursuing two mutually incompatible foreign policies in relation to France. On the one hand, the Foreign Office, under Arthur Henderson, was attempting to enlist French support for the impending World Disarmament Conference to be held in February 1932, while on the other, the Treasury and the Bank of England were intent upon pursuing financial policies in the international arena that were most calculated to upset French political and economic interests. It was hardly surprising, therefore, in view of the suspicions that existed between the two countries that in April 1931 an imaginative British proposal for international reflation (the so-called 'Norman Plan') involving the co-ordination of lending policies on the party of the major international companies and central banks, failed to enlist either American or French support.[15] International economic co-operation was breaking down and neither Paris nor New York was prepared to assume or indeed share London's former role as underwriter of the world's financial system.

A further example of the divisions between Britain and France was provided by the reaction of the two countries to the Austro-German proposals for a customs union, announced on 23 March 1931. The French, pathologically afraid that this was a manoeuvre calculated to prepare the way for an *Anschluss*, declared their implacable opposition while Henderson, anxious to maintain France's continuing interest in disarmament, fervently hoped that the proposal would come to nothing.[16] In the meantime, Austria's largest and most prestigious commercial bank, the Credit Anstalt, was encountering severe financial difficulties as a result of its heavy involvement in European industrial concerns adversely affected by the business recession. Towards the end of May, a loan for 100 million schillings was arranged from eleven countries through the Bank for International Settlements (BIS). By 5 June this credit had been exhausted and the Austrian National Bank was obliged to seek further assistance from the BIS. This was granted within a few days but on condition that the Austrian government should obtain a foreign loan for 150 million schillings for a two- to three-year period. On approaching Paris, however, the Austrian financial authorities were informed that the price of French co-operation was the abandonment of the proposed customs union. It was at this stage that the Bank of England, acting unilaterally, granted a 50 million schilling credit to the Austrian National Bank for one week. 'The gesture was a rebuke to the French for mixing finance and politics.' London may have 'thrilled to this affirmation of Britain's financial power' but 'Norman had destroyed the carefully prepared French position ... a dangerous thing to do in view of London's reliance on Paris'.[17]

In the event, the British gesture was futile: foreign confidence in Austria's financial system was shattered. The failure of the Credit Anstalt led to a complete 'standstill' on all banking assets held in Austria, a development which precipitated a general scramble for liquidity in Europe. The German banking system was the first to be affected. In the first fortnight of June the Reichsbank lost RM 720 million (about £35 million), mostly to France and the USA. Despite President Hoover's offer on 20 June of a one-year moratorium on all reparations and war-debt payments, the Reichsbank was forced to implement drastic restrictive measures, including exchange controls, on 15 July. The American intervention had been greeted with a vast surge of relief but it foundered on the rocks of French prevarication and the spectacular failure on 3 July of the Nordwolle, one of Germany's largest industrial combines.[18]

With Germany in financial chaos the crisis spread rapidly to London, the one remaining European financial centre willing to grant untrammelled accommodation to short-term investors. In the second half of July, London lost £33 million in gold, and a further £33 million in foreign exchange, mainly to Paris. By the end of the month the Bank of England had thus lost one-quarter of its official reserves and had been obliged to raise Bank Rate in successive stages, from 2½ per cent on 23 July to 4½ per cent by 30 July.[19] Earlier in the month MacDonald had invited the American, French and German governments to send representatives to a conference in London on 20 July with the dual aim of providing Germany with a substantial loan and a once-for-all settlement of the reparations issue. With the German financial situation stabilised the Bank of England hoped that the release of £90 million worth of short-term assets locked up in Germany and a further £50 million frozen in Central Europe, would restore foreign confidence in London and ease the pressure on the reserve position. Once again, however, Britain was responsible for pursuing unrealistic policy objectives in relation to France. With little prospect of French acquiescence in a general reparations settlement There could be no international loan for Germany. As Skidelsky has observed:

Of the three centres from which Germany might conceivably obtain money, London was virtually out of action, New York was unwilling to act without the others and Paris demanded political guarantees, such as the abandonment of customs union, the 'pocket battleships' programme and any claims on Danzig. France, therefore, had only to insist on its political conditions ... to reduce the conference to a nullity.[20]

Paris was indeed the arbiter of the international financial system and French intransigence was to lead ineluctably to London's collapse.

On 1 August it was announced that the Bank of England was to receive credits totalling £50 million from the Bank of France and the Federal Reserve Bank of New York. Confidence in London was temporarily restored only for it to be completely destroyed when the full implications of the May Committee report, published on 31 July, were realised. The Commitee, which painted an excessively gloomy picture of London's financial position, forecast a budget deficit of £120 million and recommended cuts in public expenditure amounting to £97 million, including a 20 per cent reduction in the rate of unemployment benefit. Two weeks earlier, on 13 July, the report of the Macmillan Committee on Finance and Industry had been published and although it was basically an optimistic document the report drew attention to the large volume of London's short-term liabilities. The two reports taken together encouraged a resumption of the drain of gold, exacerbated by the mounting current payments deficit. In the absence of appropriate action it was clear that Britain would soon be forced off the gold standard.

The May Report was an atavistic document, 'a remorseless and highly political statement', which presented a Labour government especially with the critical choice of either meeting the demands of orthodoxy or resisting them and facing the inevitable consequences of parliamentary defeat.[21] It is unnecessary to examine in detail the government's response to the report.[22] All that needs to be noted is that after long and fruitless wranglings during which various courses of action were considered (including a reduction in payments to the Sinking Fund and the introduction of a revenue tariff), the Cabinet agreed to expenditure cuts amounting to £56 million. A substantial minority of the Cabinet, however, baulked on the issue of reducing the level of unemployment benefit by 10 per cent. For the opposition parties, the national press and foreign financial opinion this was the crux of the matter involving the entire financial credibility of the government. Indeed, the implementation of the expenditure cuts recommended in the May Report came to be the *sine qua non* of the receipt of further financial assistance from Paris and New York. On 24 August the government broke up over the Cabinet's failure to agree to cuts in the dole. MacDonald then formed a National Government dominated by the Conservatives but also including the Liberals and a few loyal colleagues from his previous administration. Snowden, who remained at the Exchequer, lost no time in introducing an emergency budget and an Economy Bill. The former increased direct and indirect taxation, reduced the provision for the Sinking Fund and provided for the funding of 5 per cent War Loan when circumstances permitted. The Economy Bill proposed expenditure cuts of £70 million to be obtained from cuts in the wages and salaries of government employees and a 10 per cent reduction in the standard rate of unemployment benefit.

As a result of the economy measures new foreign credits were obtained and the drain on London was halted once more. In little under a fortnight, however, it resumed and on Monday 21 September Britain formally abandoned the gold standard. Montagu Norman, who had left England in August on a cruise to recover from a breakdown in health received a cable on Sunday 20 September from Sir Ernest Harvey, his deputy at the Bank, and Sir Edward Peacock, the Bank's first Commonwealth director. His ship was one day out from Quebec on the return voyage. It read simply: 'Old Lady goes off on Monday.' Norman, thinking that this referred to his mother's holiday plans, disembarked at Liverpool, blissfully unaware that in his absence the gold standard had been abandoned.[23] In order to avoid the embarrassment which might follow from the new government's failure to achieve its principal object, ministers in succeeding weeks, and especially during the general election campaign during October, made extensive use of the arguments prepared by Hubert Henderson, Joint Secretary of the Economic Advisory Council. Henderson argued persuasively that

> ... if the pound had gone when there was a big deficit in the Budget an internal inflation would have been almost inevitable ...It is one thing to go off the gold standard with an unbalanced Budget and uncontrolled inflation; it is quite another to take this measure, not because of internal financial difficulties, but because of excessive withdrawals of borrowed capital.[24]

It is by no means coincidental that one of the most bizarre but impressive features of the election campaign was provided by MacDonald's speeches during which he brandished a fistful of worthless German bank notes as the ultimate justification for putting the economy through 'the purifying fires of deflation'.[25]

In defence of its handling of the economy it should be emphasised that there were a number of crucial limitations on the Labour government's freedom of action.[26] In the first instance, there was the inherited intellectual constraint on policy of neo-classical orthodoxy. This is well illustrated by the Treasury's reaction to Sir Oswald Mosley's recommendation for loan-financed public works as a cure for unemployment.[27] The views of Sir Richard Hopkins, set out for the benefit of Snowden for his use in Cabinet, are worth quoting at length:

> The programme he [Mosley] has borrowed first saw the light in a political brochure, but it was hatched in the study of an

economist – a political economist. Its object must surely be a rise in the price level to be secured by the outpouring of a flood of money. That is commonly called inflation. Vast Government loans are to be raised – at what rate of interest you will – and the proceeds are to be poured with breakneck speed into the hands of quarry owners, of road contractors and of the proprietors of businesses, limited in range, which supply the goods the Government will need in unexampled quantities. And thence the gain is to spread to the shopkeepers along the routes of the roads and to those other trades who supply the needs of the working population.

What is the use of it? ... How will it benefit any depressed export trade if prices rise in this country while they remain low elsewhere? There is no doubt that the plan can make prices rise. There is no doubt that it would in the process reduce real wages. There is not the smallest prospect that it will restore the industrial equilibrium. There is every ground to think it will disturb it still more.[28]

It would be difficult to find a single statement more representative than this of Treasury attitudes towards an expansionary financial policy. It only remains to be said that Hopkins's views fell on receptive ears: as indicated already, Snowden was a Chancellor in the Gladstonian tradition who saw his prime role as being to educate his Cabinet colleagues as to the realities of Britain's increasingly straitened financial circumstances.

In addition to the constraint posed by orthodoxy there were several 'ideological' barriers in the way of the government initiating an active policy for the relief of unemployment. First, there were the political limits imposed on direct state administration of a public works programme. These had been well expressed by Sir Warren Fisher in April 1929 (see above, p. 51). Secondly, there was 'the significance attached to the investing public's judgement of the worthwhileness or otherwise of state programmes'.[29] In effect the bias of the capital market in favour of orthodoxy augmented that of the Treasury in determining the goals of economic policy. Thirdly, there was the whole question of business confidence. This was a factor to which Hubert Henderson, Keynes's co-author of the electioneering pamphlet *Can Lloyd George Do It?*, attached increasing importance during Labour's period of office. What was the point in launching a £200 million national development programme when the alarm of the business and investing classes at the government's profligacy would 'serve to counter-act fully the employment benefits of the programme'? The Treasury would ultimately find itself in a vicious circle 'requiring a still bigger programme, still more unremunerative in character with an increasing hole in the Budget, and increasing apprehension until [the authorities] were faced with either abandoning the whole policy or facing a real panic-flight from the pound'.[30] A further ideological barrier to the government's freedom of manoeuvre was provided by its sustained adherence both to free trade and the gold standard. Somewhat ironically, the Labour government emerged as a staunch, if at times reluctant, defender of the liberal international order, resistant, under Snowden's influence, to tariffs in any form (the Chancellor believed that 'it was more honest to have a straight-forward cut in the standard of life than to proceed by the indirect [and repressive] route of raising the cost of living')[31] and identifying the national interest with the defence of the existing sterling parity. It is in this latter context that the government was confronted by an excruciating double dilemma which led inexorably to its downfall in August 1931. As Janeway has concluded:

> [the Government's] continuation in office could only be secured by what MacDonald himself termed 'the negation of everything that the Labour Party stood for', but loyalty to what 'the Labour Party stood for' could be maintained only by means of a demonstration that Labour was not responsible to govern in what the Cabinet had accepted to be the national interest – i.e. maintenance of the gold standard'.[32]

Whilst a decisive majority of the Cabinet accepted the need to balance the budget in the summer of 1931, the much smaller majority in favour of the 10 per cent cut in unemployment benefit was indicative of the government's inability to raise the sectoral working-class interest from which it ultimately derived its support into the 'true' national interest.[33]

The suspension of the gold standard and the coming to power of the National Government was followed by a transformation in certain aspects of economic policy. The most important development in the field of fiscal policy was the introduction of full-scale tariff protection under the Import Duties Act of February 1932. This was followed by the inauguration of a scheme of Imperial Preference, the result of negotiations at the Imperial Economic Conference held at Ottawa in the summer of the same year.[34] The motives for introducing the tariff were basically three-fold. By the autumn of 1931 Britain was one of the few countries which had refrained from enacting a comprehensive measure of tariff protection and with contracting levels of world trade the domestic market was open to foreign dumping, whilst the opportunities for invisible earnings were becoming increasingly restricted. Thus in the early discussions protection was regarded both as a necessary safeguard of the country's international payments position and a potential contributor to economic recovery based upon the domestic market. It also brought with it the opportunity to introduce Imperial Preference. Following Joseph Chamberlain's tariff reform campaign in the early years of the century, protection, combined with Imperial Preference, was of especial significance to the Conservative Party. It was fitting that it was Neville Chamberlain, Joseph's son and Chancellor of the Exchequer in the National Government, who pressed the case for the change in direction of commercial policy and with rare emotion introduced the Import Duties Bill into Parliament, thus enabling him to fulfil partially at least, the vision of his father.[35] Nevertheless, despite Chamberlain's key role, there is little evidence to suggest that the legislation of 1932 was part of an imperial vision – a conscious British strategy for survival in a period of international economic disintegration.[36] As Skidelsky has pointed out, 'If the British delegation to Ottawa had any philosophic position, it was to restore world trade as rapidly as possible. Lowering interimperial tariff barriers was seen as a step towards this eventual aim.'[37] Indeed, the Ottawa conference served to highlight the obstacles in the way of creating an imperial autarchic bloc. The Dominions and India (the latter received fiscal autonomy in 1917) were increasingly concerned to develop their own manufacturing industries, while Britain wished to protect its domestic agriculture. Hence, from the economic perspective, there was little community of interest and the situation was further complicated by the extensive and long-standing commercial relationships between Britain, the empire and third countries.[38] The British delegation was in fact outmanoeuvred at Ottawa. The value of British exports to the empire certainly increased after 1932 but this was far outweighed by the increase in the value of imports from the empire. It is true that the agreements provided the government with a bargaining weapon for the negotiation of bilateral trading arrangements with countries with which Britain had large unfavourable balances (for example, the Baltic countries and Argentina) but although twenty such aggreements were made between 1933 and 1938 their strictly local effects barely compensated for the loss of a multilateral trading system.[39] The Ottawa agreements were therefore of negligible advantage to the British economy in the 1930s: certainly they played no role in opening up the channels of international trade.[40]

The third motive for introducing tariff protection lay in the hope, implicit in the establishment of the Import Duties Advisory Committee endowed with powers to recommend higher duties for special goods, that the tariff could be used to induce the rationalisation of industry, especially of iron and steel and cotton. The organisation of both of these industries had been the subject of critical inquiry during Labour's period of office[41] but in the absence of state compulsion little had been achieved after 1929 in the way of further concentration of output.

It is with particular reference to the reorganisation of industry, especially in the context of tariff protection, that S. H. Beer has argued persuasively that 'Governmental decisions in [the thirties] endowed Britain with a pattern of economic policy that was comprehensive and radically different from that of previous generations'.[42] Most economic historians would question the validity of this view. It is undeniable that the National Government continued and accelerated the general postwar tendency towards greater state intervention in economic and industrial activity but it would be wrong to assume that the ultimate object was the creation of a *planned* or *managed* economy as these terms are currently understood.[43] In the case of coalmining, an industry which was subjected to an increasingly restrictive regime of statutory cartelisation (see below, pp. 76-7), its experience cannot be regarded as typical of that of other industrial sectors. In the strictest sense, the only directly comparable example is that of the iron and steel industry where the granting of a 33⅓ per cent duty on imports in 1932 was on the clear understanding that the industry itself would undertake the necessary reorganisation through the establishment of a central federation.[44] If this was far removed from statutory cartelisation then the treatment of the cotton industry serves even more to illustrate the exceptional nature of the government's policy in relation to coalmining. During the course of the 1930s the industry, heavily burdened by surplus productive capacity, tried every conceivable regulatory device, but when statutory assistance was eventually forthcoming under the reorganisation Acts of 1936 and 1939 it was too late to be of real benefit to the industry.[45]

The National Government was influenced even less in its attitude towards the restructuring of industry by the amorphous groupings of planners and corporatists – those protagonists of the 'middle way' to whom Arthur Marwick and more recently, L. P. Carpenter and Trevor Smith, have drawn attention.[46] The government's reaction to the demand for a measure of corporatist industrial planning was epitomised in the response of the President of the Board of Trade, Walter Runciman, to the proposal advanced by progressive Conservatives in the spring of 1935 for a general enabling Bill to permit industries to reorganise themselves with statutory authority to coerce recalcitrant minorities. After expressing some sympathy for proposals submitted to the Board of Trade by individual industries Runciman rejected the notion that industry could be reorganised 'by any one cut-and-dried method'. There could be no question of the government granting general statutory powers for the enforcement of reorganisation.[47] All that can be said on this issue of government intervention in industrial affairs is that under the pressure of rapidly changing economic conditions ministers were compelled, without reference to a set of guiding principles, to take successive *ad hoc* steps to help those industries and interests which were least able to cope with these conditions and whose immediate plight was the most serious for the country as a whole. In coalmining the extremity of the state's response was occasioned by uniquely disastrous labour relations in an industry which could claim to lie at the very heart of the industrial system.[48]

If the case for claiming that the National Government furthered the trend towards the creation of a consciously managed economy is weak in relation to the reorganisation of industry it is only fair to point out that Beer's thesis is of greater validity when applied to the evolution of macroeconomic policy. Here the principal developments concerned the management of sterling by means of the Exchange Equalisation Account and the inauguration of a cheap money policy.[49] Following the suspension of the gold standard the pound depreciated rapidly, reaching a low of $3·23 at the beginning of December 1931. This raised the whole question of the stabilisation of the currency and led to lengthy and detailed discussions within government as to the most appropriate exchange rate policy to adopt. Broadly speaking, two views emerged, one from within the Treasury and the other from the Bank of England. The Bank, ever mindful of the spectre of inflation and anxious to repay the American and French credits, favoured a relatively high rate of stabilisation for the pound and, for substantially the same reasons, was reluctant to permit too rapid a fall in the Bank Rate. The Treasury on the other hand, was intent on promoting economic recovery and also on safeguarding the government's budgetary position. It therefore desired cheap money (that is Bank Rate held to a level of less than 3 per cent) in order to stimulate internal reflation and also as a means of reducing the level of government expenditure by lowering the cost of servicing the national debt. A low exchange rate was preferred, again to stimulate reflation and as an aid to the recovery of exports. It was the view of the Treasury which ultimately prevailed.[50]

The cheap money policy was facilitated in part by the establishment of the Exchange Equalisation Account in April 1932. The main function of the Account was 'to reduce or eliminate temporary fluctuations in the exchange rate and to insulate the internal economy from the effects of capital and gold flows'.[51] As operated by the Treasury the Account utilised its holdings of Treasury Bills to offset the purchases and sales of sterling assets by owners of funds moving into and out of London. By these means the rate of exchange to be supported was successfully controlled throughout the remainder of the 1930s. Only a few days after the establishment of the Account, Bank Rate was reduced to 3 per cent.[52] By the end of June it had fallen to 2 per cent where it remained until August 1939. On 30 June the government announced its plans for the conversion of 5 per cent War Loan (1929–1947) to 3½ per cent War Loan (1952) as the second stage of its cheap money policy. The loan, amounting to £2,088 million represented 27 per cent of the national debt and 39 per cent of quoted British securities on the London Stock Exchange.[53] The operation was an outstanding success with all but 8 per cent being taken up. The resulting budgetary relief was reflected in a fall in the cost of servicing the national debt from £281·2 million in 1932 to £228·4 million in the following year.[54] Further conversion operations at even lower rates of interest were undertaken in 1934, 1935 and 1936, and by 1938 the cost of servicing the debt as a proportion of total government expenditure had fallen to 13·4 per cent from a figure of 24·7 per cent in 1932. The final component of the cheap money policy was the embargo on new capital issues imposed in the summer of 1933 in order to facilitate the War Debt conversion and also to help the balance of payments and protect the pound. Initially the embargo applied to both home and overseas issues but later in the year the restrictions were relaxed to the extent that only non-empire overseas lending was banned. By the end of 1933 Treasury officials no longer believed that a capital export embargo was necessary but the residual restriction remained in force for the rest of the decade.[55]

One interesting by-product of the abandonment of the gold standard was the emergence of the so-called 'sterling bloc' of countries after 1931. Of all the currency areas to emerge in the 1930s with the gradual demise of the gold standard the sterling bloc was the largest and most important. It comprised all of those countries with especially close trading and financial connections with the UK and for whom there were distinct economic advantages in retaining the bulk of their foreign reserves in the form of sterling and in maintaining their exchange rates steady in relation to the British currency.[56] Thus the bloc included most of the empire, several Middle East states, the Scandinavian countries, Argentina, Brazil and even Japan. As it operated before 1939 the bloc ensured substantial exchange rate stability and permitted a reasonable degree of free trade and capital movements for the member countries, all of these being of special importance in the restrictive trading conditions of the second interwar decade. It should be noted, however, that there is little evidence to suggest that the sterling bloc was a consciously planned development. It is true that a Prime Ministerial Committee on sterling policy reported in March 1932 that stable foreign exchanges within the bloc would aid interimperial trade and that sterling itself would acquire 'a greater measure of stability and strength relatively to gold standard countries', but it seems that these views were never discussed openly in Cabinet.[57] The importance of the sterling bloc is essentially retrospective and it is worth mentioning at this stage because its existence, in modified form, was to be of considerable assistance in strengthening Britain's vulnerable payments position during the Second World War and the decade immediately following. As it was, in the context of the 1930s the bloc together with the new tariff, Imperial Preference, bilateral trading agreements and the Exchange Equalisation Account, was entirely representative of the growing mood of economic nationalism which gripped the world after 1931.

It was not until 1936 that the first tentative step was taken to restore the international economy. This took the form of a Tripartite Monetary Agreement under which Britain, France and the USA agreed to maintain a limited form of exchange rate stability. From the British perspective it was of great significance that it was only one party to the agreement – the USA – which felt strong enough to link its currency to gold. The role of sterling as 'underwriter' of the international economic system was definitely at an end: that of the dollar had just begun.[58] This modest exercise in international monetary co-operation was then followed by the Anglo-American Trade Agreement of November 1938. Towards the end of the 1930s the USA had embarked upon a policy of increasing economic internationalism which was to be of the utmost significance in the development of Anglo-American relationships after 1939 (see below, pp. 85-7). According to the American Secretary of State, Cordell Hull, the 1938 agreement 'made major breaches in the preferential wall erected around the British Empire in 1932'.[59] As one observer has concluded, 'Britain's acceptance of it was dictated by the need to gain American support in the looming conflict with Germany. By these measures, Britain took the first tentative steps back to globalism, but this time as follower rather than leader'.[60]

In their survey of the work of the Economic Advisory Council and its successor, the Committee on Economic Information, Howson and Winch have shed valuable light on the evolution of economic ideas within the academic community and their dissemination within the Treasury during the 1930s. Their principal conclusion, based upon a close examination of the numerous reports prepared by the committee after 1932, is that 'by 1937 the macroeconomic position which we associate with Keynes's *General Theory* had altered the thinking of the most important policy-making civil servants in the Treasury' (see below, pp. 78-9).[61] Leading Treasury officials, such as Sir Richard Hopkins and Sir Frederick Phillips, were continuously exposed to a barrage of argument from the academic members of the committee, dominated by Keynes, Hubert Henderson and Dennis Robertson. Keynes, in particular, was unrelenting in pressing the case for counter-cyclical loan-financed public works and low long-term interest rates, and with increasing persuasiveness in the light of Richard Kahn's multiplier hypothesis together with his own evolving views on liquidity preference.[62] In the view of Sir Austen Robinson, the Treasury 'was effectively prevented from living in a private Ivory Tower of its own. It had to defend its policies with a jury of very competent and potentially vocal outside critics, and if it could not defend them it had to change them.' In retrospect the work of the Committee on Economic Information was a factor of decisive importance in explaining 'the apparent rapidity with which Britain moved over to being a highly managed economy on Keynesian lines after 1939'.[63] It is significant that Sir Richard Hopkins, a leading advocate of the orthodox 'Treasury View' in the years 1929–31 became convinced after 1940 of the validity of the analysis contained in Keynes's *General Theory* and played a major, possibly decisive, role in securing the commitment of the wartime Coalition Government to the expansionary principles embodied in the notable 1944 White Paper on *Employment Policy* (see below, p. 103).[64]

All of this would appear to lend some support to Beer's earlier quoted thesis concerning the emergence of the managed economy in Britain before 1939. But it is essential to remember that although the Committee on Economic Information was effective in moulding and transforming opinion within the civil service, and even then, predominantly after 1935 (see below, p. 78), it was far less successful at Cabinet level. From November 1931, following Snowden's appointment as Lord Privy Seal, until his assumption of the office of Prime Minister in May 1937, the position of Chancellor of the Exchequer was held by Neville Chamberlain. A highly capable administrator and the initiator of a number of important reforms in the social services when serving as Minister of Health in Baldwin's second Cabinet in the 1920s, in economic terms Chamberlain, like his predecessor, was cast very much in an orthodox mould. In his budget speech in 1933, following a campaign conducted in various organs of the press for loan-financed public works to promote economic recovery, Chamberlain responded with the following uncompromising statement:

> Look around the world today and you see that badly unbalanced Budgets are the rule rather than the exception. Everywhere there appear Budget deficits piling up, yet they do not produce those favourable results which it is claimed would happen to us. On the contrary, I find that Budget deficits repeated year after year may be accompanied by deepening recession and by a constantly falling price level.
> ... Of all the countries passing through these difficult times with the greatest success is the United Kingdom ... We owe our freedom from [the fear that things are going to get worse] to the fact that we have balanced our Budget.[65]

At first sight this statement is vacuous and obtuse in the extreme, being based upon narrow budgetary considerations and a no longer valid preference for fiscal righteousness, in the light of the abandonment of the gold standard and the debt conversion operation. There is, however, a case for claiming that the Treasury's budgetary policy before 1935 can be explained by rational and, indeed, by the standards of the time, realistic considerations. In the first instance, there were significant political and economic barriers in the way of a break-out from the restrictions imposed by fiscal orthodoxy. The Labour government's freedom of manoeuvre had been severely restricted by them (see below, pp. 63-5) and they continued to carry weight into the 1930s. Given the small scale of the British government's budget and the dangers of serious payments deficits, an expansionary fiscal policy would undoubtedly have required a considerable growth in the level of public expenditure associated with the kind of state control over economic life which only proved to be acceptable to Britain's political and industrial establishment during the Second World War. Another limitation on Treasury fiscal policy was provided by the perceived need to maintain 'confidence' in the basic solvency of the state. This, after all, had been the fundamental issue at the centre of the 1931 crisis. In the absence of a firm commitment to balanced budgets a conservative business and financial community would have become increasingly pessimistic about future economic prospects with the added danger that the use of sterling as 'a great medium of international exchange' might be jeopardised.[66] Finally, in comparing Britain's experience in the 1930s with that of such countries as Germany and the USA where fiscal orthodoxy was abandoned, either for reasons of expediency, as in the latter, or as the deliberate result of government policy as in the former, the one factor which stands out is the 'comparative mildness' of the depression in Britain, together with the relative strength of the upswing in the level of economic activity after 1932.[67] Unemployment, though severe by historical standards was heavily localised, being concentrated in the staple export industries of south Wales, the north of England and the central lowlands of Scotland, all of these areas being well away from London, the centre of economic decision-making. The overall unemployment percentage never reached the levels of Germany and the USA, or for that matter of Sweden, Australia and Canada. In marked contrast to the experience in Germany and the USA, Britain's economic institutions remained intact and the unemployed, even after the cuts in the dole in 1931, were cushioned by a relatively expensive and comprehensive system of unemployment benefit. In the absence of any understanding of the income-generating effects of deficit financing, the need for a charitable public works programme was thereby diminished.[68]

Britain's economic recovery in the 1930s has in recent years been the subject of intense academic debate. In the present context the most interesting aspect of this particular controversy is that it has served to draw attention to the paradoxical nature of the development of the interwar economy. The debate began in the early 1960s when H. W. Richardson sought to refute the existing view that the contribution of the 'new' industries to Britain's economic growth after 1929 was of limited importance.[69] After drawing attention to their sustained technological precocity and advances in organisational structure, Richardson subsequently expanded his thesis to claim that the 'new' industries as a separate and distinct 'development block' in the economy, and with their continuing positive net investment throughout the depression years of 1929–32, were an 'important recovery-inducing force'. In this light, therefore, they should take their place alongside the housebuilding boom of the early 1930s to provide a broad-enough base to carry general economic recovery. Fundamental to the Richardson thesis is the view that since Britain had failed to participate fully in the cyclical upswing of the late 1920s, there had been no serious overbuilding of capacity. When real incomes began to rise after 1929 in response to a massive improvement in the terms of trade arising from the decline in the price of many imported primary products, consumer purchasing power, especially for those in work, was maintained. Business expectations, therefore, remained buoyant and with the boost to confidence provided by the advent of the National Government with its commitments to budget orthodoxy and the tariff, the 'new' industries not only helped to provide a vital springboard for an early and sustained economic revival, but also had an increasingly favourable impact on the structural balance of the economy as resources were reallocated away from the depressed staple trades. Thus, Britain's experience was in marked contrast to that of the USA after 1929 when business confidence was shattered in the aftermath of a catastrophic decline in the index of industrial production – partly the result of market saturation for many consumer durable goods after 1925 and the consequent exhaustion of favourable investment opportunities.

As with many new hypotheses, especially one which seriously questions an earlier, widely accepted interpretation, it was perhaps inevitable that it should, after time, be subjected to critical appraisal. In general terms, Richardson's views have been criticised on three grounds. First, it has been argued that the 'new' industries as a distinct sector within the economy were too insignificant to be an important initiator of economic recovery. At most they played a supporting role of rather limited importance.[70] With the single exception of motor vehicles all of the 'new' industries, as defined by Richardson, were disinvesting by 1932 and 'in the crucial recovery period of 1932–1934 [the 'new' industries] accounted for, at most in any one year, 3½ per cent of the total net investment undertaken and for 7 per cent of total employment. It would seem improbable that recovery on the scale apparent after 1932 could be assigned to a sector with such relatively insignificant factor shares as these.'[71] In this respect a further criticism of the Richardson hypothesis is that as far as structural change is concerned the rate at which productive factors were being transferred from the staple trades to the 'new' industries was no more rapid after 1930 than in the first interwar decade.[72] Indeed, as Richardson himself was forced to concede in his final contribution to the debate, the process of resource reallocation in favour of the new sectors of the economy slowed down during the years 1929–32.[73] There is, too, the fact that by the end of the 1930s, after a further decade of reasonably rapid economic growth based upon the expansion of the domestic market, the staple industries, as indicated by their factor shares, continued to bulk large in the economy.[74] Thus, in 1937, three of the most important of the 'new' industries, motor vehicles, electrical engineering and rayon and silk, accounted for 9·7 per cent of the capital stock of manufacturing industry, while cotton textiles alone, after two decades of almost continual decline, still accounted for 8·4 per cent.[75] Furthermore, there must be real doubts concerning the usefulness of the distinction between 'old' and 'new' industries.[76] While it is certainly true that the overall level of labour productivity (defined as output-per-man-year of employment) rose faster in the 1930s as compared with the previous decade, the variations between individual industries, both 'old' and 'new', was considerable. Most of Richardson's 'new' industries performed well in terms of productivity growth in the 1930s, but equally impressive achievements were recorded in agriculture, textiles and iron and steel. Finally, there is the danger, inherent in the approach of Richardson and his fellow 'optimists', Aldcroft and Sayers, of defining industries solely in terms of technical innovation with relatively little attention being paid to organisational and managerial standards.[77] Whilst it should be stressed that the evidence at present available is by no means extensive it would appear that the 'new' industries in general were subject to a number of the weaknesses which had characterised the staple trades in the pre-1914 period. In the sphere of marketing, examples of severe deficiencies can be quoted in such industries as rayon and aero engines.[78] But perhaps the most outstanding area of weakness is provided by the motor vehicle industry where 'in 1937 the six leading British producers, making roughly 350,000 private cars, turned out more than forty different engine types and an even greater number of chassis and body models, which was considerably more than the number offered by the three leading producers in the United States, making perhaps 3,500,000 cars'.[79] It may well be that the creation of deliberate market imperfections was an attempt to protect sales in a highly competitive situation but, as the industry's recent historians have concluded, 'The

solution to the problem of retaining a continuously successful model,
let alone of a composite range of market leaders eluded ... all [of the
motor manufacturers]' in the 1930s.[80] As for organisational standards,
once again Britain lagged noticeably behind the USA. Despite the
evidence unearthed by Hannah concerning the extent of managerial
innovation in the interwar period it remains true that there were only
two British companies, ICI and Unilever, which developed a relatively
advanced multidivisional structure on the lines of the American
General Motors and Du Pont companies as a solution to the
managerial problems posed by large-scale organisation.[81] In the
matter of labour relations Alford has maintained that the 'new'
industries, despite their technical advances, inherited many of the
deficiencies of the staple trades, with their demarcation problems and
restrictive labour practices. It is arguable that the motor vehicle
industry again provides the classic example in this respect: it was in the
interwar period that the post-1945 pattern of labour relations was
established with its multiplicity of unions and all the attendant
disadvantages associated with demarcation and wage differentials.[82]

After taking account of the most recent work on the economy in the
1930s the modest conclusion which emerges is that recovery was
initiated by a boom in housebuilding which got underway in the final
quarter of 1932 and which was sustained until the spring of 1937. This
was augmented after 1933 by an increase in investment in the 'new'
industries and, it should be stressed, the beginnings of revival in the
staple trades, especially iron and steel.[83] It was predominantly a home
market recovery: the volume of exports never reached the level of
1929 (the peak for the interwar period) before the outbreak of war and
whilst the Imperial Preference system continued to feature, superficially at least, as an important plank in the economic programme of
the National Government, it is worth re-emphasising that it merely
served to divert trade from one channel to another without increasing
the overall total.

A number of explanations have been advanced for the housebuilding boom. The key factor was undoubtedly the inauguration of
the Treasury's cheap money policy which was in turn facilitated by
the depreciation of sterling and the introduction of the tariff.[84] Other
important elements were the rise in real incomes for those in work
combined with a marked fall, after 1930, in building costs. To the
extent that the boom went some way towards improving the quality of
life for a significant section of the population it was a welcome
development. In economic terms, however, it was something of a
mixed blessing. On the one hand, it would be fair comment to say that
the building industry acted as a valuable stabilising force in the
economy, especially in the years of acute depression in 1930–2.
Thereafter its considerable expansion generated significant multiplier

effects, backwards towards the supply of building materials, and forwards towards many of the 'new' industries involved in the production of consumer durable goods.[85] On the debit side the industry experienced one of the highest rates of growth in employment in the interwar period and in so far as the level of labour productivity was relatively low, the expansion in employment helped to retard the movement of labour into higher productivity sectors.[86] Furthermore, it is arguable that the building boom had long-term disadvantages for the future growth and structure of the economy. Since the bulk of building activity was concentrated in the southern half of England, particularly in the Home Counties areas, there is a case for saying that the boom was partly responsible for the emergence after 1945 of the diseconomies of congestion in certain areas of the UK.

In some respects the service and distribution sector was comparable to housebuilding in its impact on the economy. As a group the service trades accounted for the major part of the increase in employment after 1920.[87] They therefore acted in a similar way to the building industry as a stabilising force in the economy when the level of industrial employment was subject to dramatic fluctuations. But the one thing that stands out in the performance of this sector is that its contribution to economic growth was extremely modest. It has indeed been suggested that the service trades as a whole were subject to a considerable degree of labour underemployment.[88] Certainly, they were the only major industrial sector to experience a continually declining level of labour productivity (taking the years 1924–37).[89]

Another distinctive feature of the interwar economy was the growth of imperfect competition in British industry. This is a subject on which it is impossible to generalise. Hannah's work on the rise of corporate enterprise, whilst adopting an 'agnostic' approach on its contribution to economic growth and welfare, has nevertheless presented a cogent case for the existence of a strong positive correlation between the growth in the size of enterprise and the achievement of economies of scale, expecially in those industries involved in mass-production technology.[90] But there is another side to this question which is of special relevance to the 1930s and this concerns the movement in favour of restrictive trading agreements in numerous British industries. Such agreements varied from the loosest form of trade association as in the grocery and stationery trades to the statutorily backed cartel form of organisation as in coalmining.[91] The latter does indeed provide a classic example of the dilemma confronting interwar governments in dealing with the problems of the declining industries. Accepting the need for increased efficiency and profitability and recognising the existence of surplus productive capacity should the state compel some measure of reorganisation but, at the same time, leave the industry to its own devices and the play of market forces in both national and international coal markets? Alternatively, taking into account the bitter history of labour relations in this industry, combined with the high levels of unemployment in mining districts, should the state intervene in order to preserve the existing structure of the industry by the granting of monopolistic powers?[92] As is well known the Coal Mines Act of 1930 was an attempt to seize both horns of the dilemma: Part I of the Act established a statutory cartel system while under Part II a Coal Mines Reorganisation Commission was created with statutory powers to compel the amalgamation of colliery undertakings.[93] The Act of 1930 was a remarkable piece of legislation not only because the two major objectives – the drive for efficiency and the maintenance of employment levels – were mutually inconsistent but also because, as noted above (see p. 67) it was an important element in the secular trend towards greater state intervention in industrial affairs. The significance of the experience in coalmining in the present context is that until the later 1930s there was a conflict within government as to the choice of appropriate policy objectives. Should amalgamations be imposed on the industry at the expense of employment or should the cartel system be strengthened to the detriment of further industrial concentration? In the event, the latter policy prevailed and to the extent that Part I of the Coal Mines Act slowed down the ongoing process of structural adjustment the rate of growth of the economy as a whole was adversely affected.

The coalmining industry thus provides an early example of the acute difficulties which have confronted postwar British governments in coming to terms with the secular (and occasionally precipitate) decline of major industrial sectors. That the elimination of surplus productive capacity should have received low priority is hardly surprising. With an average rate of unemployment in coalmining of 25 per cent for the 1930s as a whole and with a commensurate level of social distress it would be unreasonable to have expected the National Government of the 1930s to pursue any other but an ultra-defensive policy. Yet even here it is impossible to arrive at a firm conclusion: Hannah in his agnosticism would point to the fact that cartelisation helped to improve profit margins in a period of great trading difficulty and thereby provided some of the necessary resources to sustain further substantial mechanisation. There is also the question of the extent to which those industries burdened by overcapacity would have benefited more from exposure to the full blast of market forces or from collective schemes for the reduction of capacity. It is true that in the case of the shipbuilding industry, the National Shipbuilders Security Ltd, with its indiscriminate and ill-considered approach, was hardly a shining example of rationalisation but, as Hannah has pointed out, in the case of cotton spinning 'the financially weak firms were often those which had suffered from speculative company promotions and not necessarily those with uneconomic equipment; in this industry, therefore, the competitive process working through bankruptcy might have had adverse effects on overall productive efficiency, had it not been tempered by planned scrapping of the uneconomic equipment'.[94]

Viewed as a distinctive era in British economic history it is possible to conclude that the interwar years constituted a period of transition, first, in terms of the evolution of government economic policy, secondly as regards the structure of the domestic economy, and thirdly for Britain's role in the international economy. The increased role of the state in industrial and economic life generally can be illustrated by numerous examples. It is only necessary to point to the enforced amalgamation of the railway companies in 1922, the creation of the Central Electricity Board in 1926, the London Passenger Transport Board in 1933 and the British Overseas Airways Corporation in 1939, the passing of the Special Areas legislation in 1934, the cartelisation of coalmining and agriculture, and the intervention in the internal affairs of the iron and steel and cotton textile industries. Most, if not all, of these developments may have been *'ad hoc* and somewhat unrelated responses to immediate difficulties',[95] but this merely serves to underline the point that it was the 'mixed' rather than the 'managed' economy which had emerged by 1939.[96] There was also a transformation at governmental level in attitudes towards the running of the economy. It is instructive, for example, to note the reactions of leading Treasury officials to the fears expressed in 1937 by the Committee on Economic Information as to the damaging economic consequences which would follow on from the fading out of the domestic boom which had been underway since 1932. The economists on the committee, notably Keynes and Dennis Robertson, unhesitatingly advanced proposals for counter-cyclical regulation of public works. The response of Neville Chamberlain as Chancellor was to appoint a Committee on Public Capital Expenditure chaired by Treasury Under-Secretary Sir Frederick Phillips. Unsurprisingly, in view of the fact that Phillips was a notable convert to the views of Keynes (having read and digested the *General Theory* on its publication a year earlier), this committee recommended that public works projects unconnected with the rearmament programme should be held in abeyance with a view to their immediate implementation as soon as the economy began to sink into recession. Attention was concentrated on the Ministry of Health which was in a key position to influence the spending policies of the local authorities in England and Wales.[97] At the end of 1937, as the economy began to be adversely affected by recession in the USA and as fears mounted over the dual possibility of a cutback in the rate of housebuilding and the curtailment of rearmament expenditure, the Phillips Commitee succeeded in persuading the Chancellor (now Sir John Simon) to press the Cabinet to authorise the immediate issue of a circular by the Minister of Health requesting local authorities to prepare building programmes to be carried out in the next five years. The circular was not sent out until May 1938 due to the 'generally lukewarm reaction' of ministers but this was undoubtedly 'a great advance on anything which had been done before. There is reason to believe that it caused many local authorities to draw up long-term programmes who had never dreamed of doing so before. Some even ... gave ... serious thought to the question of works which fell outside their normal programme.'[98] The programme was never in fact implemented due to the exigencies of rearmament financing but this episode is illustrative of the erosion of the belief in financial orthodoxy at governmental level in the years immediately before the outbreak of war.

On the question of the structure of the economy, a balanced view would indicate that the interwar period witnessed a slow but continual movement away from the old staple trades towards the tertiary sector of services and distribution and the so-called 'new' industries with their capital-intensive, mass-production technology and bias towards the domestic market. Thus, after 1919, a number of the structural deficiencies of the late Victorian economy were being remedied, aided by the collapse of traditional export markets and rising living standards for those fortunate enough to remain in work. It was in the interwar period, and the 1930s in particular, that many of the typical features of modern British society began to appear – the considerable expansion in the number of motor vehicles both public and private, the introduction of an increasingly wide range of household electrical appliances, the phenomenal expansion in the number of radio licences and the beginnings of television broadcasting, the innovation of the man-made fibres industry and other dramatic advances in industrial chemicals. The 'new' industries may have been of limited importance in initiating recovery but their continued growth in the 1930s, building upon the achievements of the previous decade, was of vital importance to the health of the economy in the long term. Such developments did not go unnoticed by contemporaries. The best illustration of this is provided by J. B.Priestley's *English Journey*, published in 1934, a work which described in vivid terms the emergence of 'twentieth century England ... the England of the bustling home counties, of by-passes and the housing estates and suburban villas and cocktail bars gleaming with chromium trim'.[99] There was, of course, another side to the Britain of the 1930s – the Britain of the dole, comprising the north of England, west-central Scotland, south Wales and parts of north Wales. It has been sensitively portrayed by Mowat:

This sad unemployed Britain was only dimly known to many in the comfortable classes in the south, though it could be seen anywhere in London and in the back streets of the larger towns; nor could anyone long miss the seedy beggars selling matches or shoe laces, or the Welsh miners, with mufflers round their throats, singing 'Land of our Fathers' by the kerbside. The stricken areas were, however, a land apart: much written of but seldom visited by outsiders, save for the devoted social workers and the thoughtful undergraduates who played the Good Samaritan in the community centres and club houses. The Welsh mining valleys were numb with distress. Industrial Lancashire was at a standstill, though not officially classified as a special area. In Wigan one man in three was on the dole. The mining villages of county Durham, the steelworks and shipyards of Tyne and Tees were derelict: Gateshead, Hebburn, Jarrow, Wallsend, Crook. Of Stockton-on-Tees Priestley wrote 'the real town is finished. It is like a theatre that is kept open merely for the sale of drinks in the bars and chocolates in the corridors.' So it was in West Cumberland. So it was in Scotland: in Glasgow perhaps half the population was unemployed.[100]

It is therefore the crushing burden of unemployment, the appalling manifestation of underutilised capacity in the economy, which justifies a pessimistic conclusion on the economic achievements of interwar Britain. Although there is, as has been noted, indisputable evidence of a fundamental change in attitudes concerning unemployment policy in the final years before the war, in the absence of rearmament expenditure after 1936 unemployment in Britain might well have risen to 3 million during the recession of 1937–8. 'The depression would thus have become more severe than that of 1932 and presumably have been increased in length too.'[101] It is this sobering possibility which serves to underline the limited foundations of economic recovery in the 1930s.

Finally, the interwar period marked the passing of Britain's international economic hegemony. America had emerged from the First World War as the world's strongest economic power and in attempting to re-establish London as the premier international financial centre in the 1920s the British authorities were forced to pay constant attention to the economic policy of the USA and the condition of its domestic economy. This was reflected in the fact that from the early postwar years onwards Montagu Norman established the closest working relationship with Benjamin Strong, Governor of the Federal Reserve Bank of New York.[102] It was also highly significant that the two reparations inquiries of the 1920s – the Dawes and Young Committees – were chaired not by British nor indeed by Continental, but by American financiers. In 1931, following the abandonment of the gold standard, sterling finally ceased to be the world's key currency and it was in 1936, with the signing of the Tripartite Agreement that this role was taken over by the USA. From 1931 onwards, Britain was, in effect, an international economic power of the second rank: after 1945 it was unfortunate that the psychological legacy of a century of dominance was to take so long to disappear.

4

The Second World War and Its Aftermath: the Bankrupt State

The impact of the Second World War on the British economy was profound. The war effort, which was far more all-embracing than that of the First World War, imposed tremendous current and future burdens on the economy. The most serious legacy was the deterioration in the external position. Between the outbreak of war and the end of 1945 the cumulative current account deficit amounted to approximately £10,000 million (see Table 7, p. 143). To finance this deficit (and a £100 million rise in gold and foreign exchange reserves) Britain had received £5,400 million in lend-lease supplies and mutual aid from the USA and Canada respectively, sold £1,000 million of some of the most lucrative prewar foreign investments, requisitioned £100 million of private gold and dollar balances, and increased the volume of short-term overseas liabilities (denominated principally in sterling) by a massive £3,700 million.[1] On the domestic side the position was hardly better. To the losses sustained on external account had to be added the costs of internal disinvestment amounting to £3,100 million. Combining this with the former, approximate calculations carried out by the Treasury indicated that by the end of 1945 one-quarter of the country's prewar wealth had been liquidated as a direct consequence of Britain's commitment to the Allied war effort.[2]

The magnitude of the postwar task confronting the British economy was immense. Industry had to be reconverted to peacetime needs, physical damage repaired and new resources made available to compensate for wartime disinvestment and lack of maintenance of plant and equipment. If official wartime pledges on the creation of a welfare state and the maintenance of full employment were to be redeemed this would impose additional burdens on the country's limited resources over and above those arising from the minimum task of restoring living standards to their prewar level. If Britain was to begin to pay its way in the postwar world and meet the demands of reconstruction this would require a sustained expansion in the volume of exports, possibly as high as 75 per cent above the level of 1938. On the most optimistic view possible such an increase could not be achieved in less than three years. According to Treasury estimates in 1945 external equilibrium might be reached in 1951 but by then the cumulative adverse balance could be as high as £1,250 million (see Table 8, p. 144).[3] To meet this situation two alternative courses of action were available. First, the authorities could introduce a programme of severe external and internal retrenchment in order to reduce the size of the prospective deficit.[4] Overseas government expenditure could be reduced to a level consistent with the limited resources available, while the rationing and economic control systems inherited from the war could be intensified. In particular, the authorities could retain the policy of strict exchange control and trade discrimination. Alternatively, some form of transitional financial aid might be obtained from the USA, either in the form of an outright grant, or a loan, with or without interest, and with the minimum of strings attached. Dollar assistance would facilitate both the restoration of living standards and domestic reconstruction and also, in aiding the revival of exports, alleviate the pressure on the balance of payments.[5] In the event, the authorities opted for the latter policy, a decision which was bitterly controversial at the time and which has been the subject of debate ever since. To critics of the American loan negotiated by Lord Keynes in the autumn of 1945 its size was excessive in relation to British needs, its terms onerous and the conditions attached detrimental to essential British interests. In short, the settlement was an 'economic Munich' and the British Empire had been sold down the river for 'a pack of cigarettes'.[6]

Superficially, it would appear that the decision to seek a substantial dollar loan was forced on the authorities by circumstances beyond their control. British planning for the postwar years had been based upon the assumption that following the end of the war in Europe Britain would continue to receive lend-lease assistance from the USA until the defeat of Japan. Since it was expected that the war in the Pacific would continue for at least eighteen months after the surrender of Germany it seemed reasonable to suppose that during this transitional stage the gradual rundown of the British war effort, combined with the continuing receipt of lend-lease aid, albeit on a reduced scale, would permit domestic reconstruction to proceed and would also facilitate the revival of Britain's export trade. In this way it was envisaged that the need for further American financial aid would be minimised. Such views were certainly canvassed in the wartime Treasury, but by the spring of 1945 – before the defeat of Germany – discussions had already begun concerning the desirability of dollar assistance from the USA, independent of the continuation of lend-lease. Whilst it is true that these internal discussions had yet to be resolved at the time of Japan's sudden capitulation in August 1945 there can be little doubt that the authorities had already decided to seek substantial dollar assistance before the end of the Far Eastern War.[7]

Why did the authorities reject the policy of retrenchment and autarchy – 'starvation corner' as Keynes termed it?[8] The reasons were perhaps fourfold and were based upon both internal and external considerations. In the first instance it was felt that an intensification of domestic retrenchment would not be acceptable to public opinion. After six years of war during which the civilian population had been subjected to the rigours of rationing and extreme austerity, some easement of living standards was expected. In the circumstances of late 1945, following the election of a Labour government with a popular mandate to implement the wartime pledge on social reform, it would have been impossible to secure the nation's willing co-operation in a further round of belt-tightening. Secondly, there was a general awareness at governmental level of the massive cost of the war to Britain in purely economic terms: the scale of necessary reconversion and reconstruction together with the Treasury's estimates of the prospective balance-of-payments deficit (see Table 8, p. 144), cried out for external assistance. Thirdly, Britain emerged from the war with its status as a world power intact: to fulfil its international responsibilities, both in Europe and elsewhere – the costs of military occupation in Germany and the maintenance of a military presence in Greece and the Middle East – Britain required American financial aid. Finally, and most important of all, to intensify the wartime system of trade discrimination and exchange controls in an effort to 'go it alone' would be to invite economic warfare with the USA by departing from obligations entered into with the Roosevelt administration during the war concerning the peacetime restoration of the international economy. In the immediate aftermath of the war, Britain simply could not afford an open breach in Anglo-American economic relations. If the avoidance of 'starvation corner' required adherence to American views on the virtues of multilateralism in international trade and payments, this was a price which Britain could not refuse to pay. The difficulty was that although the British authorities, following the advice of Keynes and other academics in government employment, had come to accept the inevitability, if not the desirability, of multilaterialism, the wartime dependent relationship between Britain and America had placed considerable obstacles in the way of British adherence to a multilateral regime in trade and payments. Indeed, it was their recognition of this situation which provided much of the justification for postwar commercial bilateralism and exchange controls on the part of those who opposed both the terms of the

American loan and a return to nineteenth–century *laissez-faire* in international economic relationships.

It is one of the paradoxes of the Anglo-American alliance that whilst the two countries achieved an unparalleled degree of military collaboration the underlying political relationship was by no means harmonious. Throughout the war the American view of its ally was bedevilled by suspicions of its war aims and also by the belief that the British Empire constituted a threat to American power and prestige.[9] These antagonisms also found reflection in the economic sphere and played an important role in determining American attitudes towards British claims for financial and material assistance. What Churchill described as 'the most unsordid act' in history – the supply by the USA, under the lend-lease legislation of March 1941, of all materials necessary to sustain Britain's war effort – carried with it a number of restrictive and disadvantageous conditions which were to be a constant source of friction until the end of the war. It was not until 1943–4 that lend-lease supplies began to have a substantial logistical impact and in the meantime Britain was required to liquidate its remaining dollar holdings, sell off important capital assets in the USA at inconsiderable prices in relation to their real value, severely limit the level of its gold reserves and refrain, as far as possible, from exporting any goods incorporating lend-lease supplies.[10] All of these requirements inevitably tended to weaken Britain's long-term international position. The country's export trade was bound to suffer a severe decline in the circumstances of total war but, as the official historian of financial policy has pointed out, the British government's strict undertaking to prohibit exports containing lend-lease materials 'was very serious in its rupture of long standing connections, especially in South America, and in the difficulties imposed on the days when British traders would have to pick up the strands'.[11] Similarly, the continuing limitations placed on the size of Britain's gold and dollar reserves was a potential source of economic weakness to a country with considerable international financial obligations and heavily dependent on foreign trade and commerce. Quite apart from the necessity for 'a reasonable working balance' to finance the prospective postwar import surplus, the British authorities sought to ease the reserve position for two additional reasons. The first stemmed from Britain's role as banker to the group of countries, mainly, though not exclusively, within the empire which in 1939 had joined together to form the Sterling Area. The Area, which was a logical development of the sterling bloc of the 1930s (see above, pp. 69-70) was a system of exchange control and discrimination of which the most important part was the central reserve – the dollar pool into which all belligerent members of the Area paid in their gold and dollar earnings. In supplementing the aid derived from lend-lease the controls instituted by these formal arrangements were of vital importance to the British war effort.[12] The existence of the Sterling Area and London's role as central banker by itself required the maintenance of an adequate reserve position for, in return for the surrender of their dollar earnings, the overseas members of the Area acquired steadily mounting holdings of sterling. This was not, however, the only source of Britain's sterling indebtedness. It also arose from the normal sale of goods to Britain on the part of such countries as Brazil and Argentina, the transfer of gold to Britain by several of the Western European governments in exile, and more especially from the expenditure of empire troops stationed in the Middle East and India. By mid-1945 the grand total of Britain's sterling liabilities stood at £3,355 million. The balance accruing to the Sterling Area amounted to £2,723 million and to India alone, £1,321 million, the latter figure reflecting not just the cost of Indian defence but also the increase in the money cost of war expenditures due to inflation.[13] From the British viewpoint it was essential that adequate reserves should be held against these liabilities as a guarantee of London's creditworthiness. Unfortunately, as Britain's reserves began to expand significantly from the summer of 1943 as a result of American troop expenditures in Britain itself,[14] the United States Office of Lend Lease Administration began to make compensating reductions in lend-lease allocations and also to demand increased reciprocal aid from Britain.[15]

The question remains as to why the USA should impose these conditions on its closest ally, conditions which were at no time applied to the USSR which was also in receipt of substantial lend-lease aid. There were three principal reasons. First, the American administration betrayed every sign of failing to comprehend the economic basis of the Sterling Area – in particular, Britain's role as banker – and the special problems posed by the sterling balances. Since the balances were 'all in the family' there was, in the American view, no need to hold a gold reserve against them, and even when the case for an expansion of British reserves was accepted, the total was to be held within the range $600-1,000 million even though the volume of balances was rising rapidly.[16] The second factor encouraging American rigidity has already been indicated. As British officials found to their cost it was possible to persuade the American administration of the exhaustion of British reserves and the necessity for some easement in the reserve position but this did not always apply to the American public and its representatives in Congress who in general terms remained suspicious and distrustful of Britain in the belief that the country was not so impoverished that it required subsidisation at the expense of the US taxpayer. There can be little doubt that the need to take account of domestic public opinion was a factor of considerable importance in determining the American negotiating position over the level of British reserves and the scale of lend-lease assistance.[17] It also found reflection in the master lend-lease agreement itself. Article VII of the Mutual Aid Agreement of February 1942 stated that the final lend-lease settlement would

> include provision for agreed action by the United States of America and the United Kingdom, open to participation by all other countries of like mind, directed to the expansion by appropriate international and domestic measures, of production, employment, and the exchange and consumption of goods ... to the elimination of all forms of discriminatory treatment in international commerce, and to the reduction of tariffs and other trade barriers.[18]

What this appeared to mean was that in consideration for being let off the repayment of lend-lease goods Britain has agreed to eliminate the Imperial Preference system and hence permit American commercial penetration of the empire.[19] To the American Secretary of State, Cordell Hull, this was a cardinal principle of foreign economic policy. The 'consideration', as it came to be known, was thus a means of reconciling hostile domestic opinion to the decision of the administration to forgo payment for lend-lease supplies. The opening up of the British Empire was not, however, the sole aim of the State Department. As Hull himself subsequently commented:

> To me, unhampered trade dovetailed with peace; high tariffs, trade barriers, and unfair economic competition, with war. Though realizing that many other factors were involved, I reasoned that if we could get a freer flow of trade – freer in the sense of fewer discriminations and obstructions – so that one country would not be deadly jealous of another and the living standards of all countries might rise, thereby eliminating the economic dissatisfaction that breeds war, we might have a reasonable chance for lasting peace.[20]

The economic nationalism of the interwar years, of which the Imperial Preference system was a prime manifestation, had been a principal cause of the war. Hull, like Keynes before him, was convinced that one of the most important failures in the post-1918 peacemaking process had been the total neglect of the economic basis of a durable peace. Thus, for the State Department commercial advantage was to be tempered by political idealism.

On the British side the response to the Mutual Aid Agreement was mixed. It may have been 'good news that Britain might be able to get quit of all lend-lease obligations in return for a declaration of policy',[21] but the way in which Article VII was phrased caused misgivings among the numerous supporters in official circles of the Imperial Preference system. The position has been well summarised by Harrod:

> ... some resented the idea on sentimental grounds that we should be asked to abrogate this valuable symbol of Commonwealth and Empire unity. Others, who were reasonable men, held that Britain faced with appalling prospects on her trade balance after the War through the loss of her overseas investments could not afford to abandon any device that might assist her to retain or enlarge her export trade. Such motives were honourable and not fundamentally inconsistent with what the State Department had in mind. Most of those who held such opinions would not have deemed it a wise long-run policy to push the system of Imperial Preference further and build up a self-supporting Empire bloc. But there was a small minority which did hold this view; and these were the real enemies of the State Department doctrine.[22]

In recognition of these internal difficulties President Roosevelt went out of his way to emphasise that the working of Article VII did not mean that there was to be a trade-off between Imperial Preference and lend-lease. As far as the Americans were concerned discussions on the elimination of discrimination would take place in the context of world economic reconstruction as a whole and even then the British position would be determined 'in the light of governing economic conditions'.[23] On the basis of these assurances the British government signed the Mutual Aid Agreement. It is important to note, however, that despite Roosevelt's qualification of the Article VII conditions Britain had implicitly accepted certain limitations on its freedom of action.[24] The two countries had accepted the principle of multilateralism and Britain had undertaken to engage in negotiations on the related issues of trade and currency controls. From the perspective of those ministers and officials in Britain who wished to respond positively to the American conception, the fundamental problem centred on the restoration of a liberal international economic system endowed with sufficient liquidity to render discrimination unnecessary.

The story of the Anglo-American discussions leading to the Bretton Woods Conference of July 1944 has been told on many occasions.[25] The conference, which was attended by the delegates of forty-four nations, was the direct result of the belief on both sides of the Atlantic that multilateralism could only flourish if the international monetary system was subject to fundamental reform. On the British side the dominating figure was that of Keynes whose only official position during the war was as a member of the Consultative Council to the Chancellor of the Exchequer, a body composed of eminent authorities which had been established in mid-1940 to advise the Treasury on a range of policy issues. Keynes was, in his own words, only a 'demi-semi-official'[26] – he was not a civil servant and received no salary – yet the ascendancy he achieved over the formulation of British wartime economic policy, both internal and external, was remarkable. After a period of hesitation during which he seemed to favour a bilateralist approach to Britain's postwar problems, Keynes soon embraced the cause of economic liberalism. Fully aware of Britain's economic dependence on the USA and eager to respond positively and generously to the Article VII commitment Keynes sought to meet the view of the State Department while reserving the British position on commercial policy. The scheme which he devised (the first draft was produced in September 1941 and the final version published in April 1943) took the form of an international Clearing Union or World Central Bank.[27] Based upon the overdraft principle and with a special unit of account (Bancor) the scheme envisaged a clearing arrangement related directly to the monetary value of international trade: it permitted member countries to vary their exchange rates under certain well-defined conditions and attempted to transfer much of the responsibility for international economic adjustment on to surplus rather than deficit countries by exposing the former to a commission charge on their balances in the Union and by rendering them liable to accept Bancor up to the limit of its total issue. In sum the Clearing Union envisaged an international credit of approximately $25 billion.

The effect of the Clearing Union scheme within Whitehall was 'electrifying'. The autobiography of Lord Robbins who was at that time employed in the Economic Section of the War Cabinet Secretariat, summed up the feeling of many:

> From the time of the bimetallic controversy onwards many plans for international monetary co-operation had been produced and discussed in private or public quarters. But it is safe to say that nothing so imaginative and ambitious had ever before been discussed as a possibility of resonsible government policy. For those of us who cherished the belief that the outcome of the war might eventually permit an innovation of beneficial inter-national institutions it became as it were a banner of hope, an inspiration to the daily grind of war-time duties. What is perhaps even more remarkable is that after undergoing the detailed scrutiny of many inter-departmental official committees and discussions among ministers as regards its architectonic con-ceptions it emerged virtually unscathed as a manifesto of government proposals.[28]

In retrospect it was inevitable that the Keynesian scheme should not prove acceptable to the USA. It was not that the Americans were opposed to the plan in principle – indeed Harry White, the head of the overseas finance division of the US Treasury, went out of his way to assure Keynes and his co-negotiators that he was sympathetic and attracted to the Clearing Union. It was simply that Congress and American public opinion would never accept the principle of unlimited financial liability on the part of surplus countries which was implicit in the Union's overdraft principle.[29] Instead, it was the American plan for an International Monetary Fund, a version of the Stabilisation Fund devised by Harry White himself, which emerged from the Anglo-American negotiations and which was put forward for consideration at Bretton Woods.[30] Briefly, the plan involved member countries in contributing a quota to an international stabilisation fund – 25 per cent in gold and 75 per cent in their own currency: in return each country could purchase the currency of other members up to a limit of 200 per cent of their own contribution to the fund. In contrast to the Clearing Union, with its generous addition to international liquidity and provision for orderly exchange rate adjustments, the American plan was far less ambitious in conception and relatively inflexible. In so far as its main object was to secure stable exchange rates it bore some resemblance to the gold standard. It also provided a much smaller total of international liquidity – some £5 billion in all. Thus, the Fund, unlike the Union, would not be able to 'create credit'. The size of the Fund was to be fixed and since quotas and voting rights were to be based on the size of member countries' gold subscriptions and national income, as well as foreign trade, the management of the whole scheme would inevitably be dominated by the USA. The major concession made by the American negotiators to the British position was the so-called 'scarce currency clause' which permitted members to discriminate in their commercial policies and to introduce exchange restrictions against any member whose currency became scarce in the Fund. This clause was designed specifically for use against the USA and it was accordingly presented in Britain as being an extremely important concession – a recognition on the part of the USA that its persistent creditor position before 1939 had been a fundamental cause of international disequilibrium. Now it appeared that the Americans were admitting the principle of joint responsibility for disequilibrium on the part of the debtors *and* creditors.[31] In reality, however, the conditions under which the scarce currency clause would operate were extremely restrictive. Deficit countries were permitted to borrow from the Fund at a rate which would mean a delay of at least three years before a currency could be declared 'scarce'. Thus, 'the picture of a tremendous and immediate pressure brought to bear on an undeserving creditor was as fanciful as it was attractive'.[32]

The small initial size of the International Monetary Fund and the weaknesses in the scarce currency clause did not go unnoticed in Britain. Within official circles there were two principal sources of opposition to the Bretton Woods proposals. The first stemmed from the Bank of England where a majority of the directors regarded the Fund as a device which would lead inevitably to the enhancement of the dollar as the principal medium of international exchange to the detriment of London's position as an international financial centre.[33] The Fund would limit national sovereignty over matters of economic policy and in so far as it would tend to undermine the basis of the Sterling Area – possibly by reducing intra-area capital flows – it would weaken Britain's ability to cope with the severe financial problems that were bound to arise in the immediate aftermath of the war. The second source of opposition emanated from those members of the government, principally Lord Beaverbrook and L.S. Amery, who saw in the Fund, as they had in Article VII of the Mutual Aid Agreement (see above, p. 88), a threat to greater imperial unity. Deeply suspicious of American motives they believed that if Britain were to accept multilateralism in the financial field the way would be open to the destruction of the Imperial Preference system.[34]

Thus, the detractors of Bretton Woods were both powerful and articulate. They also received considerable support from academic opinion. Within government, Keynes's one-time collaborator, Sir Hubert Henderson, attached to the Treasury as an economic adviser, was an indefatigable opponent of economic liberalism. Indeed, Keynes's original Clearing Union proposal had produced in him a feeling of 'profound aversion'.[35] He also had little regard for Keynes's ability as a high-level negotiator.[36] Basing his arguments on an analysis of the course of international economic history in the interwar period and conscious of the weakness in Britain's balance of payments, Henderson claimed that it would be disastrous for Britain to help 'reconstruct a war-shattered world on the basis of a freely working economic system, international credits, the reduction of trade barriers, and the outlawry of quantitative regulation'.[37] In short, it was extremely dangerous and naïve to 'persist in associating the idea of international economic co-operation with the subordination of human welfare to the absolute rule of market forces, under the influence of doctrinaire abstractions, misplaced idealism, and nostalgia for the past'.[38] Henderson's views in this respect found support in outside circles from 'a small but vocal group of left-wing economists [who] expounded a foreign trade philosophy to match their programme of comprehensive planning in the domestic sphere'.[39] Dr Thomas (now Lord) Balogh was the main representative of this group and on more than one occasion he clashed openly with Keynes on the issue of multilateralism. The essence of Balogh's case lay in the need to ensure domestic full employment in a postwar world which would be subject to American economic dominance and hence the devastating effects of instability in the American economy.[40] As Balogh has retrospectively pointed out:

> The fact that inequality between the US and the rest [of the world] in investment power and therefore competitive capacity had immensely increased as a result of the war meant that a return to the unrestrained market system would inevitably lead to a cumulative upward thrust in the US and further exaggerate this discrepancy to the detriment of the victims of the war, the weaker and poorer. Far more powerful weapons than contemplated and permitted by Bretton Woods were needed to keep a balanced all-round expansion going.[41]

Thus the unifying link between those who rejected multilateralism was a belief in the need to sustain both the Sterling Area and Imperial Preference systems, and the bilateralist commercial policy of the 1930s. Only then would Britain be able to safeguard its balance-of-payments position, protect the level of domestic employment, and ensure the maintenance of sterling as an international currency. For these reasons they also opposed any proposal to block the sterling balances. In 1942, Amery in his capacity as Secretary of State for India, had argued that the growth of the sterling balances should not be a cause for concern: in fact they would be 'more likely to prove a blessing than a danger' since they would facilitate the revival of Britain's postwar export trade.[42] To the Bank of England the balances represented a solemn and binding obligation: a threat to block the balances or fund them on more or less unfavourable terms would severely damage London's credibility as a centre of international finance.[43] There were, in addition, vitally important political considerations arising from the fact that large and growing balances were held by countries with no real or vested interest in a British victory, and the largest holder of all, India, could be expected to strenuously resist any attempt at repudiation or blocking on the grounds of its impoverishment and imminent political independence.[44] This reasoning was powerful enough to persuade the government to reject an American suggestion that blocked balances should be absorbed by the stabilisation fund.[45] Although this represented a defeat for Keynes who had initially argued that India should make some contribution to the cost of the war, he continued to argue that since it would be impossible to provide unlimited convertibility for sterling after the war the balances should be blocked and only released according to a gradual timetable. To permit the free use of sterling for current account payments would be to assume 'banking undertakings beyond what we have any means to support as soon as anything goes wrong, coupled with a policy, conceived in the interests of old financial traditions, which pays no regard to the inescapable requirements of domestic policies'.[46]

Despite the undoubted strength of the opposition to the Bretton Woods proposals the government eventually decided to embrace the cause of multilateralism – at least in the financial sphere.[47] The spectre of 'starvation corner' and the political implications of Article VII were sufficient to ensure this. Nevertheless, it is important to note that one factor influencing that decision was that 'bold new measures of transitional aid' would be forthcoming from the USA. Keynes himself encouraged this view both in public and in private. In a memorandum dated 28 September 1944, for example, he had written,

> We cannot police half the world at our own expense when we have already gone into pawn to the other half. We cannot run for long a great programme of social amelioration on money lent from overseas. Unless we are willing to put ourselves financially at the mercy of America and then borrow from her on her own terms and conditions sums which we cannot confidently hope to repay, what are we expecting? Are we looking forward to a spectacular bankruptcy (not, altogether, a bad idea) from which we shall rise the next morning without a care in the world? Or are we following some star at present invisible to me?[48]

In the USA, however, a prominent feature of the administration's campaign to secure public and congressional support for ratification of the Bretton Woods final act was that the new institutions by themselves were sufficient to meet Britain's postwar needs.[49]

The final act of the Bretton Woods Conference was the result of negotiations which, with due regard to the difficulties involved on both sides of the Atlantic, had proceeded relatively smoothly. As regards commercial policy, too, it appeared at one stage that an Anglo-American understanding would be achieved according to a similar timetable of discussions. The first exploratory meeting to discuss general principles was held in Washington in September 1943. The British delegation was led by Richard Law (later Lord Coleraine), Minister of State at the Foreign Office, assisted by Sir Percival Leisching, a senior civil servant at the Board of Trade, and James Meade and Lionel Robbins of the economic section of the War Cabinet Secretariat. Both sides agreed that some form of commercial convention should be negotiated at international level embodying agreement on the reduction of tariff levels and the curbing of other direct controls on the level of multilateral trade.[50] They also agreed in the most general terms that the signatories to the convention should seek to maintain high and stable levels of employment as a direct stimulus to the liberalisation of trade. On the subject of quantitative controls on trade the negotiators were again in agreement, concurring with the view that since they were 'a particularly injurious trade barrier', they should be abolished except in circumstances of severe balance-of-payments disequilibrium and then only in accordance with strict guidelines laid down in the commercial convention. Far more contentious was the issue of tariffs and preferences: it was here that a clear divergence of opinion appeared. The American position was straightforward: on the basis of the Article VII commitment on non-discrimination it was argued that all preferences should be abolished; tariff reductions, on the other hand, would be a matter for bilateral negotiation, possibly at a large 'multilateral' conference. To the British negotiators the American attitude on this issue was as unfair as it was dogmatic. The views of Robbins, who had adopted an uncompromising free trade position in the 1930s, were representative of the British reaction:

> Why should customs unions be permissible – as they were in the US draft proposals – while anything short of complete union in the shape of mutual preferences be regarded as an ultimate iniquity? Why, in other contexts, speak of the various members of the Commonwealth as our 'colonies' whose war-time credits with us we could cancel overnight ... yet in the context of commercial policy, speak as if there were no difference between preference *within* a commonwealth and discrimination between completely independent states? Were the effects of Imperial Preference on the volume of world trade so manifestly more restrictive than those of the US tariff as to deserve treatment as if in an entirely different category of offences?[51]

From the British perspective, in order to justify the abolition of the Imperial Preference system the USA would have to offer heavy, all-round tariff reductions – probably 'much more than 50 per cent of the pre-war height of all tariffs'.[52] Although the American representatives were under no illusions that such a stipulation would encounter considerable opposition from a Congress hostile to any notion of a tariff ceiling this should not be allowed to detract from the progress that had been made in these preliminary discussions. Broad agreement had been reached on the desirablity of establishing an international commercial convention, and on the need to abolish quantitative trade restrictions and to take account of the level of employment and the balance of payments in determining national commercial policy. Finally, the Americans had shown that they were not averse to further discussion on the question of tariffs and preferences.

These hopeful auguries for a joint understanding on commercial policy were, however, more apparent than real. For more than twelve months after the return of the Law mission no further discussions, either formal or informal, took place between the two sides. The explanation for the break in negotiations lay on the British side where the proposals for commercial liberalism encountered severe opposition both from the traditional defenders of the empire and, notably, from Keynes himself, who had yet to be converted to the American viewpoint on this issue. Conscious of the limitations of the International Monetary Fund as a source of international liquidity and increasingly concerned at the prospective postwar balance-of-payments deficit Keynes, in contrast to his views on financial policy, continued to favour quantitative import restrictions.[53] By the time negotiations were resumed in earnest in the autumn of 1945 Keynes had changed his mind, but the whole issue of commercial policy was clouded by the fundamentally altered economic and political relationship between the two countries.

It has already been noted that the British authorities had decided to seek substantial dollar assistance from the USA before the end of the war in Europe (see above, p. 84). It remains to be said that the financial agreement that was negotiated bore little resemblance to the kind of settlement which the Labour government had hoped for.[54] Instead of a grant-in-aid with the minimum of conditions attached, Britain was forced to accept a loan with interest which carried with it several important 'strings' – in particular the immediate ratification of the Bretton Woods Final Act and the commitment to adhere to financial multilateralism within one year of the signing of the loan agreement rather than within the extended five-year transitional period allowed for in the original Bretton Woods agreement. What this meant was that by mid-July 1947 sterling would be made fully convertible for all current transactions both within and without the Sterling Area. Britain also undertook to end discrimination against the USA in the application of quantitative trade controls by the end of 1946. On the issue of the sterling balances, following intense American pressure for a drastic scaling down of these obligations, Britain agreed to deal with its creditors either by immediate repayment, by gradual release beginning in 1951, or by 'adjustment' in consideration of other services. Finally, in the sphere of commercial policy, the two governments formally agreed to work towards the reduction of tariffs and the elimination of preferences, these issues to be considered at an International Conference on Trade and Employment. In return for these undertakings Britain was to receive a loan of $4.4 billion from the USA of which $650 million was to settle outstanding lend-lease debts. The net credit of $3,750 million was subsequently augmented by a Canadian loan of $1,250 million. Both loans were issued on the same terms: interest was to be charged at 2 per cent and the capital sum repaid over fifty years with the first annual instalment payable in 1951.

According to Harrod the conditions on which the American loan was offered 'consisted in nothing more than the reaffirmation and application of the policy to which Britain had pledged herself by the signature of Article VII of the Mutual Aid Agreement'.[55] More recently, Moggridge has emphasised that both the terms and size of the loan 'were certainly better than the "pessimistic" Keynes of the spring of 1945 considered likely' (a loan of between $5,000–8,000 million, possibly at 2½ per cent).[56] Nevertheless, the terms of the loan – particularly the charging of interest to a wartime ally and the link between the granting of financial assistance and British conformity to American views on multilateralism – were met with a storm of protest in Britain. *The Economist*, for example, indignantly exclaimed, 'Beggars cannot be choosers. But they can by long tradition, put a curse on the ambitions of the rich' and even Keynes himself, whilst presenting an eloquent and decisive defence of the agreement in the House of Lords, went as far as to admit that as long as he lived he would never cease to regret that it was not an interest-free loan.[57] The House of Commons voted in favour of the agreement with a majority of 243 with 169 abstentions but this hardly reflected the bitterness of feeling among members of both major parties. A majority of Conservatives abstained and many voted against the agreement, while on the Labour side a three-line whip had to be applied to ensure the passage of the Bill.[58] Once again the defenders of the empire, with full exhortation from the Beaverbrook press, attacked the agreement as a threat to the Sterling Area and therefore to imperial unity, while those to the left of the political spectrum viewed the loan as a device to prevent the Labour government from 'applying socialist principles in international trade'.[59] As for the government itself, its defence of the agreement was both lukewarm and apologetic with greatest stress being laid on the dire consequences which would follow if the loan was rejected.

There were several reasons for the adverse British reaction. In the first instance, the final years of the war had witnessed a hardening of opinion in favour of the Imperial Preference system and the empire generally both as a result of sentiment in the face of shared wartime experiences and hard economic advantage.[60] Secondly, there was the problem of ignorance of the issues at stake. As Harrod pointed out:

> The fact of the matter was that many members of the new administration knew little about the implications of Article VII and that even the survivors from Coalition days had been much too immersed in the war effort to follow the developments of Anglo-American post-war planning in detail. The issues at stake were complex; the Americans had clear ideas about the evils of the discrimination, restrictionism and bilateralism that they wished to eradicate; the average British parliamentarian, conscious of the danger of too speedy a relaxation of wartime

controls and somewhat hazy, no doubt, about the implications of 'socialism' for foreign trading relations, had still much to learn about what was at stake.[61]

For the naïveté of ministers, Keynes himself was partly to blame. With his 'poetic cadences' concerning American generosity before he departed for Washington it was he who had encouraged the government to believe that a grant-in-aid could be obtained from the USA. Confident in his powers of persuasion and convinced of the justice of the British cause, Keynes seriously misjudged the state of American postwar opinion. The abrupt termination of lend-lease aid, the inauguration of a new President and changes in personnel at the White House, the nature of the campaign to secure congressional approval for the Bretton Woods settlement with its emphasis on the fact that the new institutions by themselves would be sufficient to meet Britain's postwar reconstruction needs – all of these factors should have served as a warning. The fact was that they did not, and Keynes found that despite a brilliant exposition of Britain's financial sacrifices and postwar weakness he was confronted with 'a grinding business negotiation'.[62] His major adversary on the American side was Morganthau's successor, Fred Vinson, a lawyer by training and inclination. While concerned to respond positively to the British predicament, Vinson was ever mindful of the state of domestic opinion. The two men had clashed at Bretton Woods and the difficulties in their interpersonal relationships added to the pressures on the British delegation. The only major concession Keynes obtained during his entire stay in Washington was a postponement of the date of sterling convertibility.[63]

The Anglo-American Financial Agreement was signed on 6 December 1945. On the day before Lord Halifax, British Ambassador to the USA, cabled London: 'We have all done our level best to move Americans ... I am sorry we have failed.'[64] Perhaps Lord Halifax was being a little unfair to the British negotiating team since the terms of the American loan were not ungenerous when judged as a purely financial transaction. The starting date of 1951 for the annual repayments reduced the effective rate of interest to 1.6 per cent and Britain certainly received favourable treatment in this respect as compared with other debtor countries. The difficulties lay in the limited size of the loan and the multilateral obligations. In the former case it is true that the total loan of $5 billion coincided with the estimated British transitional deficit. But, as Gardner has pointed out, the Treasury's balance-of-payments calculations ignored a number of dangerous possibilities

> ... that Britain's terms of trade might take an adverse turn and that large government expenditures might be required throughout

the transition period. It took no account of the fact that the carrying out of multilateral obligations might increase the need for financial aid. Finally, it made no allowance for the possibility that as banker for the Sterling Area Britain might have to support not only its own deficit but the deficits of other sterling countries as well. For all these reasons there was considerable doubt that the assistance was large enought to accomplish its stated objectives.[65]

As for the multilateral obligations themselves the principal difficulty lay with the commitment to sterling convertibility in relation to current transactions. To quote once more from Gardner's discussion:

> The fact is that the negotiators did not fully understand the economics of convertibility. They did not appreciate the difficulty in which Britain might find itself in the event that it went on accumulating inconvertible currencies while other countries, deliberately restricting imports from the United Kingdom, presented large sterling surpluses for conversion. Given this hazard of making one currency convertible in a generally inconvertible world, and given also the general uncertainties of the transition period, the use of a rigid time-table was certainly injudicious. It would have been much wiser if the date for implementation of convertibility could have been left to a joint Anglo-American board or even to the authorities of the International Monetary Fund.[66]

This is, of course, wisdom after the event and it is worth noting at this stage that the British negotiators did manage to insert an 'escape' clause in the articles of agreement which at least permitted the postponement or suspension of convertibility in circumstances where illegal capital transfers were taking place in order to circumvent the 'current transactions' provision. In the immediate setting, however, the loan and the conditions attached were a measure of Britain's economic dependence on the USA at the end of a war which seriously undermined the stability of the country's international financial position. In the final analysis the fact that Britain was driven to seek large-scale dollar assistance was a kind of *ex post facto* justification for the Treasury's prewar axiom that finance was indeed the fourth arm of defence.

The story of the sterling convertibility crisis of July–August 1947 is well known. According to the terms of the loan agreement, sterling was to be subject to full convertibility for all current transactions on 15 July 1947. In fact, 'convertibility had been introduced piecemeal over the last nine months'[67] so that the Chancellor of the Exchequer, Hugh Dalton, was able to assure the House of Commons on 8 July that the official date for convertibility would not impose an excessive burden on the nation's resources.[68] If it is true, as Dalton later claimed, that both he and his Treasury colleagues entertained private doubts as to the premature timing of convertibility,[69] his apparent complacency in that first week in July is reprehensible. Even at the time when he was addressing the House a run on transferable sterling was developing. In a confidential Treasury paper, dated 16 August 1947, the Cabinet was informed of the following external net drain of dollars on a week-by-week basis: 5 July – $94·6 million; 12 July – $112·1 million; 19 July – $155 million; 26 July – $91·9 million; 2 August – $114·5 million; 9 August – $124·5 million; five days ending 15 August – $175·9 million.[70] By 18 August only $700 million of the original dollar loan remained and at the current rate of withdrawal this sum would be exhausted at the latest by the end of October. In these circumstances it was obvious that convertibility would have to be suspended. This was done on 20 August and on the following day the US government reluctantly acquiesced in the British action. The government then took immediate action to introduce an 'austerity' programme mainly by cutting dollar imports and was soon joined in this policy by the other Sterling Area countries.[71] Even so, by the end of the year the level of British reserves had fallen to the bare minimum of £500 million. The question remains, what had gone wrong? Part of the answer has already been provided by Gardner (see above, pp. 97-8), but there are two further factors to taken into consideration. First, on the question of the sterling balances, it is clear that the government had made a serious miscalculation in policy. As Dow has emphasised:

> At the time of the negotiations for the Loan it had been hoped that it would be possible to persuade some of the countries holding sterling balances to agree to their partly being cancelled as war debts; and that apart from limited amounts they would agree to them being blocked. In fact only Australia and New Zealand agreed to their balances being scaled down. Starting with negotiations with Argentina in October 1944, the Government made a series of agreements with the main non-sterling countries, intended to give them convertibility for currently earned sterling but not for accumulated balances. But it appeared that only half of the total of the balances was blocked in this way. Even those countries with whom agreements were made retained access to considerable 'working balances'. With the main sterling countries, no formal agreements were thought necessary; and the countries of Western Europe also held large unblocked balances. The only safeguard was the self-restraint of the holders.[72]

In these circumstances convertibility was bound to lead to trouble. As

Dalton himself pointed out at the time of suspension, there was a massive dollar gap in international payments and 'sterling, alone of all the other currencies of the European belligerents, was freely convertible'.[73] Hence Britain alone bore the burden of the world dollar shortage.

In mitigation of the government's sterling policy in 1947 the following arguments can be offered. First, the winter fuel crisis of 1946–7 greatly reduced the country's export-earning capacity – possibly by as much as £200 million. Secondly, the terms of trade were moving against the UK and the rise in the price of dollar imports alone added as much as £300 million to the country's import bill in 1947. Thirdly, there was the mounting cost of British overseas military expenditure, especially in the eastern Mediterranean and Germany (including in the latter the cost of feeding the civilian population in the British occupation zone).[74] Finally, there were the terms of the loan agreement itself. It is true, as has been pointed out, that the agreement permitted the postponement of convertibility under certain conditions but the government did not avail itself of this concession. One reason for this (advanced subsequently by Dalton) was the likely hostile reaction of a Congress unsympathetic to Britain's profligate Labour government.[75] There were, moreover, international political considerations. At a time when American relations with the USSR were deteriorating rapidly in a situation of general Western European economic and political dislocation, the State Department was anxious to avoid any confrontation with Congress when radical changes in American foreign policy were under consideration. There is some evidence, therefore, to support the view that 'the Government abided by its promises concerning sterling convertibility in the knowledge that, while it was likely to have damaging if not catastrophic consequences, it was a necessary act to win American [Congressional] confidence, and to ensure the successful launching of Marshall Aid'.[76]

By mid-1947 the wartime American dream of a multilateral world was shattered. Western Europe as a whole was failing to achieve economic recovery and despite accusations in Congress of 'socialist extravagance' British economic weakness in particular had been unequivocally demonstrated. Nevertheless, the generous provision of dollars through the Marshall Aid programme salvaged something from the wreckage of the American conception, for the State Department initiative provided the impetus for unprecedented measures of intergovernmental co-operation in Europe. In this, the British Foreign Secretary, Ernest Bevin, played a leading role: although strongly opposed to anything approaching political and economic union between sovereign states, it was Bevin, working in close co-operation with the French, who responded most positively to the

American offer.[77] The result was the creation in April 1948 of the Organisation of European Economic Co-operation (OEEC), a body specifically designed to administer the disbursement of Marshall Aid to the recipient countries. The significance of the OEEC was twofold. First, it permitted the establishment of a region of increasingly effective economic liberalism in a world which was ill-prepared to embrace the Bretton Woods version of multilateralism and, secondly, it acted as a catalyst for further European economic integration. In this latter respect the OEEC was an important forerunner of the establishment in 1951 of the European Coal and Steel Community. Ironically, the Labour government, which in these immediate postwar years enjoyed political leadership in Europe, remained aloof from this kind of development. Bevin's much vaunted 'Europeanism' was motivated primarily by anti-communism (hence his strongly positive response to Marshall Aid and staunch support for NATO) and the Labour Party in general was highly suspicious of supranational authorities which might interfere with the running of industries which had only recently been nationalised – in the case of coalmining in an atmosphere of considerable emotion.[78] Furthermore, there was the question of Britain's pivotal role in the Sterling Area at a time of chronic dollar shortage. In the immediate postwar years Sterling Area markets, heavily concentrated in the Commonwealth, were of immense importance to the British economy. Quite apart from the fact that in 1948 three-quarters of British trade was carried on outside Europe, leadership of the Sterling Area by itself served to distance Britain from the embryonic 'European Movement' which was to lead ultimately to the founding of the European Economic Community (EEC) in 1957. Indeed, it could be argued that by the late 1940s Britain had no need for closer economic links with Europe (other than those rendered necessary by the Marshall Aid programme). By 1950, Britain's surplus of imports from America was offset by a British surplus of exports to the Sterling Area which was itself in surplus with America.[79] As Dr Balogh argued at the time, Keynes had been wrong in dismissing the value of the Sterling Area to Britain. For all member countries 'their reciprocal exchange relation gives them a stability and a common interest which has endured very severe strains and is likely to endure more'.[80] Most politicians in both of the major political parties would have agreed with Dr Balogh. The question of greater European integration was not a simple economic issue: it was politically charged and highly emotive both in Britain and on the Continent. In the late 1940s and for the greater part of the 1950s there could be no question of Britain joining any form of European Federation. The feelings of many were summed up by the newly appointed Conservative Foreign Secretary, Anthony Eden, when he stated in January 1952 that 'Britain's story and her interests lie beyond the Continent of Europe. Our thoughts move across the seas to the many communities in which our people play their part, in every corner of the world. That is our life: without it we should be no more than some millions of people living on an island off the coast of Europe.'[81]

Discounting the year 1951 when Britain's current account balance-of-payments deficit had amounted to £419 million (due largely to distortions in world commodity markets as a result of the Korean War) the country's external position seemed to be increasingly secure (see Table 9, p. 145). In 1950 Britain had enjoyed a current account surplus of £297 million: between 1946 and 1950 exports had increased by 77 per cent in real terms – a figure which would have astonished Treasury officials in 1945. There were also the beginnings of a heartening change in the composition of British exports in favour of growth sectors of world trade: this had begun in earnest in the interwar period but the trend had been further stimulated by the war.[82] Between 1936 and 1945 the amount of electrical power available to the economy had expanded by 50 per cent and at the end of the war private industry had gained considerably by the acquisition from the Ministry of Supply of $100 million's worth of machine tools (equivalent in value to about twenty times the prewar annual rate of purchase) and of 75 million square feet of factory space. As one writer has commented:

> The iron and steel, machine tool, vehicle, aircraft, chemical, plastic, electrical and electronic industries had all been expanded. The stimulus afforded by war needs to the development of radar, radio, even simple computers in anti-aircraft defence, provided an invaluable basis for much post-war civil development. Chemical substitutes for many raw materials had been known before the war, but the creation of the British petro-chemical industry really dates from 1942 ... Finally, if rail and road transport, the textile and certain other industries had suffered severe disinvestment during the war, the mechanization of both coal and agriculture had been accelerated'.[83]

The Labour government's export achievement, outstanding though it may have been, must be seen against the background of war-induced import substitution, together with the maintenance in existence into the later 1940s of those wartime economic controls which were of special relevance to the nation's export drive.[84] It should also be noted that in these years Britain was operating in a seller's market – well before the revival of the European and Japanese economies. With the failure of American-style multilateralism the Imperial Preference system came into its own and Britain undoubtedly benefited from her favoured position in colonial and Commonwealth markets. The question remains therefore as to the extent to which British industry would be able to respond to the challenge of foreign competition in an era of growing trade liberalisation in the 1950s and when European and Japanese economic recovery was well under way. Britain had been victorious in the war but there were important psychological legacies which might, in the future, serve to hamper the country's economic performance. In this respect one critical element was the all-party commitment to full employment – enshrined in the White Paper on *Employment Policy* published in 1944.[85] In an era when the trade union movement had emerged as a major force in British political life would its obsession with the memory of mass unemployment in the 1930s impose unfortunate rigidities on the economy? Secondly, there was the wartime inheritance of the welfare state. As one observer has commented, 'The idea of the Welfare State came to be identified with the war aims of a nation fighting for its life. It is not surprising that [in Britain] it wore a halo which is not to be found in other countries when in due course they undertook the task of social reconstruction.'[86] The difficulty was that with an electorate which was beginning to make increasing demands on the political parties (see below, p. 114) would the nation be able to divert sufficient resources from the 'productive' to the 'non-productive' sector in order to sustain and expand the facilities of the welfare state? Already, in April 1949, Sir Stafford Cripps was sounding a warning note:

> There is not much further immediate possibility of the redistribution of national income by way of taxation in this country: for the future, we must rely rather upon the creation of more distributable wealth than upon ... redistribution ... Total taxation, local and national, is now more than 40 per cent of the national income, and at that level the redistribution of income entailed in the payment of Social Services already falls, to a considerable extent, upon those who are the recipients of those services.
>
> We must, therefore, moderate the speed of our advance in the extended application of the existing Social Services to our progressive ability to pay for them by an increase in our national income. Otherwise, we shall not be able to avoid entrenching, to an intolerable extent, upon the liberty of spending by the private individual for his own purposes.[87]

Finally, there was the problem of the balance of payments and the role of sterling as an international currency. It is true that following the devaluation of the pound in September 1949 from $4.03 to $2.80 Britain's gold and dollar reserves rose from $1,425 million to $2,422 million in mid-1950, but this should not be regarded as evidence of a fundamental strengthening in Britain's international economic position. As Pollard has emphasised

The improvement in the current balance of payments ... plus the proceeds from loans and aid were dissipated, not in strengthening the precarious reserve, but in making foreign investments ... , in undetected exports of capital and in paying off some of the sterling balances, without, however, 'funding' the latter in any way. Thus the weakness of sterling at the beginning of the period [i.e. in 1945–6] was not yet cured at the end. With a reserve of barely £1,000 million, a swing of £200-300 million in any one year ... would cause a major crisis, and the vulnerability remained after 1951.[88]

Indeed, the continuing weakness of the reserve position goes far to explain the many precipitate changes in economic policy made by successive Chancellors from the late 1940s onwards.

5

The British Economy since 1951: the Political Economy of Failure

In surveying the development of the British economy since the early 1950s the economic historian can, perhaps, be excused for suffering from an extreme feeling of déjà vu. In historical terms several of the statistical indices of growth are impressive. Taking the years 1950–74 output-per-man-hour in British manufacturing industry increased by well over 200 per cent: gross fixed investment (other than in dwellings) was running at a rate of 15 per cent of gross national product with an acceleration in the rate (to over 17 per cent) after 1965. As for the standard of living, between 1938 and 1974 total consumers' expenditure at constant prices doubled: since 1945 the real weekly earnings of manual workers have also doubled. Taking the years 1968–9 to 1974–5 – a period noted for the growing burden of personal taxation – average real incomes, while they rose by 23 per cent before tax, still rose by a substantial 17 per cent after tax. No wonder then that despite the extent to which consumption levels have been periodically sustained by borrowing from abroad Sir Henry Phelps Brown has emphatically concluded that 'the British people today are far better supplied with the necessities and amenities of life, and more fully provided with remedial and supportive services than ever in their history before'.[1] Yet, at the same time, the postwar decades are regarded by many commentators both at home and abroad, as years of national economic decline, a period when Britain fell further and further behind its principal overseas competitors in the league table of economic growth. The literature on Britain's postwar economic ills is vast: managerial weaknesses, excessive trade union power and restrictive practices, an anachronistic social structure, an inadequate education system, the rising tide of government expenditure and weaknesses in government economic policy generally – all of these hypotheses and more, have their supporters and all of them, either singly or in some combination, are regarded as primarily responsible for Britain's alleged failure as an industrial and trading nation. The element of déjà vu lies in the fact that a substantially similar list of weaknesses can be and, as noted earlier (see Chapter 1, *passim*), has been applied to the British economy in the 1870–1914 period. And in exactly the same way that the problem of British economic decline before 1914 was a relative phenomenon *vis-à-vis* the faster growing economies of Germany and the USA, so the problem in much of the postwar era has been relative rather than absolute. Since 1950 the country's economic performance has been highly respectable in historical terms (see Table 10, p. 146), but since the mid-1950s the British economy has lagged behind a growing number of competitors. No matter which index of economic performance is taken – the rate of growth of GDP (see Table 11, p. 146), of GNP (see Table 12, p. 147), of industrial production (see Table 13, p. 147), of labour productivity (see Table 14, p. 148), Britain's share in world trade in manufactured goods (see Table 15, p. 149) – all of these statistics make depressing reading when compared with the achievements of other countries, in particular the founder members of the European Economic Community (EEC), Britain's partners in the European Free Trade Association (EFTA), and Japan. Only the USA has a comparable record of relative failure but that can be no source of comfort to Britain in so far as the absolute level of the American standard of living is so much higher. Then there has been the problem of the balance of payments, together with the progressive weakening of sterling as an international currency (see Table 16, p. 149). In historical terms this is a phenomenon which had its origins in the period following the First World War. The reduced invisible income from abroad due to the loss of overseas assets and the depressed level of international trade combined with the difficulties of Britain's staple export industries to produce a weakened balance-of-payments situation in the 1920s (see Table 5, p. 142). However, the real warning of things to come appeared in the following decade when Britain, with the level of domestic economic activity recovering from the trough of depression, recorded current account payments deficits in a number of years (1931, 1932, 1934, 1936–8).[2] In much of the post-1945 era the pursuit of 'full employment policies' has meant that instead of there being a chronic insufficiency of effective demand there has been a tendency for the growth of imports to outstrip the growth of exports. This has led to a debilitating balance-of-payments constraint as successive governments have been obliged to intervene at depressingly regular intervals to restrain the level of domestic economic activity in order to ease the problem of the foreign balance – the so-called 'stop-go' cycle (see below, pp. 117–18).

For the economic historian there is an additional factor which adds an element of irony to the déjà vu perspective. As in the pre-1914 years, when contemporaries noted the growing inroads of foreign competition in the British domestic market, there is now a small but growing body of opinion which is prepared to advocate protectionism – whether by tariffs or by quota import controls – as a solution to Britain's economic ills, both internal and external. The case for protectionism is in fact but one aspect of a wider debate of particular interest to economic historians. This concerns the so-called issue of de-industrialisation. 'De-industrialisation' is currently a vogue word, and it came to prominence in the mid-1970s primarily as a result of the work of two Oxford University economists, Robert Bacon and Walter Eltis.

The Bacon and Eltis thesis has been presented at two levels.[3] They argue first of all that Britain's relatively poor economic performance is due to the progressive shrinkage of the country's manufacturing base, a development which gathered pace in the mid-1960s due to the growing pre-emption of scarce resources – both labour and capital – by the non-productive sector of the economy. By 'non-productive' Bacon and Eltis are referring to the service sector, in particular that part which is controlled by central and local government and which does not produce 'marketable output' (unlike, say, the banking and insurance sectors of the 'City'). The 'productive' industrial economy (and this includes the nationalised industries) has been progressively starved of labour and thus obliged to compete for this factor with the service sector thus setting in motion a wage/price spiral to the detriment of Britain's international competitiveness.[4] (See Table 17, p. 150, for 'Employment in Manufacturing Industry, UK 1907-76'; Table 18, p. 150, for 'Proportions of Workforce Employed in Different Sectors, Great Britain 1931-76'; and Table 19, p. 151, for 'Ratios of Non-Industrial to Industrial Employment: Various Countries, 1961-75'). The mechanism by which this has occurred is closely related to cyclical fluctuations in the domestic economy. As Bacon and Eltis point out in their latest contribution:

> ... it is in the boom when the economy is working most nearly to full capacity that the full effects of previous growth of the non-market sector are felt. High non-market spending can often be afforded in periods of recession when, with spare resources in the economy, extra government spending will not obviously reduce the aggregate real resources available for market sector investment and the balance of payments. However, if extensive and irreversible spending decisions are taken in the slump, supply bottlenecks are reached more quickly in the subsequent boom when private spending also rises rapidly. The balance of payments then deteriorates more massively and earlier than otherwise would have been the case and the boom can therefore be allowed to last an insufficient length of time to get capacity –

creating market sector investment ... up sufficiently to raise the rate of growth of productive capacity to what is required for a faster growth rate.[5]

The second aspect of the Bacon and Eltis thesis concerns the excessive burden of taxation that the expansion of public sector employment has imposed both on British industry and those employed within it. The result has been threefold, first the debilitating effect on corporate profits which has served to limit much needed industrial investment (see Table 20, p. 151, for 'Manufacturing Investment as a Proportion of Gross Domestic Product, 1960–72'); secondly, the growing weight of personal taxation which has encouraged industrial workers, and latterly those employed in the service sector itself, to press for unprecedented wage and salary increases to compensate for the heightened tax burden; and thirdly the need to retain a higher proportion of output at home due to the resistance of wage earners to a reduction in their share of marketed output, a phenomenon which, in reducing net exports of manufactures, has worsened the balance-of-payments position.[6]

In terms of its impact on the formulation of economic policy the Bacon and Eltis thesis has found favour with a fairly broad spectrum of political opinion. Since its first presentation in a series of articles in *The Sunday Times* newspaper at the end of 1975 leading Conservative and Labour politicians have advocated policies designed to reverse the process of de-industrialisation.[7] The 1974–9 Labour government embarked upon an interventionist 'industrial strategy'[8] to raise the level of investment in manufacturing industry and attempted to negotiate an informal incomes policy with the trade union movement and to curb the growth of the non-productive sector of the economy, while the incoming Conservative government in 1979 came to office pledged to substantially reduce the public sector borrowing requirement and, having set its face against an incomes policy *per se*, to strictly control the rate of growth of the money supply. For politicians searching for a working diagnosis of Britain's economic predicament in the 1970s, the Bacon and Eltis thesis has much to offer. A combination of tax reductions and the 'rolling back' of the public sector can kill two birds with one stone – increase immediate electoral popularity and, hopefully, reverse the process of industrial decline. It is all the more important, therefore, to bear in mind that the thesis contains a number of critical weaknesses. In the first instance, on the issue of labour utilisation, it seems inappropriate to speak of the productive sector being starved of labour in a situation where British manufacturing industry is noted for overmanning and where the trend rate of unemployment over successive cycles since the early 1950s has risen inexorably.[9] (See Table 21, p. 152, for 'Rates of Male

Unemployment in Great Britain 1955–77'.) It should also be borne in mind that the expansion in service sector employment since the early 1960s has resulted in extra employment for females in the labour force, whereas the bulk of registered unemployed are males.[10] On the subject of reductions in direct taxation Bacon and Eltis are on much stronger ground. It is difficult to refute their argument that the expansion of the non-productive sector has been a prime cause of cost-push inflation to the detriment of profits in manufacturing industry (see Table 22, p.152, for 'Gross Profit Shares of UK Manufacturing and Services 1966–76'), notably in the period since 1969.[11] But even here a note of warning should be sounded. In international terms, and especially in comparison with some of the more buoyant European economies, the British people are not excessively penalised at the hands of the state.[12] Moreover, following the return to power of the Conservatives in 1951 their subsequent programme of tax reductions did not lead to an upsurge in the country's economic performance, a result which is also confirmed by experience in the fifteen years before 1914. For Phelps Brown the point to note about these years is that the highest rate of income tax was less than 7 per cent and even after 1909 the bulk of taxable earned income paid less than 4 per cent. As Phelps Brown concludes:

> Yet this was not a time of vigorous enterprise responding to incentive, or of high investment in British industry: those fifteen years were a time of stagnation, with no rise in productivity, no rise in real wages. The reason for this lay in 'other circumstances of the time': [this] may serve to indicate how minor a role taxation may play, among other forces, in the shaping of economic performance.[13]

Thus, in view of the historical record, attempts to improve the rate of economic growth by manipulating the system of taxation are more the result of an act of faith rather than being based upon any clear-cut evidence in favour of the positive effects of tax incentives.

There are two further weaknesses in the Bacon and Eltis thesis, both of them critical. The first concerns their definition of de-industrialisation. In this respect it is significant that the reduction in manufacturing employment (see Table 23, p. 153, for 'Proportions of Total Employment in Manufacturing in Various Countries 1950–75') and the rise in public expenditure are features common to a number of the advanced economies of Western Europe, Japan and the USA notably in the years after 1970.[14] It might well be asked, therefore, what so distinguishes the British experience from that of these other countries? The fact remains that Britain does not stand out as an exceptional case according to the Bacon and Eltis criteria. What then does the term 'de-industrialisation' mean in the specifically

British context? The answer to this question leads to the final criticism of the Bacon and Eltis thesis: in simple terms it is unhistorical. Britain's economic difficulties are dated from the mid-1960s following the upsurge in public expenditure and non-productive employment in the first half of the decade. Yet one of the major themes of this book is that Britain's economic decline has its origins in the past – to be precise a century ago in the final quarter of the nineteenth century. In so far as the root causes of Britain's economic predicament are long-term and hence deep-seated, one of the dangers of the Bacon and Eltis approach is that its very plausibility can be used to justify economic policy prescriptions which are either inappropriate or, alternatively, of limited effectiveness, and which are, in consequence, likely to further intensify the disillusion of the British electorate with the two main political parties. What is required, therefore, is a more precise definition of de-industrialisation, one which pays due regard to the present relative weakness of the British economy and its long-term causes. In the current debate on de-industrialisation the most appropriate definition of the phenomenon has emanated from the Faculty of Economics at the University of Cambridge. According to one of its members, in view of the historical evolution of Britain's industrial structure (a net importer of food and raw materials paid for largely, but not exclusively, by manufactured exports) 'an efficient manufacturing sector ... may be defined as one which, given the normal levels of other components of the balance of payments, yields sufficient net exports (both currently, but more importantly, potentially) to pay for import requirements at socially acceptable levels of output, employment and the exchange rate.[15] Hence, Britain can be said to be suffering from de-industrialisation to the extent that the economy, in failing to maintain its share in world trade in manufactures, and in the light of the growing import penetration of the domestic market (see Table 24, p. 154, for 'Industrial Import Penetration of the UK Home Market 1961-75'), is 'becoming increasingly unable to pay for its current [full employment] import requirements by means of exports of goods and services and property income from abroad'.[16] Thus, to improve the balance of payments merely by cutting public expenditure might result in the loss of real output with unemployment rising to unacceptable levels. If total expenditure has to be reduced – as this view concedes – it should be channelled increasingly towards British domestic production in order to maintain employment levels and to restore equilibrium in the balance of payments.[17]

It will be noted that the Cambridge definition of de-industrialisation is concerned exclusively with the contribution of manufacturing industry to the balance of payments. Bacon and Eltis, however, have argued that such emphasis on the visible trade account ignores the fact that Britain is especially strong in the provision of marketed services, primarily through the City of London. Thus, as foreign real incomes grow an increasing contribution to the balance of payments can be expected from the invisible trading account.[18] At first sight this argument is reasonable: Britain possesses a long-standing comparative advantage in the provision of international services, but it is noteworthy that as the decline in Britain's share of world manufactured exports has accelerated in the last fifteen years, so this has been matched (apart from a period of stabilisation between 1967 and 1971) by a decline in the share of invisibles (see Table 25, p. 155, for 'UK Share in World Trade in Invisibles and Private Services 1955-76'). In this light it would be wrong to place too much faith in the contribution of marketed services to the balance of payments. As one observer has pointed out:

> ... the problem facing the UK is that here exports of service already command a relatively large share of what is still a relatively small market. To illustrate this by the position in 1976, imagine that the UK's share of world exports of manufactures had been smaller than it was by one percentage point. This would have meant a loss to the current account of £3·1 billion. To compensate for this by raising exports of services by the same sum would have involved increasing the UK's share of world exports of services by about a third, from 9·7 per cent to 13·0 per cent. If allowance is made for the very low import content of services compared with exports, the magnitude of the task would be less, but it would still be considerable.[19]

In short, preoccupation with the manufacturing sector of British industry can be justified not only on the grounds of recent trends in the international market for services, but also on the relative importance of manufactured exports to the balance of payments.

Once the Cambridge definition is adopted, de-industrialisation as a phenomenon affecting the British economy, in particular, is placed in its correct historical perspective. It is in fact nothing more than a new name for a process which began a century ago – the progressive inroads of foreign competition in Britain's overseas markets and the growing import penetration of foreign manufactured goods in the domestic market. In other words, 'Britain's economic problem was not that there were too few producers. It was that the producers were not producing enough, not exporting enough and not investing enough. The problem ... , in fact was much the same as it had been for many years.'[20] The 'Cambridge' view of de-industrialisation, therefore, has the great merit of drawing attention to the historic causes of Britain's economic malaise and it is in this light that the timeliness and astuteness of the Cambridge Economic Policy Group's (CEPG) case for a return to protectionism should be judged.

The case for protectionism is based on four fundamental arguments. First, there is what can be termed the 'historical' argument as advanced by Lords Balogh and Kaldor. In their view the British economy has performed most satisfactorily in the present century when it has been insulated from external influences.[21] Thus the two world wars are noted not just for their detrimental effects on Britain's long-term financial solvency but also for their beneficial effects in encouraging the development of new industrial sectors and the modernisation of manufacturing techniques (see above pp. 31,102). Moreover, the so-called 'new' industries flourished in interwar Britain under a regime of protective duties, first under the Safeguarding of Industries legislation in the 1920s and then under the 1932 Import Duties Act (see above p. 73). In the view of Balogh and Kaldor it is the progressive liberalisation of Britain's external economic relationships since 1950,[22] including most recently (and for them notoriously) entry to the EEC, which has led to the current impasse. On the basis of Verdoorn's hypothesis on the productivity of manufacturing investment they argue, therefore, for a return to protection in order to achieve economic growth through a 'virtuous circle' – that is, a faster rate of growth of the domestic market leading to higher industrial investment with favourable effects on the rate of economic growth in the medium and longer term.[23]

The second argument in favour of protectionism is more complex: it is derived from an earlier version of the 'virtuous circle' concept. As advanced in the early 1960s the case for a virtuous circle of economic growth was based upon the desirability of sterling devaluation to promote export-led growth. The validity of this notion, which came to be associated with W. Beckerman and a number of associated economists[24] has been increasingly questioned in recent years. The reasons for this are relatively straightforward. First, the depreciation of sterling, in promoting domestic inflation (given the inelasticity of British import demand) leads in turn to a wage/price spiral thus worsening the country's foreign balance. This is indeed one of the prime reasons why the CEPG reject the case for sterling depreciation as a means of correcting the foreign balance in a situation when public expenditure needs to be cut. As indicated above (see p. 110), the balance-of-payments situation should be buttressed by means of import controls which would maintain domestic output and employment. Secondly, there is now a considerable body of empirical evidence which points to the fact that despite a substantial labour-cost advantage over its principal competitors[25] (see Table 26, p. 156, for 'International Comparison of Labour Costs'), together with an industrial structure comparable with that even of West Germany,[26] British manufacturing industry in general is incapable of responding vigorously to the advantages conferred by enhanced price competitiveness through devaluation in overseas markets. The problem here would appear to be that the world income elasticity of demand for British exports is lower than Britain's income elasticity of demand for imports.[27] It is in this context that we can refer to a 'balance-of-payments constraint' on the British growth rate. Between 1965 and 1975 productivity grew faster on average in Britain than between 1955 and 1965[28] yet the employment released by this productivity growth has been reabsorbed not by productive industry but by the non-market sector. According to Thirlwall the growth of the latter is a symptom of the inability of the 'marketable output (mainly industrial) sector to grow as fast as productivity growth without the economy coming up against a balance of payments constraint' due to the unfavourable elasticities referred to above.[29] What this suggests is that it is the handicap of non-price factors, such as delivery dates, quality of design and reliability in performance, which are a principal cause both of import penetration and the declining share of the world market for manufactures.[30] The example *par excellence* of this, at least in the public mind, is the motor vehicle industry. A recent report by the Central Policy Review Staff on the volume car production sector showed that in comparable plants in Britain, West Germany, France and Italy, output-per-man was lowest in Britain due to a combination of production-line stoppages, overmanning of identical machinery and a depressing number of quality and design faults.[31]

A further argument in favour of protectionism rests on the alleged bankruptcy of Keynesianism and the limitations, both political and economic, of the obverse policy of monetarism. With regard to the former it has long been fashionable in political and academic circles to speak of 'The End of the Keynesian Era'.[32] The postwar consensus on the conduct of economic policy – epitomised in the early 1950s by 'Butskellism' – assumed that successful economic management could be achieved through the control of demand. In the late 1950s the Keynesian approach to economic policy received a considerable boost with the appearance of the celebrated Phillips curve which purported to provide unequivocal evidence of the existence of a trade-off between the level of unemployment and the rate of change of money wages.[33] What the analysis of Professor Phillips suggested – later supported by Professor Paish[34] – was that if only the economy could be run at a lower pressure of demand (that is with an unemployment rate of 2½–3 per cent) the consequent reduction in trade union bargaining power would lessen inflationary pressure and hence increase the competitiveness of British industry thus easing the problem of the foreign balance. Experience in the late 1960s and 1970s, however, has served to discredit the Phillips curve and with it the essential basis of Keynesianism: the combination of high and rising unemployment with intensified cost-push inflation demonstrated that avoiding excessive demand was not a sufficient condition for controlling inflation.[35] No doubt there is some level of unemployment which would lead to a reduction in the rate of increase of money wages but it is difficult to envisage any government pursuing a policy on these lines to the extent required, if only to avoid the attendant political danger. The fact remains that has itself served to intensify cost inflation in the postwar economy, the public commitment to full employment. There is a school of thought which subscribes to the view that since the end of the war successive British governments have become increasingly 'irrational' and 'ineffective' in their conduct of economic policy.[36] In short, Keynesian economic policy prescriptions, which were formulated in an era when the political and administrative machine was well insulated from popular democratic pressures (despite the existence of mass unemployment), have led, since 1950, to successive governments being subjected to the competing claims of increasingly powerful pressure groups and an electorate with ever-rising expectations. It is suggested, therefore, that in the postwar era the policy-making élite has succumbed to a demanding electorate which has cast its vote according to which political party has made the most extravagant promises in favour of increased public expenditure and this has contributed powerfully towards inflationary pressure in the economy. It is precisely because of the full employment commitment, the principal legacy of the Keynesian revolution, that governments in the last twenty years have been obliged to embark on prices and incomes policies rather than by seeking to reduce inflationary pressures by means of bankruptcies and unemployment.[37] They have been drawn inexorably into the microeconomic sphere from which Keynesianism promised to keep them (see below p. 128 for the examples of Rolls Royce and UCS). Despite short-term successes the repeated failures of incomes policies since 1961 and disillusion with the 'featherbedding' of unprofitable industrial sectors has led, since 1968, to the growing popularity of 'monetarism' as a solution to Britain's economic problems.[38]

Monetarism as an economic policy is identified with the economics of the free market. Its considerable political implications are commented upon below (see p. 129). In the present context it is sufficient to note that whilst the unprecedented growth of the money supply (however defined) in the early 1970s (see Table 27, p. 157, for 'Growth Rate of UK Money Supply, 1968–73') contributed towards the rapid pace of inflation in 1974–5[39] there is a danger that the monetarist approach to economic policy (strict control of the money supply leading to a stiffening in employer resistance to 'excessive' wage claims and possibly to a rising tide of bankruptcies) will ignore the fact that there are many causes of inflationary pressure. Monetarists are in fact attempting to explain a highly complex phenomenon – the rate of price inflation – by reference to only two variables – the rate of growth of the money supply and the *expected* rate of inflation. The latter is extremely difficult to measure and although control of the former can certainly exert deflationary pressure on the economy this is to ignore the fact that inflation is the result of many different kinds of expenditure – consumers' expenditure, public expenditure, investment, imports – all of them financed in different ways, with borrowing from the banking system being only one.[40]

Thus, for the protectionist we are seemingly led to the final policy option of trade controls. Modern protectionists do not deny that exchange rate manipulation, incomes policy whether statutory or voluntary, and control of the money supply are irrelevant to the solution of Britain's ills. On the contrary, all three have a part to play and if a consensus view on the future course of economic policy were to emerge from the tripartite discussions between employer, trade union and government representatives held under the auspices of the National Economic Development Council (NEDC), so much the better.[41] But although they are legitimate and necessary tools of economic management, the protectionist would claim that whether they are applied singly or in combination they have distinct limitations.

Those who argue in favour of protectionism are not only motivated by what they regard as the inadequacies of previous and existing economic policies but also by the necessity in their view for a 'breathing space' for British manufacturing industry during which time the enhanced opportunities for expansion in a more self-sufficent home market will generate business confidence, and hence the extra industrial investment which is vitally necessary if the economy is to move to a higher rate of economic growth which can be sustained in the long term. The question remains, however, as to the form that protection would take. At the popular level protection evokes the picture of a 'siege' economy with Britain cast adrift from the mainstream of international economic life, the population experiencing a low standard of living and the economy as a whole subject to a panoply of controls reminiscent of those applied to the countries of Eastern Europe. All of this is in sharp contrast to the apparently modest proposals of the CEPG. In the first instance there would be no restriction on food and raw material imports. Secondly, controls would be operated in such a way as 'to maintain the shares of different foreign countries in semi and manufactured imports the same as they would have been'.[42] Under these circumstances the growth of manufactured imports would possibly be limited to 8 per cent per annum. Thirdly, industries would be offered equal protection except where a case for selectivity could be made on the grounds of welfare, security or efficiency. As Cripps and Godley point out, 'As a first approximation this suggests the use of uniform tariffs on imports or alternatively, some form of auction of quotas to make a predetermined amount of foreign currency available for these imports. But some selectivity may be necessary to maintain the shares of different sources of supply at roughly constant levels, or indeed to promote the most efficient development of domestic industry.'[43] Singh's analysis differs from that of Cripps and Godley to the extent that he rejects the case for selectivity on the grounds that it is little more than a euphemism for controls on manufactures from Japan and third world countries and also because of the general competitive weakness of British industry when compared, say, with West Germany.[44]

In advocating import controls as a means to full employment Cripps and Godley claim that they are a significant policy option in so far as they escape the dilemma posed by the unsatisfactory alternatives of deflation and devaluation. That may well be true in theory, but in practice it has to be said that protectionism would raise a hornets' nest of problems for Britain, both internal and external. To deal with the external first. Clearly, whether protection is obtained by tariffs or quota import restrictions, it is inconsistent with Britain's international trading obligations under GATT, commitments to the IMF and especially in relation to the EEC. As far as the Common Market is concerned the imposition of import controls by Britain, a country hardly noted for its constructive attitude towards the European ideal since obtaining membership, would call forth a storm of protest. Not only would a British government be undermining the cardinal principle of the Treaty of Rome, it would also be giving aid and comfort to those elements in other countries favouring a return to 1930s-style autarchy with all the attendant political and economic problems that this would give rise to. Such an argument would carry great weight with the USA and the other non-EEC signatories of GATT and the possibility of foreign retaliation against British manufactured exports could not be ruled out. In answer to these strictures the Cambridge response would be to point to the modesty of their proposals and the fact that under the right conditions the volume of world trade would not contract and might even expand.[45] In any case, the presumption would be that a British government would not act unilaterally on the matter, certainly not in relation to its EEC partners. It could be argued that the Western world in general and the EEC in particular has a vested interest in a strengthened British economy, and that the EEC has already demonstrated its willingness to limit trade between member states in agricultural produce (wine) where the special interests of member countries were at stake. All that can be said on this is that despite the reasonableness of these points they could well be lost in the furore which would follow the announcement of the British intention, especially in view of its timing

– when the terms of trade are moving against the manufacturing nations, and when North Sea oil is making a substantial contribution to the balance of payments.

Turning now to the internal problems and difficulties that would be raised by protection. Even if Britain were to secure international consent for its policy there must be real doubts as to the likely effectiveness of protectionism in promoting the regeneration of manufacturing industry. At first sight the protectionist case is a strong one. Reference has already been made to Lord Balogh's view that in the twentieth century the occasions when the British industrial structure underwent favourable modification were under unusual circumstances – due either to the economic exigencies of world wars, or to the protective legislation of the interwar period (see above p. 112). The favourable impact of the latter on the development of modern industrial sectors was, of course, augmented by a considerable improvement in the terms of trade in Britain's favour in the later 1920s. But even in present conditions surely it can be argued that with the growing impact of North Sea oil on the British economy in the 1980s, a similar era of special circumstances has arrived which, with the aid of protective measures, should enable the country to reconstruct its manufacturing base to meet the international competitive demands of the final quarter of the twentieth century. In answering this question it is necessary to consider certain critical aspects of Britain's postwar economic history. The first factor concerns the balance of payments and the role of sterling as an international reserve currency. Most commentators are agreed that the progressive weakening of the British balance of payments since the mid-1950s (itself the resumption of a trend which had emerged before 1939), together with the international role of sterling (assiduously promoted by the authorities in the 1950s), has acted as a major constraint on Britain's economic performance in the last thirty years.[46] This volatile combination has meant that with a weakened visible trading performance (see Table 16, p. 149) due in part to the resurgence of the West German, Japanese and to a lesser extent French and Italian economies from the mid-1950s, international speculative pressure against sterling has obliged successive British governments to intervene in the management of the economy to restrain the level of activity in order to restore equilibrium in the balance of payments and hence foreign confidence in sterling. Over a number of years, beginning in the mid-1950s, this led to the infamous phenomenon of the 'stop-go' cycle, the arrival of which was usually heralded by the introduction of a package of deflationary measures by the hapless Chancellor of the day. Prominent among these measures would be restrictions on domestic consumers' purchasing power – the manipulation of hire-purchase controls, raising of interest rates, and so on – all of which in damaging the fortunes of the consumer durable industries arguably disrupted and discouraged long-term investment programmes.[47] Now, if it is accepted that the balance of payments and the reserve role of sterling were critical factors in retarding the growth of the economy, then it can be argued that since these constraints have disappeared (the reserve role of sterling was effectively ended with the floating of the pound on 23 June 1972) or are at least diminishing (due to the North Sea oil contribution to the balance of payments), surely the economy can move forward 'with the brakes off' due to the removal of a damaging element of periodic instability. A further point to bear in mind in this context – and it is one emphasised by Susan Strange in her penetrating analysis of *Sterling and British Policy*[48] in the 1950s and 1960s is the considerable reduction in government overseas expenditure, principally for military purposes, with the retreat from empire in the late 1950s and the progressive withdrawal from East of Suez due to the country's straitened economic circumstances after 1964.

In analysing the impact of the balance of payments and the role of sterling on the economy since 1950 the major issue which requires consideration is the presumed effects of the induced instability on the domestic economy, as often as not enhanced by inappropriate government policies. When the record is analysed in rigorous detail, however, the rather surprising conclusion emerges that over the period in question fluctuations in output in the British economy were *less* marked than in most other industrial countries.[49] As one authority has concluded, this suggests

> ... that the problem with the British economy was not so much any 'stop-go' pattern imposed by government policy, but rather the slowness of the rise in the underlying trend in output. Possibly the 'stop-go' pattern appeared more marked in the UK than in most other industrial countries because in those countries output was still rising significantly when it was below trend, whereas in Britain there tended to be virtually no rise at all in the 'stop' phases.[50]

This is certainly not to suggest that 'stop-go' did not have harmful effects in discouraging long-term investment programmes, merely that there were – and are – other forces at work which have accounted for and reinforced the comparative sluggishness of Britain's rate of economic growth.[51]

Of the other causal factors offered in explanation for this phenomenon each has its own group of protagonists and what follows is a brief, critical resumé of the principal diagnoses. But before beginning this part of the analysis there is one point which requires emphasis: many of the problems of the present British economy either had their origins or were masked in the 1950s, a decade which began with a Conservative election victory under the slogan 'set the people free' and ended with an impressive victory by the same party with the electioneering rallying call 'You've never had it so good'. In retrospect the 1950s appear as a kind of golden age of increasing affluence when full recovery from postwar austerity was achieved following the fanfare of a new-found national self-confidence provided first by the Festival of Britain in 1951 and secondly by the Coronation in1953, an event which many literary pundits claimed would herald the arrival of a new 'Elizabethan Age' when Britain, in some imperfectly understood way, would reachieve the glories of a distant past. Nothing could have been further from the truth. Following the Suez debacle in 1956 the later 1950s witnessed the race for decolonisation and the decade as a whole can be interpreted from the international economic perspective as a period of failure when Britain began to fall behind its principal competitors.

One of the difficulties confronting contemporaries was the rapidity of Britain's postwar decline. In 1949, aided by the preferential trading arrangements with its Commonwealth partners and imperial territories, together with the war-induced dislocation of Japan and Western Europe, Britain, briefly, had reachieved the proportion of world exports of manufactured goods which it had enjoyed in 1913. By 1960 the proportion had fallen to 16·5 per cent (see Table 15, p. 149) with the Japanese and West German economies performing particularly well at Britain's expense. By 1970 the proportion had fallen to 10·8 per cent and although the position improved slightly thereafter this was offset by the growing import penetration of the domestic market (8 per cent in 1961; 13 per cent in 1971; 21 per cent in 1976).

In explaining the rapidity of the decline there are four factors to take into account. First and foremost was the complacency induced by the continuing importance of Commonwealth markets for British manufactures. With the benefit of hindsight we know that these markets were destined to grow only slowly,[52] a factor of considerable relevance in justifying Britain's application to join the EEC in 1961 and the country's continued interest in the European connection after General de Gaulle's original veto (see below pp. 131-2). It is important to remember, however, that even at the end of the 1950s after a decade of decline, Sterling Area markets still accounted for 43 per cent of British manufactured exports (the equivalent figure had been 50 per cent in 1953).[53] The relative neglect of markets in Europe which were destined to grow extremely rapidly after the mid-1950s can be readily understood in the light of their postwar dislocation and the temporary enhancement, due to the dollar shortage, of Sterling Area markets. There was also the reinforcement of the sentimental link with the Commonwealth countries due, in part, to shared wartime experiences, an argument powerfully articulated by Lord Balogh when he referred in the early 1950s to 'emotional relationships, which are more stable than some economists seem to give credit' and the 'solid basis of mutual interest' in the formalised Sterling Area arrangements which had emerged from the war.[54]

The second factor which should be considered in explaining the lack-lustre performance of the economy in the 1950s concerns the extremely broad area of management and trade unions. Taking the latter first, it would not be inaccurate to say that of all the elements of British society which have been singled out for special abuse in retarding the rate of economic growth, the trade union movement stands in a class of its own.[55] This view is supported by the fact that since the late 1960s the subject of trade union reform has been a major political issue and no doubt will continue to be so into the 1980s.[56] The most extreme criticism of British trade unions is that in comparison with their foreign counterparts, notably in the more buoyant European economies, they are politically motivated organ- isations with no vested interest in the success of the capitalist or, indeed, the mixed economy system, and have been prepared to use their considerable power to secure an especially privileged position in British society. These are the criticisms of the 1960s and 1970s rather than of the 1950s, but there is one important factor to note about the latter decade and it is that successive Conservative administrations embarked on policies, largely for historical and personal reasons, to appease the trade union movement thus exacerbating the problem of inflation, whether of the cost-push or demand-pull type. The prime manifestations of this are to be found in Sir Winston Churchill's injunction to his newly appointed Minister of Labour, Sir Walter Monckton, that there were to be no damaging industrial disputes during his premiership and that Monckton should use his considerable powers of conciliation to achieve this result.[57] Churchill was probably motivated by the wish to live down his 'hawkish' reputation derived primarily from his aggressive role as Chancellor of the Exchequer in 1926. Historical considerations of a personal nature seem also to have affected Harold Macmillan during his tenure of the Exchequer in the mid-1950s. Brittan, in his analysis of the Treasury under the Tories, recounts that there was an in-joke among Treasury officials at the time – to count the number of occasions in one week that the Chancellor referred to Stockton-on-Tees.[58] Macmillan had been Member of Parliament for the depressed Stockton constituency in the 1920s and, being an expansionist at heart, was simply determined that his period at the Exchequer should not be marred by monetary and fiscal restriction.[59]

Nevertheless, as far as the trade union movement is concerned, Britain is the prisoner of its past – the first industrial nation with the longest established tradition of trade union activity. As Phelps Brown has pointed out,

> Institutions like trade unions seem to have a law of their own being: as they begin, so they go on, not only in their structure, but in the perceptions they inculcate of their own function and of the environment in which they have to operate. For British trade unions that propensity has been enhanced by another feature that strikes the foreign observer of our inviolate isles – the extraordinary continuity of their history: they have had no revolution, no defeat in war and no foreign occupation to give them a fresh start. How understandable it is, then, that the structure and outlook of British trade unionism should still bear the marks of the hard world in which it fought its way up.[60]

The above factors, combined with 'the tradition of insecurity coming down from the early days of industrialisation in the UK', reinforced since 1918 by the collapse of the staple export trades and deeply imprinted collective memories of the 1930s depression, go far to explain the conservatism of British trade unions, their propensity to perpetuate overmanning and restrictive labour practices, and finally their extreme sensitivity on the issue of trade union reform by parliamentary legislation.

On the side of management, there is an almost equal volume of criticism. Probably the most penetrating and concise analysis of British managerial standards is to be found in the celebrated Brookings Institution study of the British economy published in 1968. There, British management is castigated for its poor overall quality, its amateurism and lack of professionalism, qualities exacerbated by the extensive 'old boy' network which had played a major role in perpetuating the lethargy of the managerial class.[61] This is, of course, a stereotype image: such criticisms are of long standing and go as far back as the late nineteenth century. But, as with all stereotypes, it contains a grain of truth. In international terms British managerial standards do leave much to be desired, although to be fair to management its performance (as in the late nineteenth century) cannot be divorced from the wider society in which it operates. In postwar Britain the trend was perpetuated for the most talented of the nation's youth to enter the established professions, to avoid the world of industry, and although it has been recently pointed out that the social structure of management is now much more broadly based than it once was, the same authority has conceded that 'Attitudes and perceptions formed by the old order persist and in some quarters are deliberately fostered'.[62]

Another area of weakness in the postwar economy is to be found in the allocation of scarce investment resources. The Brookings study ascribed particular importance to this issue[63] and it has received further attention more recently in the debate on de-industrialisation. In 1955 total research and development expenditure in Britain amounted to £187 million, the highest figure for any country in Western Europe, yet 63 per cent of this total was spent on defence and less than one-third funded by private industry.[64] It was not so much that Britain was neglecting research and development but that the resources involved were being misallocated. As one survey has pointed out, if British governments had proceeded with all defence projects until their completion in the period 1955–64, they would have absorbed double the amount of research and development funds available.[65]

There were, in fact, two distinctive aspects of the pattern of research and development expenditures in the 1950s and 1960s, first 'the extraordinarily high concentration of British effort in the aircraft industry compared with Germany and Japan', and secondly, 'the very high proportion of British research and development which is government-financed and directed to a few areas of high technology – especially military technology, aerospace, and military electronics'[66] (see Table 28, p. 158, for 'Estimated Industrial Distribution of Research and Development Expenditure 1962'). Two examples stand out as an indication of government short-sightedness, if not irresponsibility, in allocating scarce investment resources. In the 1950s there was the nuclear power programme, not just in its military aspect but also in the civil application of electricity generation. It may well be that under the prospective conditions of energy supply in the late twentieth century nuclear power will have an enhanced role to play, despite the vociferousness of the environmentalist lobby, but for Britain in the circumstances of the 1950s to be operating at the frontiers of technology – however successfully in the context of the times – in a high-risk, multi-million-pound industry, appears in retrospect to have been a mistake. Prestige was a luxury that postwar Britain could ill-afford: despite its early lead in electricity generation by nuclear power Britain has been unable to exploit overseas markets for nuclear power plants, and such activities were best left to those with the requisite expertise *and* financial resources.[67] The second illustration, derived from the 1960s, is located in the aircraft industry. Again, Britain, admittedly in co-operation with France, was operating at the limits of known technology in the 'race' to produce a supersonic passenger transport aircraft. All that needs to be said on the issue of Concord is that in spite of the escalating cost of the project and the extreme uncertainty as to its financial viability, many hundreds of millions of pounds were swallowed up in an exercise which must rank as 'an unmitigated commercial disaster without historical parallel in the British Isles'.[68] It may well be said in

mitigation that the excellence of such scientific and engineering
endeavours brought valuable prestige to Britain, and in the case of
Concord there were obvous difficulties in reneging on a joint contract
with a prospective (and suspicious) EEC partner. But both of the
quoted examples are exquisite illustrations of the fact that governments are motivated by criteria other than the strictly economic in
arriving at investment decisions. Although Britain did achieve some
astonishing successes in military technology, aerospace, electronics
and pharmaceuticals,[69] especially in the light of the immense competitive and financial advantages enjoyed by the USA, the counterpart of
the British effort was the relatively low proportion of research and
development expenditure devoted to the more mundane areas of
machinery and vehicles (see Table 28, p. 158), precisely the sectors of
manufacturing industry in which Germany and Japan were to have
their most important export successes. Despite the impressive British
performance in areas like radar and aeroengines, it would appear that
the overall returns were low and to make matters worse such high
prestige activities drained off the most talented scientists and engineers
who, from the strictly commercial standpoint, would have been better
employed in conventional manufacturing industry – in machinery,
vehicles and metal products.[70]

Another aspect of the same problem derives from the status of
engineering as a profession. In comparison with many continental
countries British engineers enjoy low status, both socially and
materially. This was a phenomenon which drew critical comment
from Sir John Baker, Professor of Engineering at the University of
Cambridge when he remarked in a study published in 1964, that the
most talented sixth formers were opting for pure science degree
courses while the less gifted opted for engineering.[71] The practical
results of this pattern of behaviour both in terms of research and
development expenditure and attitudes towards education can be
illustrated by the following examples – the decimation of the British
audio industry by Swedish and Japanese competition; the loss of jobs
in the television manufacturing industry; the initial neglect of digital
watches and pocket calculators; the destruction of the British motor
cycle industry beginning in the late 1950s; and finally, the growing
import penetration by foreign manufacturers of the domestic car
market.[72]

Having dealt briefly with management and trade unions, more
specific comment should be made on the activities of government.
This has already been touched upon in relation to the management of
the economy and research and development expenditures. Although
it has been noted that the British economy has been no more
susceptible to instability than other economies, nevertheless it
remains true that continual concern with the exchange rate and the

balance of payments has meant that the postwar Treasury for good or ill, has continued to occupy a position of considerable power in the formulation of economic policy. Whether or not the Treasury was a bastion of narrow conservatism is largely irrelevant in the present context: it is sufficient to note that its central role has served to direct attention away from consideration of the long-term growth prospects of the economy. It was in fact one of the most dangerous legacies of the Keynesian revolution that it implicitly assumed that if only demand was right supply could look after itself. In the circumstances of the 1930s, in conditions of mass unemployment, such a view was understandable, but in the postwar era the Keynesian consensus served to draw attention away from the supply side of the equation to the detriment of the country's long-term growth potential.[73] From time to time this fact seems to have been recognised by governments. Indeed, it is salutary to remember that Sir Stafford Cripps, before his elevation to the Exchequer in 1947, briefly held the office of Minister of Economic Affairs with specific responsiblity for 'planning'. Again in the early 1960s the creation by the Macmillan government of the NEDC, following the 'great reappraisal' of 1960,[74] was recognition of the structural weaknesses of British industry, the adverse conse-quences of 'stop-go' economic policies, and the need to enhance the economy's long-term growth prospects by introducing measures of indicative planning.[75] In 1964 the incoming Labour government established the Department of Economic Affairs which was specifi-cally designed to provide a counterweight to the Treasury in the policy-making machine.[76] As is well known, the Department's 'National Plan' published in September 1965[77] which contained targets for the growth of output, exports and incomes, was soon forgotten in the debacle surrounding the devaluation of sterling in 1967. The epitaph for the Department was written by Sir Harold Wilson himself when in retrospect he stated:

> The fact was that in the peculiar circumstances of those years, with an inherited balance of payments deficit and hostile speculative activity ... the successful asertion of positive growth policies, often involving valuable long-term industrial invest-ment but at a damaging short-term cost in demand terms was not possible.[78]

The creation of the NEDC and the Department of Economic Affairs were not, of course, the only governmental measures on the side of supply. It is possible to point to other initiatives such as the creation of the Monopolies Commission in 1948, the Restrictive Trade Practices Act of 1956, the Industrial Training Act of 1964 and the founding of the Industrial Reorganisation Corporation in 1966 as evidence of a continuing preoccupation with supply. But, as a number of observers have pointed out, continuous concern with the balance of payments and the exchange value of sterling inevitably diverted attention away from long-term policy formulation and enhanced the role of the Treasury whose primary function it was to correct the country's external imbalance.[79]

This brief review of some of the more important features of the British economy may serve to underline the fact that protectionism by itself is not a sufficient means of securing industrial regeneration. This point is readily recognised by the Cambridge economists. Singh, for example, suggests that import controls would need to be supplemented by an 'active industrial policy' with the aim of greatly increasing the volume of manufacturing investment according to 'a preconceived long-term plan'.[80] Under this strategy, therefore, import controls would, in effect, be permanent and to those who would argue that protectionism is a form of restrictive practice which 'breeds vested interests like beetles in a dung heap',[81] Singh would no doubt point out that under a Labour administration the dangers of American-style big business 'corruption' which exercised the minds of anti-protectionists in pre-1914 Britain, would be offset by 'a strengthening and greatly increased use of existing policy instruments, such as planning agreements and a far larger allocation of investment funds to the National Enterprise Board'.[82] It is at this stage, however, that political realities enter Singh's analysis for he goes on to point out that given the existing relationship between government and industry in Britain, an interventionist policy of this kind would in all probability be opposed by the business community. Certainly, in its opposition it would receive every encouragement from the Conservative Party. Singh concludes that in the event of reduced private investment and/or increased capital exports 'the government might have to undertake investment directly, impose stringent exchange controls and ultimately perhaps even nationalise the foreign multinationals'.[83] In other words, the 'command economy' beloved of the left wing of the Labour Party would have arrived.

In considering the possibility of an interventionist policy as propounded by Singh, there are two points to take into account. In political terms it is difficult to envisage the enactment of such a policy, especially the more extreme version, without a substantial Labour majority in the House of Commons elected with an interventionist mandate. The willingness to impose a 'command' or 'siege' economy would also require a fundamental change in the balance of power within the Labour Party in general and the parliamentary party in particular. It is, of course, entirely conjectural as to whether either of these conditions would ever be met. Secondly, from the economic standpoint, the presumed success of the interventionist option is based upon an act of faith, namely that the public sector is capable of mobilising capital resources and utilising them more effectively than an unsupervised private sector. Unfortunately, as has been pointed out (see above p. 123), there is little justification for believing that the state would be any more rational or effective in allocating investment resources than under the conditions of the present mixed economy. In the case of the imposition of a siege economy, presumably by a left-wing-dominated Labour government, with an enhanced role for the National Enterprise Board (NEB) enjoying a massive injection of funds derived from North Sea oil revenues, it would be naïve to assume that economic objectivity would be the order of the day. It is true that previous Labour administrations have demonstrated their willingness to run down unprofitable sectors, even within the nationalised industries – coalmining in the mid-1960s is a good, if ironic, example – but on the assumption that such a government was dependent for its parliamentary majority on Labour members elected from the old industrial heartlands of Britain – south Wales, the central industrial belt of Scotland, the north-east of England, southern Lancashire and the West Midlands – it can be presumed that it would be especially sensitive to demands for the subsidisation of unprofitable industries, especially in the era of North Sea oil. This should not be taken as an implied criticism of subsidisation policies. From the social perspective the case in their favour may be powerful, if not of overriding importance. It is merely to point to the more obvious pressures to which a Labour government, in the circumstances described, would be subjected.

Perhaps in recognition of the potential difficulties presented by the siege economy, Singh posits an alternative policy under which import controls could be introduced, with justification, by a Conservative government even of 'the extreme right wing variety'. This can be termed the protectionist 'free market' option under which import controls would be supplemented by an industrial policy designed to promote competition. As Singh points out, 'Those who believe in the beneficial influence of competition on economic activity could simply institute a stringent anti-trust policy on the supply side instead of the existing plethora of direct controls, many of which were in fact brought in by a previous Conservative administration.'[84] In view of Britain's industrial structure, it could well be that such a policy would be beneficial. One of the most impressive features of the development of British industry from the end of the nineteenth century has been the successive merger waves, both vertical and horizontal, to which it has been subjected, the first in the 1890s, the second in the 1920s and the third, after a longer interval of time, in the 1960s. The results of this activity have been dramatic (see Tables 29 and 30, p. 159, for 'The Increasing Concentration of Net Assets in UK Manufacturing

Industry 1957–69' and 'The Share of the Largest 100 Firms in UK Manufacturing Net Output 1909–70'). Even before entering the EEC, Britain possessed more giant firms (that is companies employing over 40,000 workers) than in all the rest of the EEC countries together.[85] Conversely, at the other end of the scale, Britain now has 'the most attenuated small firm sector of any major industrial nation'.[86] In the 1960s, governmental attitudes towards mergers were reflected in the establishment of the Labour government's Industrial Reorganisation Corporation, a body specifically created to promote the establishment of rationalised large-scale companies which would be in a position to obtain maximum advantage from scale economies with beneficial effects on their international competitiveness. A decade later, however, at the end of the 1970s, the benefits of such mergers are being increasingly questioned.[87] As one authority on 'the rise of the corporate economy' has emphasised, 'post mortems of the mergers of the 1960's have shown little evidence that either the social or private benefits expected from them have materialised'.[88] In the first instance, the growth in the size of firms has resulted in an increase in multiplant operation rather than in the growth of plant size. This phenomenon is more noticeable in Britain than elsewhere and provides *prima facie* evidence that technical factors were of limited importance in encouraging merger activity. Secondly, it should be borne in mind that by the early 1970s seventy-five firms accounted for 50 per cent of Britain's export trade and as few as thirty-one for 40 per cent. As one observer has remarked, 'In this kind of scenario, one has a situation where a few dozen very large companies account for half of British manufacturing output, employment and visible export trade with the clear consequence that they are also price-leaders for the dominant share of manufacturing output.'[89] This concentration in Britain's export trade helps to explain a number of interesting phenomena in the country's export performance in the last ten to fifteen years. In so far as many of these large-scale enterprises are multinational concerns it is a distinctive feature of their mode of operation that in comparison with West German and Japanese firms, their permanent overseas representation in important export markets is either very low or non-existent.[90] Secondly, a recent analysis of the response of visible exports to the 1967 sterling devaluation showed that British firms were strangely reluctant to take advantage of the situation by lowering foreign prices, increasing volume exports and enlarging their share of foreign markets.[91] It would appear that a key factor underlying this pattern of behaviour is the much greater degree of foreign production by British firms when compared with their German and Japanese competitors. Account must also be taken of the very low share of exports in the total production of multinational firms in Britain (generally less than 10 per cent).[92] Although the motor industry has a higher rate, this is due to the export of components rather than finished models and, in any case, it tends to be offset by higher import ratios. Thus, on these grounds alone, the apparent lack of interest of large-scale enterprise in exporting and its preference for multiplant operation suggests that there is an excellent case for any British government, irrespective of its political complexion, keeping a close scrutiny on the activities of giant firms. Finally, it is a point worth re-emphasising that as a result of the merger movement of the 1960s and early 1970s Britain possesses the most circumscribed small-scale manufacturing sector of all the major industrial nations and, as Kay has concluded, 'it is not implausible that the associated loss of flexibility and opportunity for individual initiative has been an element of Britain's poor industrial performance'.[93]

If an aggressive competition policy, directed against mergers of doubtful value from the national standpoint, was all that was at stake in relation to the free market option (under protectionism) then there would be little argument against it. However, those who praise the efficacy of market forces also generally support the reduction of government subsidisation and other taxation advantages as far as private industry is concerned. As a political philosophy this view of the conduct of economic policy has gained an increasing hold on the Conservative Party in the middle and later 1970s. A major component of the industrial policy of the present government is to reject the subsidisation of 'inefficient' enterprises, whether in the public or private sectors, and it has also presented a case for the running down of state financial assistance to industry generally. On the basis of past experience there are immense obstacles in the way of such a programme. First, there is the example of the 1970–4 Conservative government which came to office determined to implement its free market 'Selsdon' programme. Within two years that programme was looking very battered indeed following the state-financed reconstruction of the bankrupt aeroengine division of Rolls Royce and the attempt to retain as many jobs as possible (after a particularly effective 'work-in' by the labour force) following the collapse of Upper Clyde Shipbuilders. In retrospect, this episode in recent British economic history can be viewed as an illustration of the close interpenetration of industry and government[94] – the fact that by the early 1970s the great majority of private industrialists had become accustomed to and dependent upon extensive state intervention, especially since few of them appeared keen 'to live with the consequences of their mistakes and misfortunes'.[95] At the present time it is highly likely that there are many employers who would side with the trade union movement and the Labour Party in resisting the economics of the free market.

A further critical aspect of Conservative economic policy concerns the doctrine of monetarism (see above pp. 114). This also has considerable political implications. As one authority has pointed out

> The 'announcement effect' of a monetary target on trade union wage claims and wage awards ... might have some plausibility if the trade union movement negotiated as a whole, [but] it is less plausible as a moderating influence on each individual union, which may consider that its own position is exceptional, and that its above-average wage claim will be offset by below-average wage claims elsewhere. There is also the political question of how far the government could claim that it was the trade unions which were responsible for high unemployment; it might be argued that, if the trade union structures or negotiating procedures were such as to lead to high unemployment, then it was the government's responsibility to change them.[96]

In the final analysis, the fate of the Conservative policy could well be decided by a test of nerve. In other words, at what point in its period of office does a government committed to reversing the secular trend in favour of state collectivism by substantially reducing the level of public expenditure abandon or modify its policies in the face of unemployment levels never before experienced since the 1930s? The answer to that question clearly depends upon a variety of factors, ranging from electoral considerations of greater or lesser complexity, to the ideological bias of the Cabinet in general, and the resolve of the Prime Minister, in particular, in resisting the inevitable cries for help from employers and trade unionists alike.

The interventionist and free market options as presented by Singh illustrate the fundamental point that in terms of the conduct of economic policy in Britain, whilst there has been a consensus over the management of demand for much of the period since 1950, there has been no such agreement between the major political parties over the management of supply. In relation to the latter they are in fact drawing increasingly apart. This raises the general issue of consistency of economic policy both within and between governments which is held by some to have had a detrimental effect on Britain's economic performance in the last twenty years. The point here is that given the British predilection for adversary politics, the game of electoral swings and roundabouts in a competitive political system has militated against the continuity of economic policy and the uncertainty generated, especially in an era of growing balance-of-payments disequilibrium, has arguably inhibited manufacturing investment.[97] This is one of the central features of Blackaby's analysis of government economic policy since 1960. Citing anti-inflationary policy as the best example he comments:

There was no continuity in the attempt to establish institutions to modify the results brought about by free collective bargaining. The 1964 Labour government abolished the National Incomes Commission and created the National Board for Prices and Incomes. The 1970 Conservative government abolished the NBPI, and two years later created the Price Commission and the Pay Board. The 1974 Labour government abolished the Pay Board'.[98]

And now the incoming Conservative government has abolished the Price Commission. Anti-inflationary policy is not, however, the only area of inconsistency. To quote again from Blackaby's pertinent discussion:

... in fiscal policy, the system of corporate taxation was changed in 1958, changed back again in 1965, and changed once more in 1973; policy swung between discriminating or not discriminating against distributed profits; and there was also the change from investment allowances to investment grants and back again. In the field of indirect taxation we have the introduction and abolition of the selective employment tax. In industrial relations there were the attempts to 'bring the trade unions more within the framework of the law'; this legislation was also subsequently repealed. In policy towards the national-ised industries, there was alternation between encouraging them to act as independent commercial concerns, covering their costs, and forcing them to charge low prices in the interests of the government's anti-inflationary policy so driving them into deficit. In industrial policy, again the institution of one govern-ment – the IRC – was abolished by another.[99]

Blackaby concludes, with a distinct note of resignation, that one of the few areas of consistency between successive governments since 1960 was in their desire to join the EEC, but even here it should be noted that powerful elements within the Labour Party have attempted on more than one occasion to exploit the doubts of the electorate as to the benefits of membership for party political purposes.

On the subject of the EEC and its impact upon the British economy, it is premature to make any objective judgement. Britain has been a full member for only a comparatively short period of time, and this has coincided with immense changes in the structure of the world economy brought about not only by the dramatic rise in oil prices since 1973 but also by the increasing cost of many other imported foodstuffs and raw materials. Inevitably, therefore, the EEC – quite apart from the operation of the Common Agricultural Policy – has been blamed by many who should have known better as a prime cause of Britain's inflationary problems. At this stage it is instructive to return to the debates of the late 1950s and early 1960s to remind ourselves of the original reasons for the Macmillan government's application for entry to the EEC.

At the time of the signing of the Treaty of Rome in 1957, Britain's economic and emotional ties to the Commonwealth and Sterling Area were powerful enough to ensure that the government's response to the creation of the EEC was half-hearted and defensive. It took the form of an attempt to negotiate a free trade area without full economic integration, an approach which was particularly distasteful to the French who felt that Britain was seeking to obtain one of the principal benefits of economic integration without paying the necessary political cost in terms of the loss of national sovereignty inherent in the Rome Treaty.[100] The British approach was badly handled and, unsurprisingly, rejected. This was followed in 1959 by a successful British attempt to establish a European Free Trade Area (without harmonisation of external tariffs) to encompass a number of other European countries which had not been signatories of the Rome Treaty (the so-called 'outer seven', consisting of Britain, Sweden, Norway, Denmark, Switzerland, Austria and Portugal).[101]

In a number of respects, both political and geographical, EFTA was a much less viable entity than the EEC. The fact remains that with the formation of the latter, 'EFTA was, essentially of peripheral importance' and the core of the problem since 1957 'had always been, and would continue to be ... the relationship to be established between the United Kingdom and the Six'.[102] The fundamental point to note, however, is that the British decision to apply to join the EEC in July 1961 was motivated primarily by political and emotional rather than economic considerations. It was, in the words of two recent observers of postwar Britain, 'a means of restoring Britain to her old position at the centre of the three circles – Europe, America and the Commonwealth'.[103] The theory of interlocking circles had been the cornerstone of British foreign policy for much of the postwar period, and in the immediate circumstances of 1961 it is a fair assumption that Harold Macmillan regarded entry to the EEC not only as a means of restoring Britains's international political prestige but also as a means of reaching a new understanding with the USA in the aftermath of Suez, and especially in view of President Kennedy's desire for closer European economic union as a basis for the strengthening of NATO.[104] Viewed in this light the British application for entry was a profoundly conservative act rather than a radical departure in foreign policy.

Although political considerations were uppermost in the mind of the government in 1961 this is not to suggest that ministers were neglectful of the alleged economic benefits of entry. Macmillan himself, for example, referred publicly to the application as a 'purely economic and trading negotiation'.[105] But despite the government's attempts to present the economic case for entry to the EEC to the electorate, the factors that stand out in the debates on the merits of membership are the total bafflement of the general public as to the issues at stake and the lack of agreement among professional economists. Some economists, usually to the left of the political spectrum, shared an emotional, if at times fluctuating, antipathy to the EEC, and even where there was a willingness to countenance British membership it was, on occasion, grudging – almost to the extent of blaming the Rome signatories for having set in motion a train of events which might have disturbing effects upon Britain's international economic position which at that time appeared to be firmly linked to the Commonwealth and Sterling Area.[106]

Broadly speaking, the economic case for EEC membership resolved itself into three main issues: first, the economies which would accrue to Britain as a result of increased specialisation and large-scale production; secondly, the boost to industrial efficiency as a result of the exposure of British firms to the rigours of international (primarily West German) competition; and thirdly, the general stimulus to growth as a result of close association with a group of countries experiencing rapid economic expansion.[107] Ten years later, following the election of the Heath government and its successful attempt to join the EEC,[108] substantially the same arguments in favour of entry were presented, although in the government's White Paper on *The United Kingdom and the Economic Communities* special prominence was given to the bankruptcy of the Commonwealth option. The following paragraph appeared, significantly enough, in the section dealing with the political case for entry:

> the Commonwealth [does not] by itself offer us, or indeed wish to offer us alternative and comparable opportunities to member-ship of the European Community. The member countries of the Commonwealth are widely scattered in different regions of the world and differ widely in their political ideas and economic development. With the attainment of independence, their political and economic relations with the United Kingdom in particular have greatly changed and are still changing. They have developed and are still developing with other countries trade and investment arrangements which accord with the require-ments of their basic geographical and economic circumstances. The United Kingdom's share of the trade of the Commonwealth has declined sharply over the last decade. In absolute terms United Kingdom exports to the Commonwealth have grown only slowly, whilst our exports to the EEC have expanded much more rapidly, and in 1970 exceeded our exports to the whole of the Commonwealth. For many Commonwealth countries, too,

the European Communities increasingly appear as a more attractive trading partner than the United Kingdom. It is significant that the East African Commonwealth countries have now given the Community trade preferences over us.[109]

It is possible to look back on 100 years of British economic history and conclude that the secular trend in favour of imperial economic disintegration which began to appear even before 1914 (see above p. 22) reached its zenith in the early 1970s. In retrospect the campaign for Imperial Preference after 1903 and the 1932 Ottawa agreements were irrelevant to the long-term solution of Britain's mounting economic difficulties. The Ottawa agreements resulted merely in trade diversion and whilst Britain derived considerable economic advantages from the Commonwealth connection in the years of dollar shortage after 1945, this was a purely temporary phenomenon. Historically, a distinction has to be made between Imperial Preference and tariff protection. To contemporaries before 1914 and in the interwar period they were inextricably linked, but it is tempting to speculate on the course of British economic history, if, like other European countries and the USA, Britain had adopted a protective tariff in the generation before 1914. In an article written some years ago, Professor R.C.O. Matthews referred to the 'under-developed' nature of the pre-1914 economy which manifested itself in an excess supply of casual labour crowding into occupations where the availability of work was intermittent.[110] Although this phenomenon was diminishing in importance before 1914 due to the expansion of regular employment opportunities, it may well have been the case that 'underdevelopment' would have disappeared more rapidly with the aid of tariff protection.[111] A more buoyant domestic economy would have diminished the incentive to export such a high proportion of the nation's savings and under these circumstances Britain might well have gone further towards reducing the burden of industrial over-commitment by 1914. The possible deterioration in the invisible trade balance as a result of the loss of foreign investment income and the dislocation of the pattern of multilateral settlement might have been offset by the adoption of 'a moderate scale of infant-industry tariffs' (that is, a selective rather than a general tariff), a strengthened visible trade balance and an industrial structure which would have enabled the economy to have grown at a faster rate before 1914 and in the longer term enabled it to meet the economic difficulties of the interwar period more successfully than it did.[112] If this reasoning is accepted, then Britain has paid an exceptionally heavy price for its distinctive international economic role over many years. In this light it would be tempting to conclude that Britain has now found its rightful place in the world – a medium-rank European state located within the protective walls of the EEC. Politically, that may be the case. Certainly, the political arguments in favour of British membership as set out in the 1971 White Paper should have been sufficient to convince all but the most die-hard of insular nationalists, Commonwealth loyalists and Atlanticists. But as for the economics of EEC entry the point must be strongly reiterated that it would be premature to make any definitive pronouncements. At the time of entry in January 1973 belief in the economic benefits of membership was an act of faith: at the end of the 1970s that remains true. In the light of the analysis presented earlier in this chapter, however, the original economic arguments (in so far as they were based upon a short-term view of the likely impact of EEC membership on Britain) are beginning to look a little thin. At a time of international economic recession, the possibilities of growth stimulation arising from association with a dynamic EEC (always the weakest of the arguments for entry) are negligible, and in view of the general competitive weakness of British industry it seems highly unlikely, for the forseeable future, that advantage can be derived from scale economies. The alleged beneficial effects of the exposure of British manufacturing firms to vigorous European manufacturing competition also have a distinctly hollow ring. It is in this environment – in particular, Britain's strongly adverse balance of visible trade with the rest of the EEC – that the case for protectionism has been persuasively articulated. Yet, as argued earlier, this is a policy option which is politically unrealistic and is dependent for its validity upon what is arguably an even greater act of faith than entry to the EEC, namely the internal responsiveness of the British economy and its ability to take full advantage of the enhanced market opportunities on offer.

In his recent presidential address to the Royal Economic Society,[113] Professor A.J. Brown presented a diagnosis of Britain's economic problems on the following lines. He emphasised that since the early 1960s the economy has suffered from a constraint on the side of supply, due not to a shortage of labour, but to a low rate of manufacturing investment as a result of Britain's relatively high degree of wage and salary push. Economic expansion in 1963–4 and 1972–3 drew in large quantities of manufactured imports which resulted in permanent shifts in domestic market shares in favour of foreign suppliers.[114] Without analysing the causes of Britain's cost inflation – although his argument is consistent with a key element of the Bacon and Eltis thesis (see above pp. 107-8) – Professor Brown concluded that cost-push inflation has led to balance-of-payments difficulties and a consequentially slow rate of economic growth:

Cost-push inflation compresses profits and reduces investment both in capacity to produce tradeable goods and services and in efforts to sell them – probably in efforts to improve their design also. Productivity grows only slowly, and, given the rate of upward push of costs, this exacerbates the compression of profits. Under both fixed and floating exchange rates, slow growth of capacity and limited selling effort mean that sales respond slowly to opportunity. Meanwhile, under floating rates, the weakening of the pound [at least before 1979] on the foreign exchanges contributes to cost-push, both directly through import-prices and indirectly through the effects of these on wage demands.[115]

In conclusion, Professor Brown suggested a number of remedies which might enable Britain to escape from the associated evils of 'Inflation and the British Sickness'. First, whilst the influence of the British government is obviously limited, in view of the country's dependence on imported foodstuffs and raw materials the authorities should support all measures at international level that would reduce the rate of inflation of world prices. Secondly, there should be substantial and ongoing investment in manufacturing industry with the aim of promoting technical progress in general, with particular attention being devoted to product design, reliability and marketing. Thirdly, the state of demand in the domestic market requires careful consideration. This means that 'supply possibilities and growth targets should be agreed in advance by government, management and trade unions (through the medium of NEDC sector working parties) and that there should be some form of incomes policy in order to reduce the rate of cost-push inflation. To this list must be added two further remedies. In the era of North Sea oil the government should ensure that the revenues forthcoming are not used 'to postpone necessary increases in productivity, to preserve [Britain's] museum economy, and to continue indulging the myopia and Luddism of its management and unions'.[116] As Thirlwall has concluded:

> If the UK economy is to emerge wealthier as a result of the good fortune of North Sea oil, the oil revenue and balance of payments surplus must be used first and foremost for increasing the income elasticity of demand for UK exports. This means paying more attention to what the world wants and using both the tax revenues and balance-of-payments surplus to increase the output of the identifiable products.[117]

The final remedy is arguably the most important of all. It is the duty of politicians in general and governments in particular, irrespective of their political complexion, to educate the public as to the realities of Britain's economic position. This they signally failed to do in the twenty-five years after 1950. Their shortcomings in this regard are the essence of 'the political economy of failure' and they largely account for the fact that the deep-rooted and peculiarly British desire to achieve the fruits of economic growth, while grimly maintaining outmoded economic attitudes and institutional structures, has remained barely dented. Professor Brown is almost apologetic that his own list of remedies contains nothing new – 'only the need to do better with existing policies'. The legacy of relative economic failure is a long one and for that reason alone the task of industrial regeneration would be difficult enough. Although politicians and other interested parties might agree on the list of remedies drawn up by an academic economist there is, at present, no consensus as to the means of implementation. As one recent observer has persuasively argued, the consensus politics of the twentieth century were only established with great difficulty in the 1920s and henceforth rested on insecure foundations.[118] They were effectively undermined from the mid-1960s onwards when a social democratic Labour government failed in its attempt to curb the growing power of the trade union movement. The abandoment of 'Selsdon policies' by the Heath government after 1970, in the face of the collapse of major industrial concerns, has been followed by the emergence of a new Conservatism – that of the *petite bourgeoisie* – reflecting the ideals and aspirations of 'small businessmen and shopkeepers', politically and geographically isolated from the decaying industrial heartlands of Britain. If this analysis is correct, the outlook for the British economy is bleak in the extreme. It is no longer a question of speculating whether the British electorate will ultimately prefer the 'free market' or 'interventionist' approaches to reversing the process of industrial degeneration. In view of the historic and deep-seated nature of Britain's economic difficulties, together with the country's extreme vulnerability to international economic recession, in the absence of political consensus it is inevitable that the decline of British economic power will continue unabated.

Statistical Tables

Table 1   Balance of Payments and Export of Capital in the UK 1861–1913 (£ million in current prices)

Year (annual average for 5-year period)	Net imports (a)	Exports (b)	Balance of Commodity Trade (c) = (a) − (b)	Income from Services (d)	Income from Interest and Dividends (e)	Balance on Current Account (f) = (c) + (d) + (e)	Accumulating Balance of Credit Abroad (g)
1861–5	201·2	144·4	−56·8	57·1	21·8	22·0	490
1866–70	246·0	187·8	−58·2	67·9	30·8	40·5	692
1871–5	301·8	239·5	−62·2	86·8	50·0	74·6	1,065
1876–80	325·9	201·4	−124·5	93·0	56·3	24·9	1,189
1881–5	336·5	232·3	−104·2	101·0	64·8	61·6	1,497
1886–90	327·4	236·3	−91·1	94·6	84·2	87·6	1,935
1891–5	357·1	226·8	−130·3	88·4	94·0	52·0	2,195
1896–1900	413·3	252·7	−160·6	100·7	100·2	40·3	2,397
1901–05	471·5	297·0	−174·5	110·6	112·9	49·0	2,642
1906–10	539·6	397·5	−142·1	136·5	151·4	145·8	3,371
1911–13	623·2	488·8	−134·4	152·6	187·9	206·1	3,990

Source: Peter Mathias, The First Industrial Nation: An Economic History of Britain, 1700–1914 (1969), table 7, p. 305 (after A. H. Imlah, Economic Elements in the Pax Britannica (1958)). Table reproduced by permission of A. D. Peters & Co. Ltd.

Table 2   *World Exports of Manufactured Goods*
(Percentage Shares)

	1880	1890	1899	1913
UK	41·4	40·7	32·5	29·9
USA	2·8	4·6	11·2	12·6
France	22·2	17·1	15·8	12·9
Germany	19·3	20·1	22·2	26·5
Belgium	5·0	5·1	5·6	4·9
India	1·2	2·4	2·3	4·3
Japan	—	0·6	1·5	7·1

Source: S. B. Saul, 'The export economy 1870–1914', *Yorkshire Bulletin of Economic and Social Research,* vol. 17 (1965), table 5, p. 12

Table 3   *Average Annual Rates of Growth of Selected Indices of the UK Economy 1860–1913*

	Net National Income	Real Income per head	Output-per-man-hour	Industrial Production (including Building)	Industrial Productivity	Exports
1860–70	3·0	2·5	—	2·9	1·1	5·7
1870–80	1·9	0·8	0·9	2·4	1·2	2·8
1880–90	4·2	3·5	3·8	1·6	0·5	3·0
1890–1900	2·1	1·2	1·3	2·8	0·2	0·4
1900–13	1·1	0·4	0·6	1·6	0·2	4·2
1870–1913	2·3	1·3	1·5	2·1	0·6	2·7

Source: D. H. Aldcroft and H. W. Richardson (eds), *The British Economy, 1870–1939* (1969), table 1, p. 4. Table reproduced by permission of the Macmillan Press, London and Basingstoke.

Table 4 *Comparative Long-Term Rates of Growth 1870/1–1913 (per cent per annum)*

	Total Output	Output-per-man-hour	Industrial Production	Industrial Productivity	Exports (1880–1913)
UK	2·2	1·5	2·1	0·6	2·2
USA	4·3	2·3	4·7	1·5	3·2
Germany	2·9	2·1	4·1	2·6†	4·3
France	1·6	1·8	3·1*	N.A.	2·6

* = 1880–1913   † = rough estimate only   N.A. = not available

Source: D. H. Aldcroft (ed.), *The Development of British Industry and Foreign Competition, 1875–1914* (1968), table 2, p. 13.

Table 5   UK Balance of Payments 1920–38 (£ million)

Year	Visible Trade	Invisible Trade	Investment Income	Current Balance	Capital Flows		Balancing Item	Total Currency Flow
					Long-Term	Short-Term		
1920–9 inc.	−205	+100	+219	+114	−116	N.A.	+10	+8
1930–8 inc.	−255	+33	+183	−40	−12	−3	+87	+32
1924	−214	+74	+198	+58	−119	N.A.	+67	+6
1929	−263	+92	+247	+76	−52	−59	+27	−8
1931	−322	+41	+167	−114	−5	−252	+337	−34
1934	−220	+16	+172	−32	−36	+40	+38	+10
1937	−336	+68	+211	−57	−3	+88	+101	+129

N. A. = not available.   Short-term movements before 1928 are included in the balancing item in the absence of separate estimates.

Source: Calculated from *Bank of England Quarterly Bulletin* (March 1974), table B, p. 49. Cited in Sean Glynn and John Oxborrow, *Interwar Britain: A Social and Economic History* (1976), table 2.2, p.71.

Table 6   *Percentage Unemployed (Insured Workforce) 1920–39*

1920	2·6	1930	16·2
1921	15·6	1931	22·0
1922	13·6	1932	22·8
1923	11·5	1933	19·5
1924	9·7	1934	16·7
1925	11·2	1935	14·4
1926	14·4	1936	11·7
1927	9·2	1937	9·5
1928	11·8	1938	12·1
1929	9·7	1939	7·9

Source: D. H. Aldcroft, *The Inter-War Economy: Britain, 1919–1939* (Batsford, 1970), table 34, p. 305. For a different basis of computation see Glynn and Oxborrow, *Interwar Britain,* table 5.4, p. 149.

Table 7   *UK Balance of Visible Trade 1938–45 (£ million)*

	Exports	Imports	Visible Adverse Balance	Volume Index Exports	Imports
1938	471	858	387	100	100
1939	440	840	400	94	97
1941	365	1,132	767	56	82
1943	234	1,228	994	29	77
1945	399	1,053	654	46	62

Source: Central Statistical Office, *Statistical Digest of the War* (1951), Table 142. Table reproduced by permission of the Controller of Her Majesty's Stationery Office.

Table 8   *Treasury Estimates (mid-1945) of UK Current Account Deficit for 1946 (£ million)*

	1938	1946 estimate
Deficit on visible trade	−300	−650
Government expenditure abroad	−16	−300
Net invisible income	+248	+120
Total unfavourable balance (including some other items)	—	−750

Source: Derived from W. K. Hancock and M. M. Gowing, *British War Economy* (1949), p. 534. Table reproduced by permission of the Controller of Her Majesty's Stationery Office.

Table 9   UK Balance of Payments 1946-51 (£ million)

	Exports	Balance of Visible Trade	Total Current Balance of Payments	Change in Sterling Liabilities	Intergovernmental Transactions*	Other Capital Movements	Changes in Gold and Dollar Reserves
1946	917	−165	−295	+43	+240	+99	+87
1947	1,145	−415	−442	−112	+639	−301	−216
1948	1,602	−192	+7	−346	+437	−167	−69
1949	1,841	−137	+38	−9	+160	−207	−18
1950	2,250	−133	+297	+340	+127	−81	+683
1951	2,748	−419	+94	+94	−36	−266	−627

*+ = Receipts by UK; − = Payments by UK

Source: Cmd 9291 (1954). Table reproduced by permission of Her Majesty's Stationery Office.

Table 10   *Economic Growth in the UK, 1900–76*
(percentage increase per annum)

	GDP	GDP per man	Employed Labour Force	Capital Stock (excl. dwellings)
1900–13	1·0	0·0	1·0	1·9
1922–38	2·3	1·1	1·2	1·1
1950–60	2·6	2·2	0·4	2·8
1960–70	2·8	2·5	0·3	4·3
1970–6	1·6	1·4	0·2	3·8

Source: A. R. Prest and D. J. Coppock (eds), *The U.K. Economy: A Manual of Applied Economics* (7th edn, 1978), table 1.12, p.48. Table reproduced by permission of Weidenfeld & Nicolson Ltd.

Table 11   *Annual Growth Rates of Real Gross Domestic Product 1955–73 (per cent per annum)*

	1955–60	1960–4	1964–9	1969–73
UK	2·5	3·1	2·5	3·0
France	4·8	6·0	5·9	6·1
West Germany	6·4	5·1	4·6	4·5
Italy	5·4	5·5	5·6	4·1
EEC[a]	5·3	5·4	5·3	5·0

[a] = France, West Germany, Italy, Belgium and the Netherlands.

Source: D. T. Jones, 'Output, employment and labour productivity in Europe since 1955', *National Institute Economic Review,* no. 77 (August 1976), p. 80.

Table 12 *Annual Growth Rates of Gross National Product 1960–70 (per cent per annum)*

	1960–5	1965–8	1965–70
UK	3·4	2·3	2·4
France	5·8	4·5	5·4
West Germany	5·0	3·2	4·4
Italy	5·2	6·0	6·3
Belgium	5·1	3·3	4.2
Netherlands	5·0	4·9	4·7
Norway	5·4	4·6	4·4
USA	4·8	4·7	3·7

Source: OECD, *The Outlook for Economic Growth* (Paris, 1970)

Table 13 *Growth of Industrial Production 1957–76*

	Annual growth of industrial production 1957–76 (%)	Total growth of industrial production 1957–76 (%)
UK	2·27	57·8
France	5·03	151·2
West Germany	4·93	146·6
Italy	6·41	219·6
Belgium	3·88	106·2
Netherlands	6·08	201·6
Luxembourg	1·84	53·2
EEC (the Six)	5·32	160·4

Source: Prest and Coppock (eds), *The U.K. Economy,* table 4.3, p. 174. Table reproduced by permission of Weidenfeld & Nicolson Ltd.

Table 14　Output Per Person Employed in EEC Countries: Average Annual Rates of Increase 1955–73

| | Manufacturing | | | | GDP | | | |
	1955–60	1960–4	1964–9	1969–73	1955–60	1960–4	1964–9	1969–73
UK	2·2	3·2	3·4	4·5	1·8	2·2	2·5	2·8
Average for EEC (5 countries)	4·6	4·8	5·9	4·6	4·5	5·1	5·3	4·6

Source: Jones, 'Output, employment and labour productivity', pp. 76–82.

Table 15   *UK Share in World Trade in Manufactures
1955–76 (percentages)*

1955	19·8	1973	9·4
1960	16·5	1974	8·8
1965	13·9	1975	9·3
1970	10·8	1976	8·7

Source: C. J. F. Brown and T. D. Sheriff, 'De-industrialisation: a background paper', in F. Blackaby (ed.), *De-industrialisation* (1979), table 10.8, p. 246 (derived from *National Institute Economic Review,* Statistical Appendix, table 22 and IMF, *Balance of Payments Yearbook*). Table reproduced by permission of Heinemann Educational Books.

Table 16   *Trends in the UK Balance of Payments, Annual Averages for Selected Periods 1955–77 (£ million)*

	1955–60	1961–4	1965–7	1968–71	1972–7
Visible Balance	−94	−213	−218	−142	−2,763
Invisible Balance	+230	+182	+206	+627	+1,591
Current Account Balance	+136	−31	−75	+484	−1,171
Balance of long-term capital	−189	−139	−137	−101	+537
Basic Balance (Current Account Balance + Balance of long-term capital)	−53	−170	−212	+383	−634

Source: Prest and Coppock (eds), *The U.K. Economy,* table 3.2, p. 122. Table reproduced by permission of Weidenfeld & Nicolson Ltd.

Table 17   *Employment in Manufacturing Industry, UK*
1907–76 (thousands)

1907	4,951	1951	7,829
1924	5,383	1959	8,071
1930	5,444	1966	8,584
1935	5,694	1976	7,246
1948	7,308		

Source: A. R. Thatcher, 'Labour supply and employment trends', in Blackaby (ed.), *De-industrialisation*, table 2.6, p.32. Table reproduced by permission of Heinemann Educational Books.

Table 18   *Proportions of Workforce Employed in Different*
Sectors, Great Britain 1931–76 (percentages)

	Primary Industries	Production Industries[a]	Services	Not known
1931[b]	11·9	37·0	50·6	0·5
1951	8·9	43·6	47·4	0·1
1961	6·6	44·3	48·7	0·4
1966	5·4	44·0	50·3	0·3
1971	4·3	42·9	52·8	—
1976	3·3	39·5	57·2	—

[a] Here defined as manufacturing, construction, and gas, electricity and water.
[b] In this year there was high unemployment in industry and still many private domestic servants (included under services).

Source: Thatcher, in Blackaby (ed.), *De-industrialisation*, table 2.7, p. 33 (derived from *Department of Employment Gazette*, October 1975, p. 984). Table reproduced by permission of Heinemann Educational Books.

Table 19   *Ratios of Non-Industrial to Industrial Employment:
Various Countries 1961–75*

	1961	1974	% Change	1975	% Change
UK	0·970	1·299	33·9	1·368	41·0
USA	1·808	2·086	15·4	2·313	27·9
France	1·057	1·254	18·6	1·295	22·5
West Germany	0·758	0·866	14·2	1·007	32·8
Italy	0·806	0·889	10·3	0·908	12·6
Japan	1·374	1·353	−1·5	1·436	4·5

Source: Robert Bacon and Walter Eltis, *Britain's Economic Problem: Too Few Producers* (2nd edn, 1978), table 7.2, p. 214. Table reproduced by permission of the Macmillan Press, London and Basingstoke.

Table 20   *Manufacturing Investment as a Proportion of
Gross Domestic Product 1960–72*

	1960–4	1965–9	1970–2
UK	3·7	3·8	3·8
France[a]	6·5	6·9	7·8
West Germany	5·3	4·5	4·9
Italy	7·4	5·4	6·2
Netherlands[b]	7·9	8·9	8·2
USA	2·7	3·4	3·1
Japan	9·0	8·5	9·2

[a] Includes fishing, quarrying and construction. Figure for 1972 not available.
[b] Includes mining and quarrying, construction and gas, water and electricity

Source: NEDO, *Finance for Investment* (1975). Table reproduced by permission of Her Majesty's Stationery Office.

Table 21   *Rate of Male Unemployment in Great Britain*
1955–77 (percentages)

1955–60 (average p.a.)	1·6	1973	3·5
1961–9 (average p.a.)	2·3	1974	3·5
1970	3·4	1975	5·2
1971	4·5	1976	7·2
1972	4·9	1977	7·4

Source: Prest and Coppock (eds), *The U.K. Economy,* table 5.7, p. 274. Table
reproduced by permission of Weidenfeld & Nicolson Ltd.

Table 22   *Gross Profit Shares[a] of UK Manufacturing*
and Services 1966-76 (percentages)

| | Gross Profits[b] | | Gross Profits adjusted[c] | |
	Manufacturing	Services	Manufacturing	Services[d]
1966	26·4	35·4	20·8	33·2
1968	26·7	35·3	20·9	33·0
1970	23·0	35·0	16·7	32·4
1972	24·0	37·0	17·2	35·2
1973	21·8	38·8	14·9	36·2
1974	14·5	37·1	6·3	34·1
1975	13·2	33·9	4·1	30·5
1976	13·6	35·2	3·8	31·6

[a] Less stock appreciation; as proportions of net output.
[b] Gross profits of manufacturing include trading surpluses of public corporations; gross
profits of services include 'other income' *plus* rent.
[c] Capital consumption deducted from gross profits.
[d] Distributive trades, insurance, banking, etc. and other services.

Source: Brown and Sheriff, in Blackaby (ed.), *De-industrialisation,* table 10.13,
p. 251 (derived from Central Statistical Office, *National Income and Expenditure,
1966–76,* tables 1.11, 3.1 and 11.3). Table reproduced by permission of Heinemann
Educational Books.

Table 23   *Proportions of Total Employment in Manufacturing in Various Countries[a] 1950–75 (percentages)*

	1950	1960	1970	1973	1974	1975
UK	34·7	35·8	34·7	32·3	32·3	30·9
Belgium	32·7	33·5	32·7	31·8	31·5	30·1
France	—	27·9	27·8	27·9	28·1	27·9
West Germany	—	34·7	37·4	36·1	36·6	35·9
Italy	—	26·6	31·7	32·2	32·6	32·6
Netherlands	30·2	28·6	26·2	24·7	24·5	24·0
Japan	—	21·3	27·0	27·4	27·2	25·8
Sweden	—	32·1[b]	27·6	27·5	28·3	28·0
USA[c]	34·4	33·6	32·3	31·6	31·0	29·0

[a] The series presented is an estimated reference series which makes allowance for discontinuities in official labour statistics due to changes in industrial classification, methods of collection, etc. In some cases, particularly the UK, there are substantial differences between the series and the published inconsistent one.

[b] For 1961; 1960 not available.

[c] Industrial employment.

Source: Brown and Sheriff, in Blackaby (ed.), *De-industrialisation,* table 10.2, p. 237 (derived from OECD, *Manpower Statistics* and *Labour Force Statistics*). Table reproduced by permission of Heinemann Educational Books.

Table 24 Industrial Import Penetration of the UK Home Market 1961–75

	Exports	Home Sales (£ million, current prices)	Imports	Import Content of Exports	Imports/Home Sales	
					Remaining Imports[a] %	Total Imports %
1961	3,084	12,606	1,404	210	9·5	11·1
1962	3,156	13,045	1,440	215	9·4	11·0
1963	3,372	13,839	1,572	229	9·7	11·4
1964	3,768	15,798	2,160	286	11·9	13·7
1965	4,092	17,227	2,256	340	11·1	13·1
1966	4,392	18,138	2,472	395	11·5	13·6
1967	4,380	19,201	2,796	420	12·4	14·6
1968	5,412	21,068	3,624	563	14·5	17·2
1969	6,252	22,543	3,948	694	14·4	17·5
1970	6,804	25,314	4,560	810	14·8	18·0
1971	7,825	27,129	5,002	861	15·3	18·4
1972	8,257	29,454	6,093	793	18·0	20·7
1973	10,455	35,309	8,909	1,004	22·4	25·2
1974	13,685	38,643	11,928	1,314	27·5	30·9
1975	16,464	45,220	12,805	1,580	24·8	28·3

[a] After deducting import content of exports.

Source: Bacon and Eltis, Britain's Economic Problem, pp. 217–31. Cited in Walter Eltis, 'Comment' in Blackaby (ed.), De-industrialisation, table 9.5, p. 226. Table reproduced by permission of Heinemann Educational Books.

Table 25   *UK Share in World Trade in Invisibles and
Private Services 1955–76 (percentages)*

	Invisibles	Private Services
1955	24·9	26·3
1960	20·9	22·3
1965	17·9	17·2
1970	15·9	17·2
1973	15·3	16·0
1974	13·4	15·6
1975	13·4	15·7
1976	12·5	15·0

Source: Brown and Sheriff, in Blackaby (ed.), *De-industrialisation,* table 10.8, p. 246 (derived from *National Institute Economic Review*, Statistical Appendix, table 22, and IMF, *Balance of Payments Yearbook*). Table reproduced by permission of Heinemann Educational Books.

Table 26 International Comparison of Labour Costs[a]

Ranking	1970	DM	Indices UK = 100	1977[b]	DM	Indices UK = 100
(1)	USA	15·80	270	West Germany	18·50	231
(2)	Sweden	11·12	190	Belgium	18·50	231
(3)	West Germany	9·42	161	Sweden	18·00	225
(4)	Denmark	8·75	149	Denmark	17·50	219
(5)	Belgium	7·84	134	Switzerland	16·50	206
(6)	Switzerland	7·72	132	USA	15·50	194
(7)	Italy	6·93	118	Austria	12·00	150
(8)	France	6·45	110	France	11·00	138
(9)	UK	5·86	100	Italy	11·00	138
(10)	Austria	5·22	89	Japan	10·00	125
(11)	Japan	3·94	67	UK	8·00	100

a Total cost of labour involved in production (manufacturing) at current exchange rates.
b At exchange rates of December 1977.

Source: G. F. Ray, 'Comment' in Blackaby (ed.), De-industrialisation, table 3.5, p. 74. Table reproduced by permission of Heinemann Educational Books.

Table 27 *Growth Rate of UK Money Supply 1968–73*
(percentages)

	$M_1{}^a$	$M_3{}^b$
1968	5·0	7·3
1969	—	3·2
1970	9·3	9·4
1971	15·4	13·5
1972	14·4	28·1
1973:^{c}		
March	10·1	26·8
June	12·3	23·8
September	8·0	28·2
December	5·8	27·9

^{a} Defined to include notes and coin in circulation with the public sterling current accounts owned by the private sector.
^{b} Includes notes and coins in circulation with the public plus all UK private and public sector deposits, both sterling and other currencies, with banks and discount houses.
^{c} Percentage change on twelve months earlier.

Source: Midland Bank Review (May 1974), p. 4.

Table 28   *Estimated Industrial Distribution of Research and Development Expenditure[a] 1962 (percentages)*

	UK	France	West Germany[b]	Japan[b]	USA
Aircraft	35·4	27·7	—	—	36·3
Vehicles	3·0	2·6 }	19·2	7·4	7·4
Machinery	7·3	6·4 }		5·3	8·2
Electrical Machinery	21·7	25·7 }	33·8	28·0	21·6
Instruments	2·3	— }			3·9
Chemicals	11·6	16·8	32·9	28·3	12·6
Steel and Metal Products	2·9 }	3·2	6·6	7·0	2·0
Non-Ferrous Metals	1·2 }			2·7	0·6
Stone, Clay, Glass	1·3	1·2	0·8		1·0
Rubber	1·2 }		1·0 }		1·1
Paper	0·9 }	5·0	0·6 }	17·9	0·6
Food and Drink	1·9 }		0.6 }		0·9
Other Manufacturing	3·4 }		1·9 }		2·0
Transport, Energy	4·4	9·0	0·6	—[c]	—
Other Non-manufacturing	1·6	2·4	2·0	—[c]	1·9

[a] Analysis by Industry Group, with companies in the industry of their principal activity. Industrial Classifications vary between countries, so this table indicates broad outlines only.
[b] For 1963.
[c] Excluded from total.

Source: C. Freeman and A. Young, *The Research and Development Effort in Western Europe, North America and the Soviet Union* (Paris, 1965).

Table 29   *The Increasing Concentration of Net Assets in UK Manufacturing Industry 1957–69*

	1957	*1969*
Number of firms	1,182	744
Share of the largest 5 firms	17·0%	20·1%
Share of the largest 50 firms	48·4%	60·9%
Share of the largest 100 firms	60·1%	74·9%
Share of the largest 200 firms	73·0%	86·2%

Source: Hannah, Leslie *The Rise of the Corporate Economy* (1976), table 10.1, p. 166. Table reproduced by permission of Methuen & Co Ltd.

Table 30   *The Share of the Largest 100 Firms in UK Manufacturing Net Output 1909–70*

1909	15%	1948	21%
1919	17%	1953	26%
1924	21%	1958	33%
1930	26%	1963	38%
1935	23%	1968	42%
1939	23%	1970	45%

Source: Hannah, Leslie *The Rise of the Corporate Economy* (1976), table A.2, p. 216. Table reproduced by permission of Methuen & Co. Ltd.

Notes

The place of publication of works cited is London unless otherwise stated.

Chapter 1

1   On the Victorian boom see R. A. Church, *The Great Victorian Boom 1850–1873* (1975). For detailed studies of the performance of individual industries in the period 1825–75 see R. A. Church (ed.), *The Dynamics of Victorian Business: Problems and Perspectives to the 1870s* (1980).
2   On the contemporary case for 'fair trade' see Edward Sullivan, 'Isolated free trade', *The Nineteenth Century*, vol. 10 (1881). On the campaign against German manufactured imports see Ernest Williams, *Made in Germany* (1896)
3   Decadal rates of growth of gross domestic product (per cent per annum) were as follows: *1870–9, 1·7; 1880–9, 2·1; 1890–9, 2·4; 1900–13, 1·5.* See C. H. Feinstein, *National Income, Expenditure and Output of the United Kingdom, 1855–1965* (Cambridge, 1972), table 6.
4   D. H. Aldcroft, 'The problem of productivity in British industry, 1870–1914', in D. H. Aldcroft and H. W. Richardson, *The British Economy, 1870–1939* (1969), pp. 138–9.
5   See Roderick Floud and D. N. McCloskey (eds), *The Economic History of Britain since 1700*, 2 vols (forthcoming).
6   For discussions of the residual and of difficulties in its measurement see Aldcroft and Richardson, *The British Economy*, pp. 9–12; J. D. Gould, *Economic Growth in History: Survey and Analysis* (1972), pp. 295–320; Robert M. Solow and Peter Temin, 'Introduction: the inputs for growth', in *Cambridge Economic History of Europe*, Vol. 7, pt 1, ed. Peter Mathias and M. M. Postan (1978), pp. 22–6; D. H. Aldcroft, *The Inter-War Economy: Britain, 1919–1939* (1970), pp. 113–4.
7   Aldcroft and Richardson, *The British Economy*, pp. 14–16.
8   ibid., p. 15.
9   H. W. Richardson, 'Overcommitment in Britain before 1930', *Oxford Economic Papers*, vol. 17 (1965), p. 240. This article is reproduced in Aldcroft and Richardson, *The British Economy*, pp. 190–214.
10 ibid. See also Ingvar Svennilson, *Growth and Stagnation in the European Economy* (Geneva, 1954); W. A. Lewis, *The Deceleration of British Growth 1873–1913* (Princeton, NJ, 1967, mimeographed) and 'International competition in manufactures', *American Economic Review (Papers and Proceedings)*, vol. 47 (1957), pp. 578–87.
11 Aldcroft and Richardson, *The British Economy*, p. 14.
12 J. Saville, 'Some retarding factors in the British economy before 1914', *Yorkshire Bulletin of Economic and Social Research*, vol. 13 (1961), pp. 51–60; Peter Mathias, *The First Industrial Nation: An Economic History of Britain, 1700–1914* (1969), pp. 404–26; David Landes, *The Unbound Prometheus: Technological Change and Industrial Development in Western Europe from 1750 to the Present* (Cambridge, 1969), pp. 231–

358 *passim;* E. J. Hobsbawm, *Industry and Empire* (Pelican edn, Harmondsworth, 1969), pp. 172–94; A. M. Levine, *Industrial Retardation in Britain 1880–1914* (1967), pp. 9–25.
13 Aldcroft and Richardson, *The British Economy,* p. 5.
14 Hobsbawm, *Industry and Empire,* p. 187.
15 See D. J. Coppock, 'The climacteric of the 1890s: a critical note', *The Manchester School,* vol. 24 (1956), pp. 1–31.
16 E. H. Phelps Brown and S. J. Handfield Jones, 'The climacteric of the 1890s: a study of the expanding economy', *Oxford Economic Papers,* vol. 4 (1952), pp. 266–307.
17 See, for example, Lewis, *The Deceleration of British Growth;* W. A., Lewis, *Growth and Fluctuations* (1978), p. 117; A. H. Conrad and J. R. Meyer, *Studies in Econometric History* (1965); R. S. Sayers, *The Vicissitudes of an Export Economy: Britain since 1880* (Sydney, 1965).
18 Nicholas Kaldor, 'Capitalism and industrial development: some lessons from Britain's experience', *Cambridge Journal of Economics,* vol. 1 (1977), p. 201.
19 In its simplest form Verdoorn's law states that the higher the rate of economic growth the higher the level of average labour productivity. The original formulation is to be found in P. J. Verdoorn, 'Fattori che regolano lo sviluppo della produttività del lavoro', *L' Industria* (1949).
20 C. P. Kindleberger, 'Foreign trade and economic growth: lessons from Britain and France, 1850 to 1913', *Economic History Review,* 2nd series, vol. 14 (1961–2), pp. 289–305.
21 F. R. J. Jervis, 'The handicap of Britain's early start', *The Manchester School,* vol. 15 (1947), pp. 112–22; M. Frankel 'Obsolescence and technical change in a maturing economy', *American Economic Review,* vol. 45 (1955), pp. 296–314; C. P. Kindleberger, 'Obsolescence and technical change', *Bulletin of the Oxford University Institute of Statistics,* vol. 23 (1961), pp. 281–97; E. Ames and N. Rosenberg, 'Changing technological leadership and industrial growth', *Economic Journal,* vol. 73 (1963), pp. 13–31.
22 Svennilson, *Growth and Stagnation.*
23 S. B. Saul, *The Myth of the Great Depression, 1873–1896* (1969), p. 44. See also D. H. Aldcroft, 'The entrepreneur and the British economy, 1870–1914', *Economic History Review,* 2nd series, vol. 17 (1964), pp. 129–30; D. H. Aldcroft, 'Technical progress and British enterprise, 1875–1914', *Business History,* vol. 8 (1966), pp. 123–7. These articles are reprinted in Aldcroft and Richardson, *The British Economy,* pp. 141–67, 168–89.
24 E. Rothbarth, 'Causes of the superior efficiency of U.S.A. industry as compared with British industry', *Economic Journal,* vol. 56 (1946), pp. 383–90.
25 Aldcroft, 'The entrepreneur and the British economy'; R. J. S. Hoffman, *Great Britain and the German Trade Rivalry, 1875–1914* (1933). The former subsequently qualified his views on the shortcomings of British entrepreneurs. See his introduction to D. H. Aldcroft (ed.), *The Development of British Industry and Foreign Competition, 1875–1914* (1968), pp. 11–36.
26 M. Sanderson, 'The professor as industrial consultant: Oliver Arnold and the British steel industry, 1900–14', *Economic History Review,* 2nd series, vol. 31 (1978), pp. 585–600; S. B. Saul, 'Research and development in British industry from the end of the nineteenth century to the 1960s', in T. C. Smout (ed.), *The Search for Wealth and Stability: Essays in Economic and Social History Presented to M. W. Flinn* (1979), pp. 115–16.

27   Levine, *Industrial Retardation*, pp. 70–2; Lewis, *Growth and Fluctuations*, pp. 129–30; D. H. Aldcroft, 'Investment in and utilisation of manpower', in Barrie M. Ratcliffe (ed.), *Great Britain and Her World 1750–1914: Essays in Honours of W. O. Henderson* (Manchester, 1975), p.294.

28   For highly critical views of the education system see D. Ward, 'The public schools and industry in Britain after 1870', *Journal of Contemporary History*, vol. 2 (1967), pp. 37–52; Corelli Barnett, *The Collapse of British Power* (1972), pp. 24–43, 103–6; Levine, *Industrial Retardation*, pp. 73–6. For more balanced views see D. C. Coleman, 'Gentlemen and players', *Economic History Review,* 2nd series, vol. 26 (1973), pp. 92–116; M. Sanderson, *The Universities and British Industry 1850–1970* (1972).

29   Aldcroft, 'Investment in and utilisation of manpower', p. 292; Lewis, *Growth and Fluctuations*, p. 130.

30   Aldcroft, 'The entrepreneur and the British economy' and 'Investment in and utilisation of manpower'.

31   P. L. Payne, *British Entrepreneurship in the Nineteenth Century* (1974), p. 45. See also P. L. Payne, 'The emergence of the large-scale company in Great Britain, 1870–1914', *Economic History Review,* 2nd series, vol. 20 (1967), pp. 519–42.

32   Aldcroft, 'The entrepreneur and the British economy', pp. 125–7. See also I. W. Maclean, 'Anglo-American engineering competition, 1870–1914: some third market evidence', *Economic History Review,* 2nd series, vol. 29 (1976), pp. 452–62.

33   Aldcroft. 'Investment in and utilisation of manpower', pp. 295–9.

34   ibid., p. 299.

35   ibid., pp. 229–301.

36   ibid., pp. 301–3.

37   Lewis, *Growth and Fluctuations,* pp. 126–7.

38   Aldcroft, 'Investment in and utilisation of manpower', p. 304.

39   Aldcroft, 'The entrepreneur and the British economy', pp. 128–9; Lewis, *Growth and Fluctuations,* p. 129; Coleman, 'Gentlemen and players', *passim.*

40   Saul, *The Myth of the Great Depression*, p. 47.

41   S. B. Saul, 'The market and the development of the mechanical engineering industries in Britain, 1860–1914', *Economic History Review*, 2nd series, vol. 20 (1967), pp. 111–30. This article is reproduced in S. B. Saul (ed.), *Technological Change: The United States and Britain in the Nineteenth Century* (1970), pp. 141–70.

42   ibid.; Sidney Pollard and Paul Robertson, *The British Shipbuilding Industry 1870–1914* (Cambridge, Mass. 1979); Clive Trebilcock, *The Vickers Brothers: Armaments and Enterprise, 1854–1914* (1977). For a good general survey of British industry at this time see A. E. Musson, *The Growth of British Industry* (1978), pp. 146–255.

43   See, for example, J. B. Jeffreys, *Retail Trading in Britain* (Cambridge, 1954); W. T. C. King, *History of the London Discount Market* (1936); Sir Albert Feavearyear, *The Pound Sterling* (Oxford, 1963); R. S. Sayers, *Central Banking after Bagehot* (Oxford, 1957); T. S. Ashton and R. S. Sayers, *Papers in English Monetary History* (Oxford, 1953); R. Triffin, *Our International Monetary System: Yesterday, Today and Tomorrow* (New York, 1968); S. D. Chapman, *Jesse Boot of Boots the Chemists* (1974); W. J. Reader, *Imperial Chemical Industries: A History,* Vol. 1: *The Forerunners, 1870–1926* (1970); R. H. Campbell and R. G. Wilson, *Entrepreneurship in Britain, 1750–1939* (1975).

44 Mathias, *The First Industrial Nation*, pp. 405–6.

45 See, for example, D. N. McCloskey, *Economic Maturity and Entre-preneurial Decline: British Iron and Steel, 1870–1913* (Cambridge, Mass., 1973); Lars G. Sandberg, *Lancashire in Decline: A Study in Entrepreneurship, Technology and International Trade* (Columbus, Ohio, 1974).

46 See R. E. Tyson, 'The cotton industry', in Aldcroft (ed.), *The Development of British Industry and Foreign Competition*, pp. 100–27.

47 Lars G. Sandberg, 'American rings and English mules: the role of economic rationality', *Quarterly Journal of Economics*, vol. 83 (1969), pp. 25–43. This article is reproduced in Saul (ed.), *Technological Change*, pp. 120–40.

48 C. K. Harley, 'Skilled labour and the choice of technique in Edwardian industry', *Explorations in Economic History*, vol. 11 (1974), pp. 391–414.

49 Sandberg, 'American rings and English mules', p. 29.

50 Neil K. Buxton, *The Economic Development of the British Coal Industry: From Industrial Revolution to the Present Day* (1978), p. 91.

51 ibid., p. 94.

52 See A. J. Taylor, 'Labour productivity and technological innovation in the British coal industry, 1850–1914', *Economic History Review*, 2nd series, vol. 14 (1961), pp 48–70 and 'The coal industry', in Aldcroft (ed.), *The Development of British Industry and Foreign Competition*, pp. 37–70.

53 The following analysis is based upon M. W. Kirby, *The British Coal-mining Industry 1870–1946: A Political and Economic History* (1977), pp. 4–23.

54 Taylor, 'Labour productivity and technological innovation', p. 66.

55 H. W. Richardson, 'Chemicals', in Aldcroft (ed.), *The Development of British Industry and Foreign Competition*, p. 275.

56 ibid. See also Payne, *British Entrepreneurship*, pp. 45–56; D. N. McCloskey and Lars G. Sandberg, 'From damnation to redemption: judgements on the late Victorian entrepreneur', *Explorations in Economic History*, vol. 9 (1971), pp. 89–108; Saul, *The Myth of the Great Depression*, p.46.

57 Kirby, *The British Coalmining Industry*, p. 23.

58 Saul, *The Myth of the Great Depression*, p. 46.

59 A. G. Kenwood, and A. L. Lougheed, *The Growth of the International Economy, 1820–1960* (1971), table 3, p. 43.

60 King, *History of the London Discount Market*, p. 271.

61 Robert J. A. Skidelsky, 'Retreat from leadership: the evolution of British foreign economic policy, 1870–1939', in Benjamin J. Rowland (ed.), *Balance of Power or Hegemony: The Interwar Monetary System* (New York, 1976), p. 160.

62 W. P. Kennedy, 'Foreign investment, trade and growth in the United Kingdom, 1870–1913', *Explorations in Economic History*, vol. 11 (1974), pp. 415–44; A. J. Brown, 'Britain and the world economy, 1870–1914', *Yorkshire Bulletin of Economic and Social Research*, vol. 17 (1965), pp. 46–60.

63 See Floud and McCloskey (eds), *The Economic History of Britain*.

64 P. L. Cottrell, *British Overseas Investment in the Nineteenth Century* (1975), pp. 54–5.

65 S. B. Saul, 'The motor industry in Britain to 1914', *Business History*, vol. 5 (1962), pp. 22–44.

66 Richardson, 'Overcommitment in Britain', p. 246.

67   Kennedy, 'Foreign investment, trade and growth', pp. 436–9. Part of this
      article takes the form of an effective refutation of McCloskey's argument
      that British overseas investment did not lead to 'capital starvation' in the
      home economy. For McCloskey's views see his article 'Did Victorian
      Britain fail?', *Economic History Review*, 2nd series, vol. 23, (1970), pp.
      446–59. See also the debate between Crafts and McCloskey: N. F. R.
      Crafts, 'Victorian Britain did fail', *Economic History Review,* 2nd series,
      vol. 32 (1979), pp. 533–7; D. M. McCloskey, 'No it did not, a reply to
      Crafts', ibid., pp. 538–41.
68   See G. M. Meier, 'Long period determinants of Britain's terms of trade,
      1880–1913', *Review of Economic Studies*, vol. 20 (1952–3), pp. 115–30.
69   A. K. Cairncross, *Home and Foreign Investment, 1870–1913* (Cambridge,
      1953), pp. 2, 225, 232–3.
70   The analysis contained in the following section has been heavily influenced
      by S. B. Saul's monograph. *Studies in British Overseas Trade 1870–1914*
      (Liverpool, 1960) and his article 'The export economy, 1870–1914',
      Yorkshire Bulletin of Economic and Social Research, vol. 17 (1965), pp.
      5–18.
71   Saul, *Studies in British Overseas Trade*, pp. 45–56; Francois Crouzet,
      'Trade and empire: the British experience from the establishment of free
      trade until the First World War', in Ratcliffe (ed.), *Great Britain and Her
      World*, p. 222.
72   Saul, *Studies in British Overseas Trade,* pp. 107, 109, 114–5, 117, 120–1,
      129–31.
73   W. M. Scammell, 'The working of the gold standard', *Yorkshire Bulletin of
      Economic and Social Research*, vol. 17 (1965), pp. 32–45.
74   For an exposition of the classical analysis of the gold standard see C. A. E.
      Goodhart *The Business of Banking, 1891–1914* (1972), pp. 195–208.
      See also Kenwood and Lougheed, *Growth of the International Economy,*
      pp. 124–7.
75   Scammell, 'The working of the gold standard', p. 33. For further comment
      on the complexity of the pre-1914 international monetary system see D. J.
      Williams, 'The evolution of the sterling system', in C. R. Whittlesey and J.
      S. S. Wilson (eds), *Essays in Money and Banking in Honour of R. S.
      Sayers* (1968), pp. 266–84; A. I. Bloomfield, *Monetary Policy under the
      International Gold Standard, 1880–1914* (New York, 1959); A. G. Ford,
      The Gold Standard 1880–1914: Britain and Argentina (1962).
76   Saul, *Studies in British Overseas Trade*, p. 63.
77   J. M. Keynes, *The Economic Consequences of the Peace* (New York,
      1920), pp. 10–11.
78   Saul, *Studies in British Overseas Trade*, pp. 60–1. See also M. de Cecco
      and P. H. Lindert, *Key Currencies and Gold 1900–1913* (1969), pp. 76–7.
79   Saul, *Studies in British Overseas Trade*, p. 62. See also E. Monroe,
      Britain's Moment in the Middle East (1963), p. 11. For an alternative
      view stressing the unimportance of India to the British economy see M. and
      T. Zinkin *Britain and India* (1964), pp. 51–3.
80   Saul, *Studies in British Overseas Trade,* pp. 62–3.
81   See, for example, Alfred Gollin, *Balfour's Burden: Arthur Balfour and
      Imperial Preference* (1965), pp. 3–50; William L. Strauss, *Joseph
      Chamberlain and the Theory of Imperialism* (New York, 1971), pp. 96–
      115; Richard A. Rempel, *Unionist Divided: Arthur Balfour, Joseph
      Chamberlain and the Unionist Free Traders* (Newton Abbott, 1972); A.
      F. Madden, 'Changing attitudes and widening responsibilities, 1895–
      1914', in *Cambridge History of the British Empire,* Vol. 3: *The Empire-*

Commonwealth 1870–1919, ed. E. A. Benians, Sir James Butler and C. E. Carrington (Cambridge, 1959), pp. 338–405; G. S. Graham, 'Imperial finance, trade and communications, 1895–1914', ibid., pp. 438–89.

82 Bernard Semmel, *Imperialism and Social Reform: English Social-Imperial Thought 1895–1914* (Anchor Books edn, New York, 1968), p. 142.

83 ibid., pp. 136–8. See also A. P. Thornton, *The Imperial Idea and Its Enemies* (1959), pp. 99–100.

84 Cited in Semmel, *Imperialism and Social Reform*, pp. 51, 160.

85 Saul, *Studies in British Overseas Trade*, pp. 226–9; Crouzet, 'Trade and empire', p. 223; Graham, 'Imperial finance, trade and communications', pp. 483–4.

86 Matthew Simon, 'The pattern of new British portfolio investment, 1865–1914', in A. R. Hall (ed.) *The Export of Capital from Britain, 1870–1914* (1968), pp. 15–44.

87 Crouzet, 'Trade and empire', p. 227; E. A. Benians, 'Finance, trade and communications 1870–1895', in *Cambridge History of the British Empire*, pp. 181–229.

88 Mathias, *The First Industrial Nation*, p. 405.

89 See Semmel, *Imperialism and Social Reform*, p. 147.

90 For a more optimistic view of Britian's international position in 1913 see Benians, 'Finance, trade and communications', pp. 224–5.

Chapter 2

1 Keynes, *The Economic Consequences of the Peace.*

2 R. S. Sayers, 'The young Keynes', *Economic Journal,* vol. 82 (1972), p. 597.

3 J. S. Davis, *The World between the Wars 1919–1939: An Economist's View* (1975), p. 39.

4 R. F. Harrod, *The Life of John Maynard Keynes* (Penguin edn, Harmondsworth, 1972), pp. 308–10.

5 Keynes, *The Economic Consequences of the Peace,* p. 1.

6 D. E. Moggridge, *Keynes* (Fontana edn, 1976), pp. 60–1.

7 Harrod, *The Life of John Maynard Keynes*, p. 316.

8 Howard Elcock, *Portrait of a Decision: The Council of Four and the Treaty of Versailles* (1972), pp. 208–10, 286–7, 316–22. For further criticisms of Keynes see especially Etienne Mantoux, *The Carthaginian Peace or The Economic Consequences of Mr Keynes* (1946). See also Thomas Balogh, *Unequal Partners*, Vol. 2: *Historical Episodes* (Oxford, 1963), pp. 137–8; Lord Balogh, 'Keynes and the International Monetary Fund' in A. P. Thirlwall (ed.), *Keynes and International Monetary Relations* (1976), pp. 70–2; Douglas C. McIntosh, 'Mantoux versus Keynes: a note on German income and the Reparations Commission', *Economic Journal,* vol. 87 (1977), pp. 756–7; Robert Skidelsky, 'Verdicts on Versailles', *The Times Literary Supplement* (15 September 1978).

9 Keynes, *The Economic Consequences of the Peace*, p. 254.

10 Svennilson, *Growth and Stagnation*, pp. 45–6; D. H. Aldcroft, *From Versailles to Wall Street, 1919–29* (1977), pp. 37–8; D. E. Moggridge, *British Monetary Policy, 1924–1931: The Norman Conquest of $4.86* (Cambridge, 1972), pp. 16–36.

11 Aldcroft, *From Versailles to Wall Street*, pp. 38–43.

12 Svennilson, *Growth and Stagnation*, p. 46. See also H. Tyszinski, 'World

trade in manufactured commodities 1899–1950', *The Manchester School*, vol. 19 (1951), pp. 272–304.

13   W. Ashworth, *An Economic History of England, 1870–1939* (1960), p. 319.

14   ibid., p. 302.

15   For war-debt statistics see Harold G. Moulton and Leo Pasvolsky, *War Debts and World Prosperity* (Washington, DC, 1932).

16   Aldcroft, *From Versailles to Wall Street*, p. 240.

17   Moggridge, *British Monetary Policy*, p. 36.

18   Aldcroft, *From Versailles to Wall Street,* pp. 218–38, *passim.*

19   Aldcroft, *The Inter-War Economy*, p. 18; Aldcroft and Richardson, *The British Economy*, pp. 5–9; J. A. Dowie, 'Growth in the inter-war period: some more arithmetic', *Economic History Review*, 2nd series, vol. 21 (1968), p. 97; Feinstein, *National Income, Expenditure and Output*, table 6.

20   The main exception to the depressing trend of the immediate prewar years was the rate of growth of exports – 1·6 per cent annum in the period 1920–9 as compared with 4·2 per cent per annum in the period 1900–13. See Aldcroft, *The Inter-War Economy*, p. 17.

21   ibid., pp. 114–15.

22   D. H. Aldcroft, 'Economic progress in Britain in the 1920s', *Scottish Journal of Political Economy*, vol. 13 (1966), p. 298. This article is reproduced in Aldcroft and Richardson, *The British Economy*, pp. 219–38. See also R. S. Sayers, 'The springs of technical progress in Britain, 1919–39', *Economic Journal,* vol. 60 (1950), pp. 275–91; D. H. Aldcroft, 'Economic growth in Britain in the inter-war years: a reassessment', *Economic History Review,* 2nd series, vol. 20 (1967), pp. 311–26. The latter article is reproduced in D. H. Aldcroft and Peter Fearon, (eds), *Economic Growth in Twentieth Century Britain* (1969), pp. 34–54.

23   Aldcroft. 'Economic progress in Britain', pp. 298–9.

24   ibid., p. 306.

25   For developments in company organisation see Leslie Hannah, *The Rise of the Corporate Economy* (1976), pp. 30–1 and 'Managerial innovation and the rise of the large-scale company in interwar Britain', *Economic History Review*, 2nd series, vol. 27 (1974), pp. 252–70.

26   Aldcroft. 'Economic progress in Britain', p. 306.

27   ibid., pp. 307–8. For a useful survey of British industrial performance between the wars in both 'new' and 'old' industries see N. K. Buxton and D. H. Aldcroft (eds), *British Industry between the Wars: Instability and Industrial Development* (1979).

28   Sidney Pollard, *The Development of the British Economy, 1914–1967* (2nd edn, 1969), pp. 54–7; Sayers, 'The springs of technical progress'.

29   Pollard, *The Development of the British Economy*, p. 54.

30   ibid. See also Saul, 'Research and development in British industry', pp. 118–9; Sir Frank Heath and A. L. Heatherington, *Industrial Research and Development in the United Kingdom: A Survey* (1945); J. M. Sanderson, 'Research and the firm in British industry, 1919–1939', *Science Studies,* vol. 2 (1972), pp. 107–51.

31   *Report of the Departmental Committee Appointed by the Board of Trade To Consider the Position of the Shipping and Shipbuilding Industry after the War,* Cd 9062 (1918), para 89–90, p. 31.

32   Kirby, *The British Coalmining Industry,* pp. 40–1.

33   Aldcroft, 'Economic progress in Britain', p. 309.

34   The description 'The Doldrums' in relation to the 1920s was first coined by

A. C. Pigou. See A. C. Pigou, *Aspects of British Economic History, 1918–1925* (1948).

35   B. W. E. Alford, *Depression and Recovery? British Economic Growth 1918–1939* (1972), p. 82.

36   Aldcroft, 'Economic progress in Britain', p. 312

37   Ashworth, *An Economic History of England*, p. 320.

38   Committee on Currency and Foreign Exchanges after the War, *First Interim Report*, Cd 9182 (1918).

39   Committee on Currency and Foreign Exchanges, *Final Report,* Cmd 464 (1919).

40   Susan Howson, *Domestic Monetary Management in Britain 1919–38* (Cambridge, 1975), p. 11. On the postwar labour unrest see P. B. Johnson, *Land Fit for Heroes: The Planning of British Reconstruction 1916–1919* (Chicago, Ill., 1968), pp. 375, 394–402; Charles Loch Mowat, *Britain between the Wars 1918–1940* (1955), pp. 30–43; Alan Bullock, *The Life and Times of Ernest Bevin,* Vol. 1 (1960), pp. 89–115; S. M. H. Armitage, *The Politics of Decontrol: Britain and the United States* (1969).

41   Howson, *Domestic Monetary Management*, pp. 17–23.

42   Committee on Currency and Foreign Exchanges, *Final Report.*

43   Howson, *Domestic Monetary Management*, p. 24.

44   See J. A. Dowie, '1919 is in need of attention', *Economic History Review,* 2nd series, vol. 28 (1975), pp. 429–50 for an attempt to redress the balance on existing interpretations of the impact of the boom. Dowie is concerned to highlight the effect of the general reduction in working hours in industry (1919–20) 'in assessing and interpreting the reflation of the immediate postwar period'.

45   Pigou, *Aspects of British Economic History*, p. 172.

46   *The Economist* (29 November 1919), p. 979. See also A. J. Youngson, *Britain's Economic Growth, 1920–1966* (1967), p. 45.

47   Pollard, *The Development of the British Economy*, p. 114. See also A. Slaven, 'A shipyard in depression: John Browns of Clydebank, 1919–1938', *Business History*, vol. 19 (1977), p. 209; Peter L. Payne, 'Rationality and personality: a study of mergers in the Scottish iron and steel industry', *Business History*, vol. 19 (1977), pp. 166–7. See also Peter L. Payne, *Colvilles and the Scottish Steel Industry* (Oxford, 1979), pp. 146–7; John R. Hume and Michael Moss, *Beardmore: The History of a Scottish Industrial Giant* (1979), pp. 163–79.

48   Aldcroft, *The Inter-War Economy*, p. 36.

49   *The Economist* (22 November 1919), p. 939.

50   See Kirby, *The British Coalmining Industry*, pp. 49–65.

51   Public Record Office, T M2/1208, 'Treasury Memoranda on the Unemployment Situation, 1921'. I am grateful to Professor R. H. Campbell for this reference.

52   See Peter Rowland, *Lloyd George* (1975), p. 544.

53   Committee on Currency and Foreign Exchanges, *Interim Report.*

54   R. S. Sayers, *The Bank of England, 1891–1944*, Vol. 1 (1976), pp. 121–2.

55   ibid., p. 122.

56   On the Genoa deliberations see S. V. O. Clarke, *The Reconstruction of the International Monetary System: The Attempts of 1922 and 1933* (1973) and *Central Bank Co-operation 1924–31* (New York, 1967), pp. 34–40; Sir Henry Clay, *Lord Norman* (1957), pp. 137–9; J. M. Keynes, *Collected Writings*, Vol. 17: *Activities 1920–22: Treaty Revision and Reconstruction* (1977), pp. 354–425. The following section is based on the analysis provided by Frank C. Costigliola, 'Anglo-American financial

rivalry in the 1920s', *Journal of Economic History,* vol. 37 (1977), pp. 911–33.

57   ibid., p. 918.

58   ibid., p. 915.

59   ibid., p. 919.

60   On the German hyper-inflation see Fritz K. Ringer, *The German Inflation of 1923* (1969). On the policy of the German government during the Ruhr occupation see Charles S. Maier, *Recasting Bourgeois Europe: Stabilization in France, Germany and Italy in the Decade after World War I* (Princeton, NJ, 1975), pp. 355–87 and Karl Erich Born, 'The German inflation after the First World War', *Journal of European Economic History,* vol. 6 (1977), pp. 109–16.

61   See Clay, *Lord Norman,* ch. 5 *passim;* Sayers, *The Bank of England,* Vol. 1, pp. 174–83; Clarke, *Central Bank Co-operation,* pp. 53–67, 115.

62   Costigliola, 'Anglo-American financial rivalry, pp. 923–7; L. S. Pressnell, '1925: the burden of sterling', *Economic History Review,* 2nd series, vol. 31 (1978), pp. 71, 79–80.

63   See D. E. Moggridge, *The Return to Gold, 1925: The Formulation of Policy and Its Critics* (Cambridge, 1969) and *British Monetary Policy,* ch. 3; Sayers, *The Bank of England,* Vol. 1, pp. 133–42; Howson, *Domestic Monetary Management,* pp. 30–63; Costigliola, 'Anglo-American financial rivalry'. See also Sidney Pollard (ed.), *The Gold Standard and Employment Policies between the Wars* (1970) – note especially the editor's introduction and the articles by Sayers and L. J. Hume; Ralph Hawtrey, 'The return to gold in 1925', *Bankers' Magazine,* vol. 208 (1970), pp. 61–7; W. B. Reddaway, 'Was $4·86 inevitable in 1925?', *Lloyds Bank Review* (April 1970), pp. 15–28; D. Williams, 'Montagu Norman and banking policy in the 1920s', *Yorkshire Bulletin of Economic and Social Research,* vol. 11 (1959), pp. 38–55; John Foster, 'Imperialism and the labour aristocracy', in Jeffrey Skelley (ed.), *The General Strike* (1976), pp. 3–57.

64   Moggridge, *British Monetary Policy,* pp. 84–6, 111.

65   Costigliola, 'Anglo-American financial rivalry', pp. 920–1, 926.

66   ibid., p. 927.

67   See Bloomfield, *Monetary Policy under the International Gold Standard;* A. G. Ford, 'The truth about gold', *Lloyds Bank Review* (July 1965), pp. 1–18; D. Williams, 'London and the 1931 financial crisis', *Economic History Review,* 2nd series, vol. 15 (1962–3), pp. 513–28.

68   Moggridge, *British Monetary Policy,* pp. 34, 127–8.

69   ibid., p. 34.

70   Moggridge, *The Return to Gold,* p. 48; P. J. Grigg, *Prejudice and Judgement* (1948), p. 185; Moggridge, *British Monetary Policy,* pp. 91, 92.

71   See J. M. Keynes, *Essays in Persuasion* (1931), pp. 225–36.

72   J. M. Keynes, *The Economic Consequences of Mr Churchill* (1925).

73   ibid.

74   Moggridge, *British Monetary Policy,* pp. 92, 110.

75   See Neil K. Buxton, 'Entrepreneurial efficiency in the British coal industry between the wars', *Economic History Review,* 2nd series, vol. 23 (1970), p. 495.

76   See Kirby, *The British Coalmining Industry,* pp. 66–107 *passim.*

77   Reddaway, 'Was $4·86 inevitable in 1925?', pp. 26–7.

78   G. A. Phillips, *The General Strike: The Politics of Industrial Conflict* (1976), p. 294.

79   Kirby, *The British Coalmining Industry,* p. 106.
80   For an excellent analysis of the rationalisation movement see Hannah, *The Rise of the Corporate Economy*, pp. 29–60.
81   See Sir Alfred Mond, *Industry and Politics* (1927), pp. 210–22.
82   Kirby, *The British Coalmining Industry*, pp. 108–23 and 'The politics of state coercion in inter-war Britain: The Mines Department of the Board of Trade, 1920–1942', *Historical Journal*, vol. 22 (1979), pp. 380–5.
83   M. W. Kirby, 'The Lancashire cotton industry in the inter-war years: a study in organisational change', *Business History,* vol. 16 (1974), p. 151.
84   Hannah, 'Managerial innovation and the rise of the large-scale company', pp. 266–7.
85   See Payne, *Colvilles and the Scottish Steel Industry*, pp. 163–210.
86   ibid. See also Slaven, 'A shipyard in depression'.
87   See R. H. Campbell, 'The North British Locomotive Company between the wars', *Business History*, vol. 20 (1978), pp. 201–34.
88   See R. H. Campbell, *The Rise and Fall of Scottish Industry* (Edinburgh, 1980).
89   Campbell, 'The North British Locomotive Company', p. 218.
90   Hannah, *The Rise of the Corporate Economy*, pp. 101–15.
91   ibid., p. 41. The Samuel Commission on the coal industry had been highly impressed by the degree of integration in the German Ruhr industry. See *Report of the Royal Commission on the Coal Industry (1925),* Vol. 1, Cmd 2600 (1926), p. 57. Mond's case for rationalisation was based partly on the need to create larger industrial units as 'a united front' against the 'foreign giants'. See Kirby, *The British Coalmining Industry,* p. 110.
92   Hannah, *The Rise of the Corporate Economy*, pp. 42–3, 125–6, 131–2.
93   See Committee on Industry and Trade, *Factors in Industrial and Commercial Efficiency* (1927), *Survey of Textile Industries* (1928), *Survey of Metal Industries* (1928) and, in particular, *Final Report*, Cmd 3282 (1929), pp. 175–94.
94   For government views on the issue of rationalisation see Hannah, *The Rise of the Corporate Economy,* pp. 45–60; Kirby, *The British Coalmining Industry,* pp. 108–23.
95   Hannah, *The Rise of the Corporate Economy,* p. 56.
96   Moggridge, *British Monetary Policy,* pp. 125–6. See also Aldcroft, *The Inter-War Economy*, p. 265.
97   ibid.
98   See J. Atkin, 'Official regulation of British overseas investment, 1914–31', *Economic History Review*, 2nd series, vol. 23 (1970), pp. 325–35.
99   Feavearyear, *The Pound Sterling,* p. 362.
100   Kenwood and Lougheed, *The Growth of the International Economy*, pp. 197, 199.
101   Aldcroft, *From Versailles to Wall Street,* p. 169.
102   ibid., pp. 174–5; L. J. Williams, *Britain and the World Economy 1919–1970* (1971); Peter Fearon, *The Origins and Nature of the Great Slump 1929–1932* (1979), p. 19.
103   Aldcroft, *From Versailles to Wall Street,* p. 169.
104   L. J. Williams, *Britain and the World Economy*, p. 103.
105   Kenwood and Lougheed, *The Growth of the International Economy*, p. 199.
106   ibid., p. 200; Fearon, *The Origins and Nature of the Great Slump*, p. 24.
107   Aldcroft, *From Versailles to Wall Street*, p. 172. See also Clarke, *Central Bank Co-operation, passim*; R. Nurkse, *International Currency Experience* (Geneva, 1944).

108   Kenwood and Lougheed, *The Growth of the International Economy*, p. 108.
109   Sayers, *The Bank of England,* Vol. 1, p. 219.
110   Moggridge, *British Monetary Policy*, p. 237.
111   ibid., p. 238; Aldcroft, *From Versailles to Wall Street,* pp. 171–3.
112   Defence expenditure fell from £520 million in 1920 to an annual average of £131 million in the period 1923–9. See Alan T. Peacock and Jack Wiseman, *The Growth of Public Expenditure in the United Kingdom* (rev. 2nd edn, 1967), table A-7, p. 168.
113   Donald Winch *Economics and Policy: An Historical Study* (Fontana edn of 1972), p. 106.
114   ibid., pp. 113–4
115   See D. E. Pitfield, 'Labour Migration and the Regional Problem in Britain 1920–1939' (unpublished PhD thesis, University of Stirling, 1973), pp. 157–80; I. M. Drummond, *Imperial Economic Policy 1917–1939* (1974), pp. 99–108.
116   Liberal Party, *Britain's Industrial Future* (1928). This is commonly referred to as the Liberal 'Yellow Book'.
117   *Memoranda on Certain Proposals relating to Unemployment*, Cmd 3331 (1929), pp. 50–1.
118   On the 'Treasury View' see Winch, *Economics and Policy*, pp. 118–19; Youngson, *Britain's Economic Growth*, pp. 195–6; Henry Roseveare, *The Treasury: The Evolution of a British Institution* (1969), pp. 266–7.
119   See W. H. Janeway, 'The Economic Policy of the Second Labour Government 1919–31' (unpublished PhD thesis, University of Cambridge, 1971), p. 276; *Report of the Committee on Finance and Industry,* Cmd 3897 (1931) and *Minutes of Evidence,* Q. 5565, 5685–6 (1931).
120   J. M. Keynes, *The General Theory of Employment, Interest and Money* (1936). On the evolution of Keynes's ideas see J. M. Keynes, *Collected Writings,* ed. D. E. Moggridge, Vol. 13: *The General Theory and After: Part I: Preparation* (1973); Harrod, *The Life of John Maynard Keynes*, pp. 436–574; Moggridge, *Keynes,* pp. 88–112; James Meade, 'The Keynesian revolution', in Milo Keynes (ed.), *Essays on John Maynard Keynes* (1975), pp.82–8.
121   Sean Glynn and John Oxborrow, *Interwar Britain: A Social and Economic History* (1976), pp. 132–3.
122   Public Record Office, Cab 24/203, CP204(29), 2 April 1929.
123   Winch, *Economics and Policy, pp. 121–2.*
124   Aldcroft, *The Inter-War Economy,* pp. 330–4.
125   Howson, *Domestic Monetary Management,* p. 52.
126   ibid., p. 54.
127   Moggridge, *British Monetary Policy*, p. 233.
128   Howson, *Domestic Monetary Management,* p. 63.
129   Moggridge, *British Monetary Policy*, pp. 228-44, *passim.*
130   Pressnell, '1925', p. 83.
131   Skidelsky in B. J. Rowland (ed.), *Balance of Power or Hegemony*, p. 174.
132   Kenwood and Lougheed, *The Growth of the International Economy,* p. 196.
133   Aldcroft, *From Versailles to Wall Street*, p. 188.
134   See Kenwood and Lougheed, *The Growth of the International Economy*, pp. 194–7. For a critical view of American overseas lending at this time see Fearon, *The Origins and Nature of the Great Slump*, pp. 19–21.
135   On the difficulties of the primary producing countries see W. A. Lewis, *World Economic Survey* (1949), pp. 149–56; Aldcroft, *From Versailles*

to Wall Street, pp. 218–38; C. P. Kindleberger, *The World in Depression 1929–1939* (1973), pp. 190–2; Fearon, *The Origins and Nature of the Great Slump,* pp. 26–7.

136 Moggridge, *British Monetary Policy*, p. 125.

Chapter 3

1 Aldcroft, *From Versailles to Wall Street,* p. 263.

2 Kindleberger, *The World in Depression,* pp. 97, 144–5.

3 Fearon, *The Origins and Nature of the Great Slump,* pp. 31–9, 41–2; Aldcroft, *From Versailles to Wall Street, pp. 270, 284.*

4 ibid., p. 266; C. H. Lee, 'The effects of the depression on primary producing countries', *Journal of Contemporary History,* vol. 4 (1969), pp. 139–55; Fearon, *The Origins and Nature of the Great Slump,* pp. 49–52.

5 Aldcroft, *From Inter-War Economy,* table 33, p. 261.

6 ibid., p. 147.

7 See David Marquand, *Ramsay MacDonald* (1977), pp. 518–637, *passim;* Robert Skidelsky, *Politicians and the Slump: The Labour Government, 1929–31* (Pelican edn, Harmondsworth, 1970), pp. 39–40, 80–1; Ross Mckibbin, 'The Economic Policy of the Second Labour Government 1929–31', *Past and Present,* no. 68 (1975), pp. 95–123; Janeway, 'The Economic Policy of the Second Labour Government' pp. 271–97, *passim.*

8 See McKibbin, 'The Economic Policy of the Second Labour Government', pp. 112–13.

9 Winch, *Economics and Policy,* p. 135; McKibben 'The Economic Policy of the Second Labour Government', p. 113.

10 ibid., p. 112.

11 ibid., p. 114.

12 *Report of the Committee on National Expenditure,* Cmd 3920 (1931).

13 Alford, *Depression and Recovery?,* p. 88.

14 Skidelsky, *Politicians and the Slump,* p. 107.

15 ibid., pp. 315–16, 318, 370–1; Kindleberger, *The World in Depression,* p. 151.

16 Skidelsky, *Politicians and the Slump,* p. 316.

17 Kindleberger, *The World in Depression,* p. 151; Winch, *Economics and Policy,* pp. 370–1. See also Clarke, *Central Bank Co-operation,* p. 189.

18 Kindleberger, *The World in Depression,* p. 155.

19 Howson, *Domestic Monetary Management,* p. 75; Susan Howson and Donald Winch, *The Economic Advisory Council 1930–1939: A Study in Economic Advice during Depression and Recovery* (Cambridge, 1977), p. 85.

20 Skidelsky, *Politicians and the Slump,* p. 378.

21 McKibbin, 'The Economic Policy of the Second Labour Government', p. 113.

22 See Marquand, *Ramsay MacDonald,* pp. 610–12; Skidelsky, *Politicians and the Slump,* pp. 389–421.

23 Andrew Boyle, *Montagu Norman: A Biography* (1967), pp. 268–9.

24 Howson and Winch, *The Economic Advisory Council,* p. 95. Kindleberger, *The World in Depression,* p. 37. For further comment on the 1931 financial crisis see D. Williams, 'London and the 1931 financial crisis' and 'The 1931 financial crisis', *Yorkshire Bulletin of Economic and Social Research,* vol. 15 (1963), pp. 91–110.

26 The next section has been heavily influenced by the views presented in

Janeway, 'The Economic Policy of the Second Labour Government', pp. 271–97.

27   On the 'Mosley Memorandum' see Sir Oswald Mosley, *My Life* (1968), pp. 229–63, *passim;* Robert Skidelsky, *Oswald Mosley* (1975), pp. 191–220, *passim;* Skidelsky, *Politicians and the Slump*, pp. 445–50; Marquand, *Ramsay MacDonald* pp. 534–7, 539–41. See also Mosley's resignation speech in the House of Commons, Hansard, *Parliamentary Debates* (Commons), fifth series, vol. 239, cols 1348–72, 28 May 1930.

28   Public Record Office, 'Notes on Sir Oswald Mosley's speech in the House of Commons', T 175/42, p. 28, 16 June 1930, cited in Janeway, 'The Economic Policy of the Second Labour Government, p. 275. A factor emphasised by Marquand in his analysis of the economic record of the second Labour government is the consistent and firm opposition of the Ministry of Transport to an extensive trunk-road building programme. See Marquand, *Ramsay MacDonald*, pp. 552–4.

29   Janeway, 'The Economic Policy of the Second Labour Government p. 278.

30   ibid., p. 280.

31   Skidelsky, *Politicians and the Slump*, p. 403. See Marquand, *Ramsay MacDonald* pp. 571–2 for Snowden's 'brutal intransigence' on the issue of tariff protection.

32   Janeway, 'The Economic Policy of the Second Labour Government', p. 283. See also Marquand, *Ramsay MacDonald,* pp. 623, 634.

33   Janeway, 'The Economic Policy of the Second Labour Government', p. 296.

34   On the Ottawa Conference see Drummond, *Imperial Economic Policy* chs 5–6.

35   Mowat, *Britain between the Wars*, p. 416.

36   This is the argument advanced by Hobsbawm. See Hobsbawm, *Industry and Empire*, pp. 149–50.

37   Skidelsky in B. J. Rowland (ed.), *Balance of Power or Hegemoney*, p. 180.

38   ibid., p. 181.

39   Pollard, *The Development of the British Economy*, pp. 198–9.

40   Skidelsky in B. J. Rowland (ed.), *Balance of Power or Hegemony*, p. 180.

41   On the iron and steel industry see Janeway, 'The Economic Policy of the Second Labour Government', pp. 117–24. On the cotton industry see Economic Advisory Council, *Cotton Industry Report,* Cmd 3615 (1928–30).

42   S. H. Beer, *Modern British Politics* (1965), p. 279.

43   See Winch, *Economics and Policy,* pp. 212–18; Alford, *Depression and Recovery?,* p. 69.

44   See D. Abel, *A History of British Tariffs, 1923–1942* (1945); H. Hutchinson, *Tariff-Making and Industrial Reconstruction* (1965).

45   See Kirby, 'The Lancashire cotton industry', pp. 155–6.

46   Arthur Marwick, 'Middle opinion in the thirties: planning, progress and "political agreement"', *English Historical Review,* Vol. 79 (1964), pp. 285–98; L. P. Carpenter, 'Corporatism in Britain, 1930–45', *Journal of Contemporary History,* vol. 11 (1976), pp. 3–25; Trevor Smith, *The Politics of the Corporate Economy* (1979), pp 6–92, *passim.*

47   Hansard, *Parliamentary Debates* (Commons), fifth series, vol. 300, cols 432–3, 3 April 1935.

48   Kirby, *The British Coalmining Industry,* p. 168.

49   Aldcroft, *The Inter-War Economy,* pp. 334–44; Howson, Domestic *Monetary Management,* pp. 88–95; Howson and Winch, *The Economic Advisory Council,* pp. 109–14.

50   ibid.
51   Aldcroft, *The Inter-War Economy*, p. 335.
52   Howson, *Domestic Monetary Management*, p. 88.
53   Kindleberger, *The World in Depression*, p. 180.
54   Peacock and Wiseman, *The Growth of Public Expenditure* table A-7, p. 169.
55   Howson, *Domestic Monetary Management*, p. 196.
56   Howson and Winch, *The Economic Advisory Council*, p. 257; Drummond, *Imperial Economic Policy*, pp. 213, 423, 444.
57   Howson and Winch, *The Economic Advisory Council*, p. 258.
58   Skidelsky in Rowland(ed.), *Balance of Power or Hegemony*, p. 187.
59   Cordell Hull, *Memoirs*, Vol. 1 (1948), p. 530.
60   Skidelsky in Rowland(ed.), *Balance of Power or Hegemony*, p. 187.
61   Howson and Winch, *The Economic Advisory Council*, p. 109.
62   ibid.
63   ibid.
64   See *Employment Policy after the War*, Cmd 6527 (1944). On Hopkins's views see Howson and Winch, *The Economic Advisory Council*, p. 152.
65   Cited in Winch, *Economics and Policy*, pp. 217–18.
66   McKibbin, 'The economic policy of the second Labour government', p. 105; Howson and Winch, *The Economic Advisory Council*, p. 122.
67   H. W. Richardson 'The economic significance of the depression in Britain', *Journal of Contemporary History*, vol. 4 (1969), p. 4
68   See McKibbin, 'The economic policy of the second Labour government', pp. 104, 106; Frederic M. Miller, 'The unemployment policy of the National Government, 1931–1936', *Historical Journal*, vol. 19 (1976), pp. 453–76.
69   On the evolution of Richardson's views see H. W. Richardson, 'The new industries between the wars', *Oxford Economic Papers*, vol. 13 (1961), pp. 360–84; H. W. Richardson, 'The basis of economic recovery in the 1930s: a review and a new interpretation', *Economic History Review*, 2nd series, vol. 15 (1962), pp. 344–63. These articles are reproduced in Aldcroft and Richardson, *The British Economy*, pp. 239–88 Richardson's final contributions were *Economic Recovery in Britain, 1932–1939* (1967) and 'The economic significance of the depression'.
70   See Neil K. Buxton, 'The role of the "new" industries in Britain during the 1930s: a reinterpretation', *Business History Review*, vol. 49 (1975), pp. 205–22; Buxton, editor's introduction in Buxton and Aldcroft (eds), *British Industry between the Wars*, pp. 9–23; Dowie, 'Growth in the inter-war period'; Alford, *Depression and Recovery?*, p. 47.
71   Buxton, 'The role of the "new" industries', pp. 208–14.
72   ibid.
73   Richardson, 'The economic significance of the depression', p. 3.
74   Dowie, 'Growth in the inter-war', p. 111.
75   Alford, *Depression and Recovery?*, p. 47.
76   Dowie, 'Growth in the inter-war period', p. 111.
77   Alford, *Depression and Recovery?*, p. 47.
78   See D. C. Coleman, *Courtaulds: An Economic and Social History*, Vol. 2: *Rayon* (Oxford, 1969), chs 11 and 13; Richardson, 'The new industries between the wars', p. 371.
79   A. E. Kahn, *Great Britain and the World Economy* (1946), pp. 112–13
80   R. A. Church and Michael Miller, 'The big three: competition, management and marketing in the British motor industry, 1922–1939', in Barry Supple (ed.), *Essays in British Business History* (Oxford, 1977), p. 183.

81   Barry Supple, 'A framework for British business history', in Supple (ed.), *Essays in British Business History*, pp. 24–5.
82   Alford, *Depression and Recovery?*, p. 79; B. W. E. Alford, 'Entrepreneurship, business performance and industrial development', *Business History*, vol. 19 (1977), p. 130.
83   Howson, *Domestic Monetary Management*, pp. 108–19.
84   ibid., pp. 112–16.
85   Aldcroft, *The Inter-War Economy*, pp. 203–4.
86   Alford, *Depression and Recovery?*, p. 47.
87   Dowie, 'Growth in the inter-war period', statistical appendix, pp 108–11.
88   R. C. O. Matthews, 'Some aspects of post-war growth in the British economy in relation to historical experience', *Transactions of the Manchester Statistical Society* (1964), pp. 17–18; Alford, *Depression and Recovery?*, p. 56.
89   Dowie, 'Growth in the inter-war period', table 1, p. 108.
90   Hannah, *The Rise of the Corporate Economy, passim.*
91   See A. F. Lucas, *Industrial Reconstruction and the Control of Competition* (1937), p. 209.
92   M. W. Kirby, 'Government intervention in industrial organization: coal mining in the nineteen thirties', *Business History*, vol. 15 (1973), p. 160.
93   For an analysis of the operation of the Coal Mines Act see Kirby, *The British Coalmining Industry*, pp. 139–68,
94   Hannah, *The Rise of the Corporate Economy*, p. 158.
95   Alford, *Depression and Recovery?*, p. 65. For an excellent study of the electricity supply industry which provides much insight into the evolving relationship between government and private industry see Leslie Hannah, *Electricity before Nationalisation: A Study of the Electricity Supply Industry in Britain to 1948* (1979).
96   Winch, *Economics and Policy*, p. 229.
97   Howson and Winch, *The Economic Advisory Council*, pp. 141–2.
98   R. F. Bretherton, F. A. Burchardt and R. S. G. Rutherford, *Public Investment and the Trade Cycle in Great Britain* (Oxford, 1941), pp. 198–9. Cited in Howson and Winch, *The Economic Advisory Council*, p. 142.
99   Mowat, *Britain between the Wars*, p. 481 borrowing from J. B. Priestley, *English Journey* (1934), pp. 397–408.
100   Mowat, *Britain between the Wars*, p. 481.
101   Bretherton, Burchardt and Rutherford, *Public Investment and the Trade Cycle*, pp. 83–93. Cited in Howson, *Domestic Monetary Management*, p. 139. For an attempt to explain the extent of interwar unemployment by reference to the unemployment insurance scheme see Daniel K. Benjamin and Levis A. Kochin 'Searching for an explanation of unemployment in interwar Britain', *Journal of Political Economy*, vol. 8 (1979), pp. 441–78. This is an unconvincing econometric study, noteworthy for its lack of any historical perspective.
102   Susan Strange, *Sterling and British Policy: A Political Study of an International Currency in Decline* (Oxford, 1971), p. 36.

Chapter 4

1   See D. E. Moggridge, 'From war to peace – the sterling balances', *The Banker*, vol. 122 (1972), p. 1,032; W. K. Hancock and M. M. Gowing *British War Economy* (1949), p. 548; Pollard, *The Development of the British Economy*, pp. 331–2.
2   Hancock and Gowing, *British War Economy*, p. 551.

3 ibid., p. 549; Pollard, *The Development of the British Economy*, p. 354.

4 Hancock and Gowing, *British War Economy*, p. 533.

5 For succinct summaries of the options available to Britain see D. E. Moggridge, 'From war to peace – how much overseas assistance?' *The Banker*, vol 122 (1972), p. 1, 167; R. S. Sayers, *Financial Policy 1939–1945* (1956), p. 484. The various options – 'starvation corner', 'temptation' and 'justice' were formulated by Keynes. See J. M. Keynes, *Collected Writings*, ed. D. E. Moggridge, Vol. 24: *Activities 1944–46: The Transition to Peace* (1979), pp. 276–9.

6 See Lord Boothby, *My Yesterday, Your Tomorrow* (1962), p. 154; Balogh,*Unequal Partners*, Vol. 2, pp. 140–59.

7 See Moggridge, 'From war to peace', pp. 1,165–6. The authorities were heavily influenced by a paper prepared by Keynes in June 1944 and circulated to the Cabinet in July. See Keynes, *Collected Writings*, vol. 24, pp. 34–65.

8 ibid., pp. 270–5.

9 See, for example, G. Kolko, *The Politics of War* (New York, 1968), pp. 280–94; William Roger Louis, *Imperialism at Bay 1941–1945: The United States and the Decolonisation of the British Empire* (Oxford, 1977), *passim*.

10 See Armand Van Dormael, *Bretton Woods: Birth of a Monetary System* (1978), pp. 13–15; Sayers, *Financial Policy*, table 7, p. 496, table 14, p. 503.

11 ibid., p. 403.

12 Keynes, *Collected Writings*, Vol. 24, *passim*.

13 Harrod, *The Life of John Maynard Keynes*, p. 680,

14 Sayers, *Financial Policy*, table 7, p. 496.

15 ibid., p. 435.

16 ibid., pp. 429–30

17 ibid., pp. 429–37.

18 *Agreement on the Principles of Mutual Aid*, Cmd 6341 (1942).

19 Sayers, *Financial Policy*, p. 413.

20 Alfred E. Eckes Jr, *A Search for Solvency: Bretton Woods and the International Monetary System* (1975), p. 34.

21 Harrod, *The Life of John Maynard Keynes*, p. 609.

22 ibid.

23 D. E. Moggridge, 'New light on post-war plans', *The Banker*, vol. 122 (1972), p. 340.

24 Lord Robbins, *Autobiography of an Economist* (1971), p. 192

25 The definitive account has been provided by Van Dormael, *Bretton Woods*. See also R. N. Gardner, *Sterling Dollar Diplomacy;* Eckes, *A Search for Solvency;* Harrod, *The Life of John Maynard Keynes*, pp. 621–92; J. M. Keynes, *Collected Writings*, ed. D. E. Moggridge Vol. 25: *Activities 1940–44: Shaping the Post-War World: The Clearing Union* (1980); Marcello de Cecco, 'Origins of the post-war payments system', *Cambridge Journal of Economics*, vol. 3 (1979). pp. 49–61.

26 Harrod, *The Life of John Maynard Keynes*, p. 588; Moggridge, *Keynes*, p. 114.

27 For the evolution of Keynes's ideas see Keynes, *Collected Writings*, Vol. 25,*passim;* Van Dormael,*Bretton Woods*, pp. 29–39; Harrod,*The Life of John Maynard Keynes*, pp. 622–9, 640–4.

28 Robbins, *Autobiography*, p. 196.

29 ibid., p. 199.

30 For the evolution of White's ideas and the Anglo-US negotiations before

the Bretton Woods conference see Van Dormael, *Bretton Woods*, pp. 40–7, 59–75, 99–126.

31   Harrod, *The Life of John Maynard Keynes*, pp. 643–9.
32   T. Balogh, 'The International Aspect', in G. D. N. Worswick and P. H. Ady(eds) *The British Economy 1945–50* (Oxford, 1952), p. 502.
33   Harrod, *The Life of John Maynard Keynes*, pp. 626–7; Moggridge, 'New light on post-war plans', pp. 341–2.
34   ibid.; Van Dormael, *Bretton Woods*, pp. 131, 133.
35   Lord Kahn, 'Historical origins of the International Monetary Fund', in Thirlwall (ed.), *Keynes and International Monetary Relations*, p. 12. See also Van Dormael, *Bretton Woods*, pp. 127–30.
36   For a contrary view stressing Keynes's knowledge of American negotiating tactics see Sayers, 'The young Keynes's p. 596.
37   Sir Hubert Henderson, *The Inter-War Years and Other Papers* (Oxford, 1955), p. 290.
38   ibid., p. 295.
39   Gardner, *Sterling Dollar Diplomacy*, p. 122.
40   Balogh, *Unequal Partners*, Vol. 2, pp. 152–9.
41   Lord Balogh, 'Keynes and the Internal Monetary Fund', in Thirlwall (ed.), *Keynes and International Monetary Relations*, p. 76.
42   Moggridge, 'From war to peace', p. 1,033.
43   ibid., p. 1,034.
44   Sayers, *Financial Policy*, p. 259.
45   Moggridge, From war to peace', p. 1,034.
46   ibid.
47   Robbins, *Autobiography*, p. 203.
48   Public Record Office, T 160/1375/F1 7942/01015, Keynes's memorandum, 28 September 1944. Cited in Van Dormael, *Bretton Woods*, p. 267.
49   Gardner, *Sterling Dollar Diplomacy*, pp. 127, 143. For detailed discussion of the American congressional debates and the difficulties of the Roosevelt administration in securing the passing of the final Bretton Woods Act see Van Dormael, *Bretton Woods*, pp. 251–65.
50   Gardner, *Sterling Dollar Diplomacy*, pp. 103–4.
51   Robbins, *Autobiography*, pp. 202–3.
52   Gardner, *Sterling Dollar Diplomacy*, p. 108.
53   Harrod, *The Life of John Maynard Keynes*, pp. 671–2.
54   On the financial negotiations see Keynes, *Collected Writings*, Vol. 24, pp. 420–628; Harrod, *The Life of John Maynard Keynes*, pp. 693–738.
55   ibid., p. 716.
56   Moggridge, 'From war to peace', p. 1,168.
57   *The Economist* (15 December 1945); Van Dormael, *Bretton Woods*, p. 283.
58   For a summary of the parliamentary debates see Van Dormael, *Bretton Woods*, pp. 275–85.
59   Gardner, *Sterling Dollar Diplomacy*, p. 221.
60   ibid., pp. 154–5.
61   Harrod, *The Life of John Maynard Keynes*, p. 716.
62   Robbins, *Autobiography*, p. 207; Van Dormael, *Bretton Woods*, pp. 272–85.
63   ibid., p. 273.
64   Public Record Office, FO 371/45713, Halifax to Churchill and Eden, 5 December 1945. Cited in Van Dormael, *Bretton Woods*, p. 275.
65   Gardner, *Sterling Dollar Diplomacy*, p. 211.
66   ibid., p. 218.

67   J. C. R. Dow, *The Management of the British Economy 1945–60* (1964), p. 23.
68   Hansard, *Parliamentary Debates* (Commons), fifth series, vol. 441, col. 1673, 7 August 1947.
69   Dow, *The Management of the British Economy,* note 2, p. 25.
70   Public Record Office, Treasury Papers, CP(47), 233, 16 August 1947, Annexe 1. Cited in *The Times* (4 January 1978).
71   Dow, *The Management of the British Economy*, p. 26.
72   ibid., p. 23.
73   ibid., p. 24.
74   See Worswick and Ady (eds), *The British Economy*, table 1, p. 479. The cost of relief expenditure in Germany jumped from £40 million in 1946 to £81 million in 1947.
75   See Dow, *The Management of the British Economy,* note 3, p. 25.
76   C. J. Bartlett, *A History of Postwar Britain 1945–74* (1977), p. 37.
77   See Francis Williams, *Ernest Bevin* (1952), p. 267.
78   Roger Eatwell, *The 1945–1951 Labour Governments* (1979), p. 106; Bartlett, *A History of Postwar Britain,* p. 78.
79   Worswick and Ady (eds), *The British Economy,* p. 559.
80   ibid., p. 483.
81   Bartlett, *A History of Postwar Britain,* p. 79.
82   See P. D. Henderson, 'Britain's international position', in Worswick and Ady (eds), *The British Economy,* p. 70.
83   ibid., p. 48.
84   See Pollard, *The Development of the British Economy,* pp. 364–91, *passim*; Dow, *The Management of the British Economy,* pp. 153–4, 159, 162–72.
85   *Employment Policy after the War,* Cmd 6527 (1944).
86   T. H. Marshall, *Social Policy in the Twentieth Century* (1975), p. 83.
87   Bartlett, *A History of Postwar Britain,* pp. 68–9.
88   Pollard, *The Development of the British Economy*, pp. 363–4.

Chapter 5

1   Sir Henry Phelps Brown, 'What is the British predicament?', *The Three Banks Review* (December 1977), pp. 4–5. For an exceptionally lucid and penetrating analysis of the course of Britain's postwar economic history see J. F. Wright, *Britain in the Age of Economic Management: An Economic History since 1939* (Oxford, 1979).
2   Aldcroft, *The Inter-War Economy,* table 33, p. 261.
3   On the Bacon and Eltis thesis see *The Sunday Times* (10 November 1974; 2, 9, 16 November 1975); Robert Bacon and Walter Eltis, 'Stop-go and de-industrialisation', *National Westminster Bank Quarterly Review* (November 1975), pp. 31–43; Robert Bacon and Walter Eltis, *Britain's Economic Problem: Too Few Producers* (2nd edn, 1978); Walter Eltis 'How rapid public sector growth can undermine the growth of the national product', in Wilfred Beckerman (ed.) *Slow Growth in Britain: Causes and Consequences,* (Oxford, 1979), pp. 118–39.
4   Bacon and Eltis, *Britain's Economic Problem.*
5   G. Hadjimatheou, A. Skouras, R. Bacon and W. Eltis, 'Britain's economic problem: the growth of the non-market sector: an interchange', *Economic Journal,* vol. 89 (1979), p. 405.
6   Bacon and Eltis, *Britain's Economic Problem;* Alan Peacock, *The Economic Analysis of Government and Related Themes* (Oxford, 1979),

pp. 113–14; A. R. Prest and D. J. Coppock, *The U. K. Economy: A Manual of Applied Economics* (7th edn, 1978), table A-11, p. 299. See, for example, Ajit Singh, 'U.K. industry and the world economy: a case of de-industrialisation?', *Cambridge Journal of Economics*, vol. 1 (1977), p. 113; Bacon and Eltis, *Britain's Economic Problem*, p. 177.

8   See *The Regeneration of British Industry*, Cmnd 5710 (1974); *An Approach to Industrial Strategy*, Cmnd 6315 (1975) and Alan Lord, *A Strategy for Industry* (York, 1976).

9   Taking the five postwar peak years, 1955, 1960, 1964, 1969 and 1973, unemployment rates in Great Britain were 1·0, 1·5, 1·6, 2·3 and 2·6 per cent respectively. For the argument that manufacturing industry has been *releasing* labour since 1966 see B. Moore, and J. Rhodes, 'The relative decline of the U.K. manufacturing sector', *Economic Policy Review*, no. 2 (1976). On 'overmanning' see Edward F. Denison, 'Economic growth', in Richard E. Caves and associates, *Britain's Economic Prospects* (1968), pp. 330–1; M. Lipton, *Assessing Economic Performance* (1968), pp. 138–9; Central Policy Review Staff, *The Future of the British Car Industry* 1975); C. F. Pratten and A. C. Atkinson, 'The use of manpower in British manufacturing industry', *Department of Employment Gazette* (June 1976); D. K. Stout, 'De-industrialisation and industrial policy', in F. Blackaby (ed.) *De-industrialisation* (1979), pp. 171–96. The views of Bacon and Eltis on the supply of 'productive' labour are not inconsistent with those presented by N. Kaldor, in *Causes of the Slow Rate of Growth of the United Kingdom* (Cambridge, 1966). For criticisms of Kaldor, see R. E. Rowthorn, 'What remains of Kaldor's law?', *Economic Journal*, vol. 85 (1975), pp. 10–19. Kaldor himself now believes that the UK is hampered more by a lack of international competitiveness than the inability of manufacturing industry to recruit sufficient labour.

10   A. R. Thatcher, 'Labour supply and employment trends', in Blackaby (ed.), *De-industrialisation*, p. 31.

11   See G. Hadjimatheou, *et al.*, 'Britain's economic problem', p. 408 and C. J. F. Brown and T. D. Sheriff, 'De-industrialisation: a background paper', in Blackaby (ed.) *De-industrialisation*, pp. 233–62.

12   See R. Neild and T. Ward, *The Budgetary Situation: An Appraisal* (Cambridge, 1976).

13   Phelps Brown, 'What is the British predicament?', pp. 10–13.

14   Neild and Ward, *The Budgetary Situation*, p. 19; Brown and Sheriff, 'De-industrialisation', pp. 237–40.

15   A. Singh, 'North sea oil and the reconstruction of U.K. industry,' in Blackaby (ed.), *De-industrialisation*, p. 204.

16   Singh, 'U.K. industry and the world economy', p. 129.

17   W. M. Corden, I. M. D. Little and M. Fg. Scott, *Import Controls Versus Devaluation and Britain's Economic Prospects* (1975), pp. 3–4.

18   Robert Bacon and Walter Eltis, 'The non-market sector and the balance of payments', *National Westminster Bank Quarterly Review* (May 1978), pp. 67.

19   J. R. Sargent, 'U.K. performance in services,' in Blackaby (ed.), *De-industrialisation*, p. 508; Singh, 'U.K. industry and the world economy', p. 121–2.

20   Michael Stewart, *The Jekyll and Hyde Years: Politics and Economic Policy since 1964* (1977), p. 227. See also Singh, 'U.K. industry and the world economy', p. 133; Frank Blackaby, 'Report on the discussion', in Blackaby (ed.), *De-industrialisation*, pp. 263–8.

21   Nicholas Kaldor, 'Comment'; Thomas Balogh, 'Comment', in Blackaby (ed.), *De-industrialisation*, pp. 22–3, 198–9.

22 On UK trade liberalisation see A. D. Morgan and D. Martin, 'Tariff reductions and U.K. imports of manufactures, 1955–1977', *National Institute Economic Review*, no. 72 (May 1975); M. F. W. Hemming, C. M. Miles and G. F. Ray, 'A statistical summary of the extent of import controls in the U.K. since the war', *Review of Economic Studies*, vol. 26 (1958–9), pp. 75–109.

23 Kaldor, 'Comment'; Balogh, 'Comment', in Blackaby (ed.), *De-industrialisation*, pp. 23, 199–200. On Verdoorn's law see note 19, p. 161 above.

24 Wilfred Beckerman, 'Projecting Europe's growth', *Economic Journal*, vol. 72 (1962), pp. 912–25; Wilfred Beckerman and associates, *The British Economy in 1975* (Cambridge, 1965). See also Alexandre Lamfalussy, *Investment and Growth in Mature Economies* (1961) and Nicholas Kaldor, 'Conflicts in national economic objectives', *Economic Journal*, vol. 81 (1971), pp. 1–16.

25 G. F. Ray, 'Comment', in Blackaby (ed.) *De-industrialisation*, pp. 73–7. See also G. F. Ray, 'Labour costs in OECD countries 1964–75', *National Institute Economic Review*, no. 78 (November 1976), pp. 58–62.

26 M. Panic, *The U.K. and West German Manufacturing Industry* (1976).

27 Brown and Sheriff, 'De-industrialisation', p. 258. See also M. Panic, 'Why the U.K. propensity to import is high', *Lloyds Bank Review* (January 1975), pp. 1–12; A. P. Thirlwall, 'The U.K.'s economic problem; a balance of payments constraint?', *National Westminster Bank Quarterly Review* (February 1978), pp. 24–32.

28 See D. T. Jones, 'Output, employment and labour productivity in Europe since 1955', *National Institute Economic Review*, no. 77 (August 1976), pp. 72–85; I. B. Kravis, 'A survey of international comparisons of productivity', *Economic Journal*, vol. 86 (1976), pp. 1–44; Pratten and Atkinson, 'The use of manpower in British manufacturing industry'.

29 Thirlwall, 'The U.K.'s economic problem'.

30 D. K. Stout, *International Price Competitiveness, Non-price Factors and Export Performance* (1977); M. V. Posner and A. Steer, 'Price Competitiveness and performance of manufacturing industry', in Blackaby (ed.), *De-industrialisation*, pp. 141–65; Panic, 'Why the U.K. propensity to import is high'.

31 Central Policy Review Staff, *The Future of the British Car Industry;* C. F. Pratten, *Labour Productivity Differentials within International Companies* (Cambridge, 1976); R. W. Bacon and W. A. Eltis, *The Age of U.S. and U.K. Machinery* (1974).

32 See Robert Skidelsky (ed.), *The End of the Keynesian Era* (1977).

33 A. W. Phillips, 'The relationship between unemployment and the rate of change of money wage rates in the UK., 1861–1957', *Economica*, vol. 25 (1958), pp. 283–99.

34 F. W. Paish, *Studies in an Inflationary Economy* (1966), pp. 309–62; F. W. Paish and J. Hennessy, *Policy for Incomes* (1964).

35 Prest and Coppock, (eds), *The U.K. Economy*, pp. 42–4; Stewart, *The Jekyll and Hyde Years*, p. 158.

36 See Robert Skidelsky, 'The political meaning of the Keynesian revolution' and Samuel Brittan, 'Can democracy manage an economy?,' in Skidelsky (ed.), *The End of the Keynesian Era*, pp. 33–40, 41–9.

37 ibid., p. 39.

38 For expositions of the monetarist position see Milton Friedman, *Money and Economic Development* (1973); M. Parkin, 'Where is Britain's inflation rate going?', *Lloyds Bank Review* (July 1975), pp. 1–13; D. Laidler, 'Inflation in Britain: a monetarist perspective', *American Economic Review*, vol. 66 (1976), pp. 485–500.

39   But see F. T. Blackaby (ed.), *British Economic Policy 1960–74: Demand Management* (Cambridge, 1978), pp. 285–7 for qualifications on this issue.

40   See ibid.; Stewart, *The Jekyll and Hyde Years,* pp. 159–64; Sir John Hicks, 'What is wrong with monetarism', *Lloyds Bank Review* (October 1975), pp. 1–13; E. H. Phelps Brown, 'A non-monetarist view of the pay explosion', *The Three Banks Review* (March 1975), pp. 3–24.

41   On the tripartite discussions see Lord, *A Strategy for Industry.* For a pessimistic view on 'tripartism' see Trevor Smith, *The Politics of the Corporate Economy,* pp. 178–80.

42   F. Cripps and W. Godley, 'Control of imports as a means to full employment and the expansion of world trade: the U.K.'s case', *Cambridge Journal of Economics,* vol. 2 (1978), p. 329. See also W. Godley, 'Britain's chronic recession: can anything be done?', in Beckerman (ed.), *Slow Growth in Britain,* pp. 226–33.

43   Cripps and Godley, 'Control of imports.' See also W. Godley and R. M. May, 'The macroeconomic implications of devaluation and import restrictions', *Economic Policy Review* (March 1977).

44   Singh, 'North sea oil and the reconstruction of U.K. industry', pp. 220–1.

45   Cripps and Godley, 'Control of imports', pp. 332–4.

46   See, for example, Strange, *Sterling and British Policy,* chs 9–10; Richard N. Cooper, 'The balance of payments', in Caves and associates, *Britain's Economic Prospects,* pp. 147–97; G. D. N. Worswick, 'Trade and payments', in Sir Alec Cairncross (ed.), *Britain's Economic Prospects Reconsidered,* (1971), pp. 61–100; L. J. Williams *Britain and the World Economy,* pp. 74–80. On the 1964–70 Labour government's trauma over the 1967 sterling devaluation see Samuel Brittan, *Steering the Economy: the Role of the Treasury* (1971), ch. 8; Richard Crossman, *The Diaries of a Cabinet Minister, 1964–8,* 2 vols (1967–8), Vol. 1, pp. 94–5, 117, 354; Vol. 2, pp. 156, 182–4; Harold Wilson, *The Labour Government 1964–70; A Personal Record* (Pelican edn Harmondsworth, 1974), pp. 570–86, 588–616.

47   On 'stop-go' see Brittan, *Steering the Economy,* pp. 448–56; Richard A. and Peggy B. Musgrave, 'Fiscal Policy', in Caves and associates. *Britain's Economic Prospects,* pp. 42–3; Stewart, *The Jekyll and Hyde Years, passim;* Blackaby (ed.), *British Economic Policy, passim;* Pollard, *The Development of the British Economy,* pp. 468–84.

48   Strange, *Sterling and British Policy.*

49   NEDO, *Cyclical Fluctuations in the United Kingdom Economy* (1976).

50   Blackaby (ed.), *British Economic Policy,* p. 421. The final 'General appraisal' chapter of this work is reproduced in *National Institute Economic Review,* no. 80 (May 1977), pp. 38–57.

51   See T. Wilson, 'Instability and economic growth: an international comparison 1950–65', in Aldcroft and Fearon (eds), *Economic Growth,* pp. 184–95.

52   For evidence of early disintegrative trends in intra-Commonwealth economic relationships see Phillip W. Bell, *The Sterling Area in the Postwar World: Internal Mechanism and Cohesion* (Oxford, 1956), pp. 396–427; J. D. B. Miller *Survey of Commonwealth Affairs 1953–69* (Oxford, 1974), pp. 275–6. See also Cooper, in Caves and associates. *Britain's Economic Prospects,* pp. 180–4.

53   See A. R. Conan, *The Rationale of the Sterling Area* (1961) for the statement made to the House of Commons in April 1958 (Hansard, *Parliamentary Debates,* fifth series, vol. 586, cols 51–2, 15 April 1958) by

the Chancellor of the Exchequer defending the Sterling Area and sterling's international role. The statement was made partly in response to mounting attacks on the 'sterling system' in the late 1950s.

54 Worswick and Ady, *The British Economy*, p. 483. See also Strange, *Sterling and British Policy*, pp. 66–7, 69, 128, for analysis of factors facilitating the survival of the Sterling Area and Commonwealth economic ties.

55 For early criticisms of the trade union movement see Andrew Shonfield, *British Economic Policy since the War* (1958), pp. 15–29; Michael Shanks, *The Stagnant Society* (1961, reissued and revised 1972); Eric Wigham, *What's Wrong with the Unions? (1961)*. For a general survey see Robert Taylor, 'Scapegoats for national decline: the trade unions since 1945,' in Chris Cook and John Ramsden (eds.), *Trends in British Politics since 1945* (1978), pp. 88–108.

56 On the 1964–70 Labour government's attempts to introduce a measure of trade union reform see *In Place of Strife*, Cmnd 3888 (1969); H. Wilson, *The Labour Government*, pp. 806–10, 817–33; Peter Jenkins, *The Battle of Downing Street* (1970). On the 1970–4 Conservative government's Industrial Relations Act see Michael Moran, *The Politics of Industrial Relations: The Origins, Life and Death of the 1971 Industrial Relations Act* (1977); Brian Weekes, Michael Mellish, Linda Dickens and John Lloyd, *Industrial Relations and the Limits of the Law* (Oxford, 1975); A. W. J. Thomson and S. R. Engleman, *The Industrial Relations Act: A Review and Analysis* (1975); H. A. Clegg, *The Changing System of Industrial Relations in Great Britain* (Oxford, 1979), pp. 319–28. See also generally Gerald A. Dorfman, *Government Versus Trade Unionism in British Politics since 1968* (1979).

57 See Lord Birkenhead, *Monckton: The Life of Lord Monckton of Blenchley* (1969), p. 276; Brittan, *Steering the Economy*, p. 193.

58 ibid., p. 203.

59 For an early insight into Macmillan's views on the running of the economy see Harold Macmillan, *The Middle Way* (1938).

60 Phelps Brown, 'What is the British predicament?', p. 20. See also R. P. Dore, *British Factory – Japanese Factory: The Origins of National Diversity in Industrial Relations* (1973); J. E. T. Eldridge, *Industrial Disputes* (1968).

61 Richard E. Caves, 'Market organization, performance and public policy,' in Caves and associates, *Britain's Economic Prospects*, pp. 300–6. See also Cairncross (ed.), *Britain's Economic Prospects Reconsidered*, pp. 30–4; Graham Turner, *Business in Britain* (1971); Bacon and Eltis, *The Age of U.S. and U.K. Machinery;* Derek F. Channon, *The Strategy and Structure of British Enterprise* (1973), pp. 21–49, 211–13, 218–35, *passim.*

62 Phelps Brown, 'What is the British predicament?, p. 19. On management and shop-floor divisions from the perspective of the 1950s see Henry Pelling, *America and the British Left* (1956).

63 Merton J. Peck, 'Science and technology', in Caves and associates, *Britain's Economic Prospects,* pp. 448–84. See also Sir Solly Zuckerman, *Scientists at War* (1966), p. 45; John and Anne-Marie Hackett *The British Economy: Problems and Prospects* (1967), pp. 224–7; F. V. Meyer *et al.*, *Problems of a Mature Economy* (1970), pp. 275–7.

64 Saul, in Smout (ed.), *The Search for Wealth and Stability,* p. 125.

65 Christopher Layton, *European Advanced Technology* (1969), p. 53. The

result was a predictable series of cancellations: in the first half of the 1960s the Blue Streak Rocket (£84 million); the Skybolt missile (£27 million); the TSR2 aircraft (£195 million). See also Victor Keegan, 'Industry and technology', in David McKie and Chris Cook (eds), *The Decade of Disillusion: British Politics in the Sixties,* (1972), pp. 137–48.

66   C. F. Freeman, 'Technical innovation and British trade performance', in Blackaby(ed.), *De-industrialisation,* p. 66; Channon, *The Strategy and Structure of British Enterprise,* p. 231.

67   D. Burn, *Nuclear Power and the Energy Crisis* (1978).

68   Peter Sinclair, 'Economic debates' in Cook and Ramsden (eds), *Trends in British Politics,* p. 84.

69   Saul, in Smout (ed.), *The Search for Wealth and Stability,* pp. 129, 130–1.

70   Freeman, in Blackaby (ed.), *De-industrialisation,* pp. 65–72.

71   Sir John Baker, 'The engineer in the U.K.', *Progress* (1964), pp. 182–4

72   G. F. Ray, 'Comment', in Blackaby (ed.), *De-industrialisation,* p. 75.

73   See Skidelsky, in Skidelsky (ed.), *The End of the Keynesian Era,* p. 39.

74   Brittan, *Steering the Economy,* pp. 230–5. On the NEDC see Richard Bailey, *Managing the British Economy: A Guide to Economic Planning in Britain since 1962* (1968), *passim;* Stewart, *The Jekyll and Hyde Years,* pp. 48–50. See also Jacques Leruez, 'Macro-economic planning in mixed economies: the French and British experience', in Jack Hayward and Olga A. Narkiewicz (eds), *Planning in Europe,* (1978), pp. 26–52; Smith, *The Politics of the Corporate Economy,* pp. 149–60.

75   See J. E. Meade, *The Theory of Indicative Planning* (Manchester, 1970) for a rigorous theoretical analysis.

76   See Blackaby (ed.), *British Economic Policy,* pp. 30–1; Stewart, *The Jekyll and Hyde Years,* pp. 36–7; Wilson, *The Labour Government,* p. 24; George Brown, *In My Way: The Political Memoirs of Lord George-Brown* (1971), pp. 95–109; Frank Broadway, *State Intervention in British Industry 1964–68* (1969), pp. 15–26.

77   *The National Plan,* Cmnd 2764 (1965).

78   Wilson, *The Labour Government,* p. 893. See also Roger Opie, 'Economic planning and growth', in W. Beckerman (ed.), *The Labour Government's Economic Record, 1964–70,* (1972), pp. 170–2.

79   National Institute of Economic and Social Research, *The United Kingdom Economy* (3rd edn, 1977), pp. 109–10.

80   Singh, in Blackaby (ed.), *De-industrialisation,* p. 222.

81   Corden, Little and Scott, *Import Controls Versus Devaluation,* p. 10.

82   Singh, in Blackaby (ed.), *De-industrialisation,* p. 222.

83   ibid., p. 223.

84   ibid., p. 221.

85   A. K. Cairncross, J. A. Kay and A. Silberston, 'The regeneration of manufacturing industry', *Midland Bank Review* (Autumn 1977), p. 17. On the growth of 'big business' in Britain and S. Aaronovitch and M. C. Sawyer, *Big Business* (1975); Leslie Hannah and J. A. Kay *Concentration in Modern Industry* (1977); S. J. Prais, 'A new look at the growth of industrial concentration', *Oxford Economic Papers,* vol. 26 (1974), pp. 273–88; S. J. Prais, *The Evolution of Giant Firms in Britain: A Study of the Growth of Concentration in Manufacturing Industry in Britain, 1909–70* (Cambridge, 1976); G. Meeks and G. Whittington, 'Giant companies in the United Kingdom 1948–1969', *Economic Journal,* vol. 85 (1975), pp. 824–43.

86   Kay, in Cairncross, Kay and Silberston, 'The regeneration of manufacturing industry', p. 18.

87 Hannah and Kay, *Concentration in Modern Industry,* pp. 23–40, 118–25; K. D. George and T. S. Ward, *The Structure of Industry within the EEC* (Cambridge, 1975). See also Hannah, *The Rise of the Corporate Economy,* pp. 178–99. For an extremely critical view of the growth of 'big business' (in so far as it is equated with multinational enterprise) written from a committed socialist standpoint see Stuart Holland, *The Socialist Challenge* (1975). Holland advocates the nationalisation of multinational firms (the 'mesoeconomic' sector) wherever it can be shown that their activities subvert a country's social and economic objectives.

88 Kay, in Cairncross, Kay and Silberston, 'The regeneration of manufacturing industry', p. 17.

89 Stuart Holland, 'Comment', in Blackaby (ed.), *De-industrialisation,* p. 96.

90 British Export Trade Association, *Export Concentration* (1975).

91 D. C. Hague, E. Oakeshott and A. Strain, *Devaluation and Pricing Decisions* (1974).

92 Labour Research Department, *Multinational Companies* (1975).

93 Kay, in Cairncross, Kay and Silberston, 'The regeneration of manufacturing industry', p. 18.

94 On the issue of interpenetration see Sir Alec Cairncross, *Essays in Economic Management* (1971), pp. 9–25; Smith, *The Politics of the Corporate Economy;* S. Young and A. V. Lowe, *Intervention in the Mixed Economony: The Evolution of British Industrial Policy 1964–72* (1974); S. Young, 'Industrial policy in Britain, 1972–77,' in Hayward and Narkiewicz (eds), *Planning in Europe,* pp. 79–100.

95 Taylor, in Cook and Ramsden (eds), *Trends in British Politics,* pp. 130–1.

96 Blackaby (ed.), *British Economic Policy,* p. 417. See also G. D. N. Worswick, 'The end of demand management?', *Lloyds Bank Review* (January 1977), pp. 1–18.

97 The memoirs of Harold Macmillan, Harold Wilson and the diaries of Richard Crossman provide considerable evidence of the amount of time and nervous energy leading politicians are obliged to devote to the 'parliamentary-electoral battle'.

98 Blackaby (ed.), *British Economic Policy,* p. 438.

99 ibid.

100 Lord Gladwyn, *The Memoirs of Lord Gladwyn* (1972), pp. 288ff.

101 Miriam Camps, *Britain and the European Community 1955–1963* (Oxford, 1964), chs 1–7. See also Miriam Camps, *European Unification in the Sixties: From the Veto to the Crisis* (Oxford, 1967).

102 Camps, *Britain and the European Community,* p. 276.

103 Alan Sked and Chris Cook, *Post-War Britain: A Political History* (1979), p. 190.

104 On Macmillan's own views on the decision to apply for entry to the EEC see Harold Macmillan, *At the End of the Day 1961–1963* (1973), pp. 5–9, 16–18.

105 Sked and Cook, *Post-War Britain,* p. 190.

106 T. W. Hutchison, *Economics and Economic Policy in Britain 1946–1966* (1968), pp. 165–74, 190–206, 250–1.

107 ibid., *passim.*

108 Uwe Kitzinger, *Diplomacy and Persuasion: How Britain Joined the Common Market* (1973).

109 *The United Kingdom and the European Communities,* Cmnd 4715 (1971), para. 37, pp. 10–11. See also J. D. B. Miller *Survey of Commonwealth Affairs,* pp. 442–50.

110 R. C. O. Matthews, 'Why has Britain had full employment since the war?', *Economic Journal,* vol. 78 (1968), pp. 565–6.

111   See Lewis, *Growth and Fluctuations*, pp. 131–2.
112   Richardson, 'Overcommitment in Britain before 1930', p. 258.
113   A. J. Brown, 'Inflation and the British sickness', *Economic Journal*, vol. 89 (1979), pp. 1–12.
114   For the results of the 1963–4 expansion see F. Brechling and J. N. Wolfe 'The end of stop-go', *Lloyds Bank Review* (January 1965), pp. 23–30.
115   A. J. Brown, 'Inflation and the British sickness', p. 9.
116   Sinclair, in Cook and Ramsden (eds), *Trends in British Politics*, p. 83.
117   Thirlwall, 'The U.K.'s economic problem', pp. 30–1.
118   Keith Middlemas, *Politics in Industrial Society* (1979).

Bibliography

The place of publication is London unless otherwise stated.

Aaronovitch, S. and Sawyer, M. C., *Big Business* (1975).

Abel, D., *A History of British Tariffs, 1923–1942* (1945).

Aldcroft, D. H., 'Economic growth in Britain in the inter-war years: a reassessment', *Economic History Review*, 2nd Series, vol. 20 (1967).

Aldcroft, D. H., 'Economic Progress in Britain in the 1920s', *Scottish Journal of Political Economy,* vol. 13 (1966).

Aldcroft, D. H., *From Versailles to Wall Street, 1919–29* (1977).

Aldcroft, D. H., 'Investment in and utilisation of manpower', in Barrie M. Ratcliffe (ed.) *Great Britain and Her World 1750–1914* (Manchester, 1975).

Aldcroft, D. H., 'Technical progress and British enterprise, 1875–1914', *Business History,* vol. 8 (1966).

Aldcroft, D. H. (ed.), *The Development of British Industry and Foreign Competition, 1875–1914* (1968).

Aldcroft, D. H., 'The entrepreneur and the British economy, 1870–1914', *Economic History Review,* 2nd series, vol. 17 (1964).

Aldcroft, D. H., *The Inter-War Economy: Britain, 1919–1939* (1970).

Aldcroft, D. H., 'The problem of productivity in British industry 1870–1914', D. H. Aldcroft and H. W. Richardson (eds), *The British Economy, 1870–1939* (1969).

Aldcroft, D. H. and Fearon, Peter (eds), *Economic Growth in Twentieth Century Britain* (1969).

Aldcroft, D. H. and Richardson, H. W., (eds), *The British Economy, 1870–1939* (1969).

Alford, B. W. E., *Depression and Recovery? British Economic Growth 1918–1939* (1972).

Alford, B. W. E., 'Entrepreneurship, business performance and industrial development', *Business History*, vol. 19 (1977).

Ames, E. and Rosenberg, N., 'Changing technological leadership and industrial growth', *Economic Journal*, vol. 73 (1963).

Armitage, S. M. H., *The Politics of Decontrol: Britain and the United States* (1969)

Ashton, T. S. and Sayers, R. S., *Papers in English Monetary History* (Oxford, 1953).

Ashworth, W., *An Economic History of England, 1870–1939* (1960).

Atkin, J., 'Official regulation of British overseas investment, 1914–31', *Economic History Review,* 2nd series, vol. 23 (1970).

Bacon, Robert and Eltis, Walter, *Britain's Economic Problem: Too Few Producers* (2nd edn, 1978).

Bacon, Robert and Eltis, Walter, 'Stop-go and de-industrialisation', *National Westminster Bank Quarterly Review* (November 1975).

Bacon, R. W. and Eltis, W. A., *The Age of U.S. and U.K. Machinery* (1974).

Bacon, Robert and Eltis, Walter, 'The non-market sector and the balance of payments', *National Westminster Bank Quarterly Review* (May 1978).

Bailey, Richard, *Managing the British Economy: A Guide to Economic Planning in Britain since 1962* (1968).

Baker, Sir John, 'The engineer in the U.K.', *Progress* (1964).

Balogh, Lord, 'Keynes and the International Monetary Fund', in A. P. Thirlwall (ed.), (1976).

Balogh, T., 'The international aspect', in G. D. N. Worswick and P. H. Ady (eds), *The British Economy, 1945–50* (Oxford, 1952).

Balogh, Thomas, *Unequal Partners,* Vol. 2: *Historical Episodes* (Oxford, 1963).

Barnett, Corelli, *The Collapse of British Power* (1972).

Bartlett, C. J., *A History of Postwar Britain 1945–74* (1977).

Beckerman, Wilfred, 'Projecting Europe's growth', *Economic Journal*, vol. 72 (1962).

Beckerman, Wilfred (ed.), *Slow Growth in Britain: Causes and Consequences* (Oxford, 1979).

Beckerman, W. (ed.), *The Labour Government's Economic Record, 1964–70* (1972).

Beckerman, Wilfred and associates, *The British Economy in 1975* (Cambridge, 1965).

Beer, S. H., *Modern British Politics* (1965).

Bell, Phillip W., *The Sterling Area in the Postwar World: Internal Mechanism and Cohesion* (Oxford, 1956).

Benians, E. A., Butler, Sir James and Carrington, C. E. (eds), *Cambridge History of the British Empire,* Vol. 3: *The Empire-Commonwealth 1870–1919* (Cambridge, 1959).

Benjamin, Daniel K. and Kochin, Levis A., 'Searching for an explanation of unemployment in interwar Britain', *Journal of Political Economy*, vol. 8 (1979).

Birkenhead, Lord, *Walter Monckton: The Life of Lord Monckton of Blenchley* (1969).

Blackaby, F. T. (ed.), *British Economic Policy 1960–74: Demand Management* (Cambridge, 1978).

Blackaby, Frank (ed.), *De-industrialisation* (1979).

Bloomfield, A. I., *Monetary Policy under the International Gold Standard, 1880–1914* (New York, 1959).

Boothby, Lord, *My Yesterday, Your Tomorrow* (1962).

Born, Karl Erich, 'The German inflation after the First World War', *Journal of European Economic History*, vol. 6 (1977).

Boyle, Andrew, *Montagu Norman: A Biography* (1967).

Brechling, F. and Wolfe, J. N., 'The end of stop-go', *Lloyds Bank Review* (January 1965).

Bretherton, R. F., Burchardt, F. A. and Rutherford, R. S. G., *Public Investment and the Trade Cycle in Great Britain* (Oxford, 1941).

British Export Trade Association, *Export Concentration* (1975).

Brittan, Samuel, 'Can democracy manage an economy?, in Robert Skidelsky (ed.), *The End of the Keynesian Era* (1977).

Brittan, Samuel, *Steering the Economy: The Role of the Treasury* (1971).

Broadway, Frank, *State Intervention in British Industry 1964–68* (1969).

Brown, A. J., 'Britain and the world economy, 1870–1914', *Yorkshire Bulletin of Economic and Social Research,* vol. 17 (1965).

Brown, A. J., 'Inflation and the British sickness', *Economic Journal,* vol. 89 (1979).

Brown, C. J. F. and Sheriff, T. D., 'De-industrialisation: a background paper', in Frank Blackaby (ed.), *De-industrialisation* (1979).

Brown, George, *In My Way: The Political Memoirs of Lord George-Brown* (1971).

Bullock, Alan, *The Life and Times of Ernest Bevin,* Vol. 1 (1960).

Burn, D., *Nuclear Power and the Energy Crisis* (1978).

Buxton, Neil K., 'Enterprenerurial efficiency in the British coal industry between the wars', *Economic History Review,* 2nd series, vol 23 (1970).

Buxton, Neil K., *The Economic Development of the British Coal Industry: From Industrial Revolution to the Present Day* (1978).

Buxton, Neil K., 'The role of the "new" industries in Britain during the 1930s: a reinterpretation', *Business History Review,* vol. 49 (1975).

Buxton, N. K. and Aldcroft, D. H. (eds), *British Industry between the Wars: Instability and Industrial Development* (1979).

Cairncross, Sir Alec, *Essays in Economic Management* (1971).

Cairncross, Sir Alec (ed.), *Britain's Economic Prospects Reconsidered* (1971).

Cairncross, A. K., *Home and Foreign Investment, 1870–1913* (Cambridge, 1953).

Cairncross, A. K., Kay, J. A. and Silberston, A., 'The regeneration of manufacturing industry', *Midland bank Review* (Autumn 1977).

Campbell, R. H., 'The North British Locomotive Company between the wars', *Business History,* vol. 20 (1978).

Campbell, R. H., *The Rise and Fall of Scottish Industry* (Edinburgh, 1980).

Campbell, R. H. and Wilson, R. G., *Enterpreneurship in Britain, 1750–1939* (1975).

Camps, Miriam, *Britain and the European Community 1955–1963* (Oxford, 1964).

Camps, Miriam, *European Unification in the Sixties: From the Veto to the Crisis* (Oxford, 1967).

Carpenter, L. P., 'Corporatism in Britain, 1930–45', *Journal of Contemporary History,* vol. 11 (1976).

Caves, Richard E., 'Market organization, performance and public policy', in Richard E. Caves and associates, *Britain's Economic Prospects* (1968).

Caves, Richard E. and associates, *Britain's Economic Prospects* (1968).

Cecco, Marcello de, 'Origins of the post-war payments system', *Cambridge Journal of Economics,* vol. 3 (1979).

Cecco, Marcello de and Lindert, P. H., *Key Currencies and Gold 1900–1913* (1969).

Central Policy Review Staff, *The Future of the British Car Industry* (1975).

Channon, Derek F., *The Strategy and Structure of British Enterprise* (1973).

Chapman, S. D., *Jesse Boot of Boots the Chemist* (1974).

Church, R. A. (ed.), *The Dynamics of Victorian Business: Problems and Perspectives to the 1870s* (1980).

Church, R. A., *The Great Victorian Boom 1850–1873* (1975).

Church, R. A. and Miller, Michael, 'The big three: competition, management and marketing in the British motor industry, 1922–1939', in Barry Supple (ed.), *Essays in British Business History* (Oxford, 1977).

Clarke, S. V. O., *Central Bank Co-operation 1924–31* (New York, 1967).

Clarke, S. V. O., *The Reconstruction of the International Monetary System: The Attempts of 1922 and 1933)* (1973).

Clay, Sir Henry, *Lord Norman* (1957).

Clegg, H. A., *The Changing System of Industrial Relations in Great Britain* (Oxford, 1979).

Coleman, D. C., *Courtaulds: An Economic and Social History,* Vol. 2: *Rayon* (Oxford, 1969).

Coleman, D. C., 'Gentlemen and players', *Economic History Review,* 2nd series, vol. 26 (1973).

Conan, A. R., *The Rationale of the Sterling Area* (1961).

Conrad, A. H. and Meyer, J. R., *Studies in Econometric History* (1965).

Cook, Chris and Ramsden, John (eds), *Trends in British Politics since 1945* (1978).

Cooper, Richard N., 'The balance of payments', in Richard E. Caves and associates, *Britain's Economic Prospects, (1968).*

Copock, D. J., 'The climacteric of the 1890s: a critical note', *The Manchester School,* vol. 24 (1956).

Corden, W. M., Little, I. M. D. and Scott, M. Fg., *Import Controls Versus Devaluation and Britain's Economic Prospects* (1975).

Costigliola, Frank C., 'Anglo-American financial rivalry in the 1920s', *Journal of Economic History,* vol. 37 (1977).

Cottrell. P. L., *British Overseas Investment in the Nineteenth Century* (1975).

Crafts, N. F. R. and McCloskey, D. N., 'Victorian Britain did fail'[a debate], *Economic History Review,* 2nd series, vol. 32 (1979).

Cripps, F. and Godley, W., 'Control of imports as a means to full employment and the expansion of world trade: the U.K.'s case', *Cambridge Journal of Economics*, vol. 2 (1978).

Crossman, Richard, *The Diaries of a Cabinet Minister, 1964–8*, 2 vols (1967–8).

Crouzet, François, 'Trade and empire: the British experience from the establishment of free trade until the First World War', in Barrie M. Ratcliffe (ed.), *Great Britain and Her World 1750–1914* (Manchester, 1975).

Davis, J. S., *The World between the Wars 1919–1939: An Economist's View* (1975).

Denison, Edward F., 'Economic growth', in Richard E. Caves and associates, *Britain's Economic Prospects* (1968).

Dore, R. P., *British Factory – Japanese Factory: The Origins of National Diversity in Industrial Relations* (1973).

Dorfman, Gerald, *Government Versus Trade Unionism in British Politics since 1968* (1979).

Dow, J. C. R., *The Management of the British Economy 1945–60* (1964).

Dowie, J. A., 'Growth in the inter-war period: some more arithmetic', *Economic History Review,* 2nd series, vol. 21 (1968).

Dowie, J. A., '1919 is in need of attention', *Economic History Review,* 2nd series, vol. 28 (1975).

Drummond, I. M., *Imperial Economy Policy 1917–1939* (1974).

Eatwell, Roger, *The 1945–1951 Labour Governments* (1979).

Eckes, Alfred E. Jr, *A Search for Solvency: Bretton Woods and the International Monetary System* (1975).

Elcock, Howard, *Portrait of a Decision: The Council of Four and the Treaty of Versailles* (1972).

Eldridge, J. E. T., *Industrial Disputes* (1968).

Eltis, Walter, 'How rapid public sector growth can undermine the growth of the national product', in Wilfred Beckerman (ed.), *Slow Growth in Britain: Causes and Consequences* (Oxford, 1979).

Fearon, Peter, *The Origins and Nature of the Great Slump 1929–1932* (1979).

Feavearyear, Sir Albert, *The Pound Sterling* (Oxford, 1963).

Feinstein, C. H., *National Income, Expenditure and Output of the United Kingdom, 1855–1965* (Cambridge, 1972).

Floud, Roderick and McCloskey, D. N. (eds), *The Economic History of Britain since 1700* (forthcoming).

Ford, A. G., *The Gold Standard 1880–1914: Britain and Argentina* (1962).

Ford, A. G., 'The truth about gold', *Lloyds Bank Review* (July 1965).

Foster, John, 'Imperialism and the labour aristocracy', in Jeffrey Skelley (ed.), *The General Strike,* (1976).

Frankel, M., 'Obsolescence and technical change in a maturing economy', *American Economic Review,* vol. 45 (1955).

Freeman, C. F., 'Technical innovation and British trade performance, in Frank Blackaby (ed.), *De-industrialisation* (1979).

Freeman, C. and Young, A., *The Research and Development Effort in Western Europe, North America and the Soviet Union* (Paris, 1965).

Friedman, Milton, *Money and Economic Development* (1973).

Gardner, R. N., *Sterling Dollar Diplomacy* (1956).

George, K. D., and Ward, T. S., *The Structure of Industry within the EEC* (Cambridge, 1975).

Gladwyn, Lord, *The Memoirs of Lord Gladwyn* (1972).

Glynn, Sean and Oxborrow, John, *Interwar Britain: A Social and Economic History* (1976).

Godley, W., 'Britain's chronic recession: can anything be done?', in Wilfred Beckerman (ed.), *Slow Growth in Britain: Causes and Consequences* (Oxford, 1979).

Godley, W. and May, R. M., 'The macroeconomic implications of devaluation and import restrictions', *Economic Policy Review* (March 1977).

Gollin, Alfred, *Balfour's Burden: Arthur Balfour and Imperial Preferences* (1965).

Goodhard, C. A. E., *The Business of Banking, 1891–1914* (1972).

Gould, J. D., *Economic Growth in History: Survey and Analysis* (1972).

Graham, G. S., 'Imperial finance, trade and communications, 1895–1914', in *Cambridge History of the British Empire,* Vol. 3, ed. E. A. Benians *et al.*

Grigg, P. J., *Prejudice and Judgement* (1948).

Hackett, John and Anne-Marie, *The British Economy: Problems and Prospects* (1967).

Hadjimatheou, G., Skouras, A., Bacon, R. and Eltis, W., 'Britain's economic problem: the growth of the non-market sector: an interchange', *Economic Journal*, vol. 89 (1979).

Hague, D. C., Oakeshott, E. and Strain, A., *Devaluation and Pricing Decisions* (1974).

Hancock, W. K. and Gowing, M. M., *British War Economy* (1949).

Hannah, Leslie, 'Managerial innovation and the rise of the large-scale company in interwar Britain', *Economic History Review,* 2nd series, vol. 27 (1974).

Hannah, Leslie, *The Rise of the Corporate Economy* (1976).

Hannah, Leslie and Kay, J. A., *Concentration in Modern Industry* (1977).

Harley, C. K., 'Skilled labour and the choice of technique in Edwardian industry', *Explorations in Economic History,* vol. 11 (1974).

Harrod, R. F., *The Life of John Maynard Keynes* (Penguin edn, Harmondsworth, 1972).

Hawtrey, Ralph, 'The return to gold in 1925', *Bankers' Magazine,* vol. 208 (1970).

Hayward, Jack and Narkiewicz, Olga (eds), *Planning in Europe* (1978).

Heath, Sir Frank and Heatherington, A. L., *Industrial Research and Development in the United Kingdom: A Survey* (1945).

Hemming, M. F. W., Miles, C. M. and Ray, G. F., 'A statistical summary of the extent of import controls in the U.K. since the war', *Review of Economic Studies,* vol. 26 (1958–9).

Henderson, Sir Hubert, *The Inter-War Years and Other Papers* (Oxford, 1955).

Hicks, Sir John, 'What is wrong with monetarism', *Lloyds Bank Review* (October 1975).

Hobsbawn, E. J., *Industry and Empire* (Pelican edn, Harmondsworth, 1969).

Hoffman, R. J. S., *Great Britain and the German Trade Rivalry, 1875–1914* (1933).

Holland, Stuart, *The Socialist Challenge* (1975).

Howson, Susan, *Domestic Monetary Management in Britain 1919–38* (Cambridge, 1975).

Howson, Susan and Winch, Donald, *The Economic Advisory Council 1930–1939: A Study in Economic Advice during Depression and Recovery* (Cambridge, 1977).

Hull, Cordell, *Memoirs,* Vol. 1 (1948).

Hume, John R. and Moss, Michael, *Beardmore: The History of a Scottish Industrial Giant* (1979).

Hutchinson, H., *Tariff-Making and Industrial Reconstruction* (1965).

Hutchison, T. W., *Economics and Economic Policy in Britain 1946–1966* (1968).

Janeway, W. H., 'The Economic Policy of the Second Labour Government 1929–31' (unpublished PhD thesis, University of Cambridge, 1971).

Jeffreys, J. B., *Retail Trading in Britain* (Cambridge 1954).

Jenkins, Peter, *The Battle of Downing Street,* (1970).

Jervis, F. R. J., 'The handicap of Britain's early start', *The Manchester School,* vol. 15 (1947).

Johnson, P. B., *Land Fit for Heroes: The Planning of British Reconstruction, 1916–1919* (Chicago, Ill., 1968).

Jones, D. T., 'Output, employment and labour productivity in Europe since 1965', *National Institute Economic Review* (August 1976).

Kahn, A. E., *Great Britain and the World Economy* (1946).

Kahn, Lord, 'Historical origins of the International Monetary Fund', in A. P. Thirlwall (ed.), *Keynes and International Monetary Relations* (1976).

Kaldor, Nicholas, 'Capitalism and industrial development: some lessons from Britain's experience', *Cambridge Journal of Economics,* vol. 1 (1977).

Kaldor, N., *Causes of the Slow Rate of Growth of the United Kingdom* (Cambridge, 1966).

Kaldor, N., 'Conflicts in national economic objectives', *Economic Journal,* vol. 81 (1971).

Keegan, Victor, 'Industry and technology', in David McKie and Chris Cook, (eds), *The Decade of Disillusion: British Politics in the Sixties* (1972).

Kennedy, W. P., 'Foreign investment, trade and growth in the United Kingdom, 1870–1913', *Explorations in Economic History,* vol. 11 (1974).

Kenwood, A. G. and Lougheed, A. L., *The Growth of the International Economy, 1820–1960* (1971).

Keynes, J. M., *Collected Writings,* Vol. 13: *The General Theory and After: Part I: Preparation* (1973); Vol. 17: *Activities 1920–22: Treaty Revision and Reconstruction* (1977); Vol. 23: *Activities 1940–44: External War Finance* (1978); Vol. 24: *Activities 1944–46: The Transition to Peace* (1979); Vol. 25: *Activities 1940–44: Shaping the Post-War World: The Clearing Union* (1980).

Keynes, J. M., *Essays in Persuasion* (1931).

Keynes, J. M., *The Economic Consequences of Mr Churchill* (1925).

Keynes, J. M., *The Economic Consequences of the Peace* (New York, 1920).

Keynes, J. M., *The General Theory of Employment, Interest and Money* (1936).

Keynes, Milo (ed.), *Essays on John Maynard Keynes* (1975).

Kindleberger, C. P., 'Foreign trade and economic growth: lessons from Britain and France, 1850 to 1913', *Economic History Review,* 2nd series, vol. 14 (1961–2).

Kindleberger, C. P., 'Obsolescence and technical change', *Bulletin of the Oxford University Institute of Statistics,* vol. 23 (1961).

Kindleberger, C. P., *The World in Depression 1929–1939* (1973).

King, W. T. C., *History of the London Discount Market* (1936).

Kirby, M. W., 'Government intervention in industrial organisation: coal-mining in the nineteen thirties', *Business History,* vol. 15 (1973).

Kirby, M. W., *The British Coalmining Industry 1870–1946: A Political and Economic History* (1977).

Kirby, M. W., 'The Lancashire cotton industry in the inter-war years: a study in organisational change', *Business History*, vol. 16 (1974).

Kirby, M. W., 'The politics of state coercion in inter-war Britain: the Mines Department of the Board of Trade, 1920–1942', *Historical Journal,* vol. 22 (1979).

Kitzinger, Uwe, *Diplomacy and Persuasion: How Britain Joined the Common Market* (1973).

Kolko, G., *The Politics of War* (New York, 1968).

Kravis, I. B., 'A survey of international comparisons of productivity', *Economic Journal,* vol. 86 (1976).

Labour Research Department, *Multinational Companies* (1975).

Laidler, D., 'Inflation in Britain: a monetarist perspective', *American Economic Review,* vol. 66 (1976).

Lamfalussy, Alexandre, *Investment and Growth in Mature Economies* (1961).

Landes, David, *The Unbound Prometheus: Technological Change and Industrial Development in Western Europe from 1750 to the Present* (Cambridge, 1969).

Layton, Christopher, *European Advanced Technology* (1969).

Lee, C. H., 'The effects of the depression on primary producing countries', *Journal of Contemporary History,* vol. 4 (1969).

Luruez, Jacques, 'Macro-economic planning in mixed economies: the French and British experience', in Jack Hayward and Olga Narkiewicz (eds), *Planning in Europe* (1978).

Levine, A. M., *Industrial Retardation in Britain 1880–1914* (1967).

Lewis, W. A., *Growth and Fluctuations* (1978).

Lewis, W. A., 'International competition in manufactures', *American Economic Review (Papers and Proceedings),* vol. 47 (1957).

Lewis, W. A., *The Deceleration of British Growth 1873–1913* (Princeton, NJ, 1967; mimeographed).

Lewis, W. A., *World Economic Survey* (1949).

Liberal Party, *Britain's Industrial Future* (1928).

Lipton, M., *Assessing Economic Performance* (1968).

Lord, Alan, *A Strategy for Industry* (Sir Ellis Hunter Memorial Lecture University of York, 1976).

Louis, William Roger, *Imperialism at Bay 1941–1945: The United States and the Decolonisation of the British Empire* (Oxford, 1977).

Lucas, A. F., *Industrial Reconstruction and the Control of Competition* (1937).

McCloskey, D. N., 'Did Victorian Britain fail?', *Economic History Review,* 2nd series, vol. 23 (1970).

McCloskey, D. N., *Economic Maturity and Entrepreneurial Decline: British Iron and Steel, 1870–1913* (Cambridge, Mass., 1973).

McCloskey, D. N. and Sandberg, Lars G., 'From damnation to redemption: judgements on the late Victorian entrepreneur', *Explorations in Economic History*, vol. 9 (1971).

McIntosh, Douglas, C., 'Mantoux versus Keynes: a note on German income and the Reparations Commission'. *Economic Journal*, vol. 87 (1977).

McKibbin, Ross, 'The economic policy of the second Labour government', *Past and Present*, no. 68 (1975).

McKie, David and Cook, Chris (eds), *The Decade of Disillusion: British Politics in the Sixties* (1972).

Maclean, I. W., 'Anglo-American engineering competition, 1870–1914: some third market evidence', *Economic History Review*, 2nd series, vol. 29 (1976).

Macmillan, Harold, *At the End of the Day 1961–1963* (1973).

Macmillan, Harold, *The Middle Way* (1938).

Madden, A. F., 'Changing attitudes and widening responsibilities, 1895–1914', in *Cambridge History of the British Empire*, Vol. 3, ed. E. A. Benians *et al.*

Maier, Charles S., *Recasting Bourgeois Europe: Stabilization in France, Germany and Italy in the Decade after World War I* (Princeton, NJ, 1975).

Mantoux, Etienne, *The Carthaginian Peace or The Economic Consequences of Mr Keynes* (1946).

Marquand, David, *Ramsay MacDonald* (1977).

Marshall, T. H., *Social Policy in the Twentieth Century* (1975).

Marwick, Arthur, 'Middle opinion in the thirties: planning, progress and "political agreement" ', *English Historical Review*, vol. 79 (1964).

Mathias, Peter, *The First Industrial Nation: An Economic History of Britain, 1700–1914* (1969).

Mathias, Peter and Postan, M. M. (eds), *Cambridge Economic History of Europe*, vol. 7, pt 1 (1978).

Matthews, R. C. O., 'Some aspects of post-war growth in the British economy in relation to historical experience', *Transactions of the Manchester Statistical Society* (1964).

Matthews, R. C. O., 'Why has Britain had full employment since the war?', *Economic Journal*, vol. 78 (1968).

Meade, J. E., *The Theory of Indicative Planning* (Manchester, 1970).

Meeks, G. and Whittington, G., 'Giant companies in the United Kingdom 1948–1969', *Economic Journal*, vol. 85 (1975).

Meier, G. M., 'Long period determinants of Britain's terms of trade, 1880–1913', *Review of Economic Studies*, vol. 20 (1962–3).

Meyer, F. V. *et al.*, *Problems of a Mature Economy* (1970).

Middlemas, Keith, *Politics in Industrial Society* (1979).

Miller, Frederic M., 'The unemployment policy of the National Government, 1931–1936', *Historical Journal*, vol. 19 (1976).

Miller, J. D. B., *Survey of Commonwealth Affairs 1953–69* (Oxford, 1974).

Moggridge, D. E., *British Monetary Policy, 1924–1931: The Norman Conquest of $4.86* (Cambridge, 1972).

Moggridge, D. E., 'From war to peace – how much overseas assistance?', *The Banker,* vol. 122 (1972).

Moggridge, D. E., 'From war to peace – the sterling balances', *The Banker,* vol. 122 (1972).

Moggridge, D. E., *Keynes* (Fontana edn, 1976).

Moggridge, D. E., 'New light on post-war plans', *The Banker*, vol, 122 (1972).

Moggridge, D. E., *The Return to Gold, 1925: The Formulation of Policy and Its Critics* (Cambridge, 1969).

Mond, Sir Alfred, *Industry and Politics* (1927).

Monroe, E., *Britain's Moment in the Middle East* (1963).

Moore, B. and Rhodes, J., 'The relative decline of the U.K. manufacturing sector', *Economic Policy Review,* no. 2 (1976).

Moran, Michael, *The Politics of Industrial Relations: The Origins, Life and Death of the 1971 Industrial Relations Act* (1974).

Morgan, A. D. and Martin, D., Tariff reductions and U.K. imports of manufactures, 1955–1977', *National Institute Economic Review,* no. 72 (May 1975).

Mosley, Sir Oswald, *My Life* (1968).

Moulton, Harold G. and Pasvolsky, Leo, *War Debts and World Prosperity* (Washington, DC, 1932).

Mowat, Charles Loch, *Britain between the Wars 1918–1940* (1955).

Musgrave, Richard A. and Peggy B., 'Fiscal policy', in Richard E. Caves and associates, *Britain's Economic Prospects* (1968).

Musson, A. E., *The Growth of British Industry* (1978).

National Economic Development Office, *Cyclical Fluctuations in the United Kingdom Economy* (1976).

National Institute of Economic and Social Research, *The United Kingdom Economy* (3rd edn, 1977).

National Economic Development Office, *Finance for Investment* (1975).

Nield, R. and Ward, T., *The Budgetary Situation: An Appraisal* (Cambridge, 1976).

Nurkse, R., *International Currency Experience* (Geneva, 1944).

OECD, *The Outlook for Economic Growth* (Paris, 1970).

Opie, Roger, 'Economic planning and growth', in W. Beckerman (ed.), *The Labour Government's Economic, Record, 1964–70* (1972).

Paish, F. W., *Studies in an Inflationary Economy* (1966).

Paish, F. W. and Hennessy, J., *Policy for Incomes* (1964).

Panic, M., *The U.K. and West German Manufacturing Industry* (1976).

Panic, M., 'Why the U.K. propensity to import is high', *Lloyds Bank Review* (January 1975).

Parkin, M., 'Where is Britain's inflation rate going?', *Lloyds Bank Review* (July 1975).

Payne, Peter L., *British Entrepreneurship in the Nineteenth Century* (1974).

Payne, Peter L., *Colvilles and the Scottish Steel Industry* (Oxford, 1979).

Payne, Peter L., 'Rationality and personality: a study of mergers in the Scottish iron and steel industry', *Business History,* vol. 19 (1977).

Payne, P. L., 'The emergence of the large-scale company in Great Britain, 1870–1914', *Economic History Review,* 2nd series, vol. 20 (1967).

Peacock, Alan, *The Economic Analysis of Government and Related Themes* (Oxford, 1979).

Peacock, Alan T. and Wiseman, Jack, *The Growth of Public Expenditure in the United Kingdom* (rev. 2nd edn, 1967).

Peck, Merton, J., 'Science and technology', in Richard E. Caves and associates, *Britain's Economic Prospects* (1968).

Pelling, Henry, *America and the British Left* (1956).

Phelps Brown, E. H., 'A non-monetarist view of the pay explosion', *The Three Banks Review* (March 1975).

Phelps Brown, Sir Henry, 'What is the British predicament?', *The Three Banks Review* (December 1977).

Phelps Brown, E. H. and Handfield Jones, S. J., 'The climacteric of the 1890s: a study of the expanding economy', *Oxford Economic Papers,* vol. 4 (1952).

Phillips, A. W., 'The relationship between unemployment and the rate of change of money wage rates in the U.K., 1861–1957', *Economica,* vol. 25 (1958).

Phillips, G. A., *The General Strike: The Politics of Industrial Conflict* (1976)

Pigou, A. C., *Aspects of British Economic History, 1918–1925* (1948).

Pitfield, D. E., 'Labour Migration and the Regional Problem in Britain 1920–1939', (unpublished PhD thesis, University of Stirling, 1973).

Pollard, Sidney, *The Development of the British Economy 1914–1967* (2nd edn, 1969).

Pollard, Sidney (ed.), *The Gold Standard and Employment Policies between the Wars* (1970).

Pollard, Sidney and Robertson, Paul, *The British Shipbuilding Industry 1870–1914* (Cambridge, Mass. 1979).

Posner, M. V. and Steer, A., 'Price competitiveness and performance of manufacturing industry', in Frank Blackaby (ed.), *De-industrialisation* (1979).

Prais, S. J., 'A new look at the growth of industrial concentration', *Oxford Economic Papers,* vol. 26 (1974).

Prais, S. J., *The Evolution of Giant Firms in Britain: A Study of the Growth of Concentration in Manufacturing Industry in Britain, 1909–70* (Cambridge, 1976).

Pratten C. F., *Labour Productivity Differentials within International Companies* (Cambridge, 1976).

Pratten, C. F. and Atkinson, A. C., 'The use of manpower in British manufacturing industry', *Department of Employment Gazette* (June 1976).

Pressnell, L. S., '1925; the burden of sterling', *Economic History Review,* 2nd series, vol. 31 (1978).

Prest, A. R. and Coppock, D. J. (eds), *The U.K. Economy: A Manual of Applied Economics* (7th edn, 1978).

Priestley, J. B., *English Journey* (1934).

Ratcliffe, Barrie M., *Great Britain and Her World 1750–1914: Essays in Honour of W. O. Henderson* (Manchester, 1975).

Ray, G. F., 'Labour costs in OECD countries, 1964–75', *National Institute Economic Review,* no. 78 (November 1976).

Reader, W. J. *Imperial Chemical Industries: A History*, Vol. 1: *The Forerunners, 1870–1926* (1970).

Reddaway, W. B., 'Was $4.86 inevitable in 1925?', *Lloyds Bank Review* (April 1970).

Rempel, Richard A., *Unionists Divided: Arthur Balfour, Joseph Chamberlain and the Unionist Free Traders* (Newton Abbott, 1972).

Richardson, H. W., 'Chemicals', in D. H. Aldcroft (ed.), *The Development of British Industry and Foreign Competition, 1875–1914* (1968).

Richardson, H. W., *Economic Recovery in Britain 1932–1939* (1967).

Richardson, H. W., 'Overcommitment in Britain before 1930', *Oxford Economic Papers*, vol. 17 (1965).

Richardson, H. W., 'The basis of economic recovery in the 1930s: a review and a new interpretation', *Economic History Review*, 2nd series, vol. 15 (1962).

Richardson, H. W., 'The economic significance of the depression in Britain', *Journal of Contemporary History*, vol. 4 (1969).

Richardson, H. W., 'The new industries between the wars', *Oxford Economic Papers*, vol. 13 (1961).

Ringer, Fritz K., *The German Inflation of 1923* (1969).

Robbins, Lord, *Autobiography of an Economist* (1971).

Roseveare, Henry, *The Treasury: The Evolution of a British Institution* (1969).

Rothbarth, E., 'Causes of the superior efficiency of U.S.A. industry as compared with British industry', *Economic Journal*, vol. 56 (1946).

Rowland, Benjamin J. (ed.), *Balance of Power or Hegemony. The Interwar Monetary System* (New York, 1976).

Rowland, Peter, *Lloyd George* (1975).

Rowthorn, R. E., 'What remains of Kaldor's law?', *Economic Journal*, vol. 85 (1975).

Sandberg, Lars G., 'American rings and English mules: the role of economic rationality', *Quarterly Journal of Economics*, vol. 83 (1969).

Sandberg, Lars G., *Lancashire in Decline: A Study in Entrepreneurship, Technology and International Trade* (Columbus, Ohio, 1974).

Sanderson, J. M., 'Research and the firm in British industry, 1919–1939', *Science Studies*, vol. 2 (1972).

Sanderson, M., 'The professor as industrial consultant: Oliver Arnold and the British steel industry, 1900–14', *Economic History review*, 2nd series vol. 31 (1978).

Sanderson, M., *The Universities and British Industry 1850–1970* (1972).

Sargent, J. R., 'U.K. performance in services', in Frank Blackaby (ed.), *Deindustrialisation* (1979).

Saul, S. B., 'Research and development in British industry from the end of the nineteenth century to the 1960s', in T. C. Smout (ed.), *The Search for Wealth and Stability* (1979).

Saul, S. B., *Studies in British Overseas Trade 1870–1914* (Liverpool, 1960).

Saul, S. B. (ed.), *Technological Change: The United States and Britain in the Nineteenth Century* (1970).

Saul, S. B., 'The export economy 1870–1914', *Yorkshire Bulletin of Economic and Social Research*, vol. 17 (1965).

Saul, S. B., 'The market and the development of the mechanical engineering industries in Britain, 1860–1914', *Economic History Review,* 2nd series, vol. 20 (1967).

Saul, S. B., 'The motor industry in Britain to 1914', *Business History,* vol. 5 (1962).

Saul, S. B., *The Myth of the Great Depression, 1873–1896* (1969).

Saville, J., 'Some retarding factors in the British economy before 1914', *Yorkshire Bulletin of Economic and Social Research,* vol. 13 (1961).

Sayers, R. S., *Central Banking after Bagehot* (Oxford, 1957).

Sayers, R. S., *Financial Policy 1939–1945* (1956).

Sayers, R. S., *The Bank of England, 1891–1944,* 3 vols (1976).

Sayers, R, S., 'The springs of technical progress in Britain, 1919–1939', *Economic Journal,* vol. 60 (1950).

Sayers, R. S., *The Vicissitudes of an Export Economy: Britain since 1880* (Sydney, 1965).

Sayers, R. S., 'The young Keynes', *Economic Journal,* vol. 82 (1972).

Scammell, W. M., 'The working of the gold standard', *Yorkshire Bulletin of Economic and Social Research,* vol. 17 (1965).

Semmel, Bernard, *Imperialism and Social Reform: English Social-Imperial Thought 1895–1914* (Anchor Books edn, New York, 1968).

Shanks, Michael, *The Stagnant Society* (1961, revised and reissued 1972).

Shonfield, Andrew, *British Economic Policy since the War* (1958).

Simon, Matthew, 'The pattern of new British portfolio investment, 1865–1914', in A. R. Hall (ed.), *The Export of Capital from Britain, 1875–1914.*

Sinclair, Peter, 'Economic debates', in Chris Cook and John Ramsden (eds), *Trends in British Politics since 1945* (1978).

Singh, A., 'North sea oil and the reconstruction of U.K. industry in Frank Blackaby (ed.), *De-industrialisation* (1979).

Singh, A., 'U.K. industry and the world economy; a case of de-industrialisation?', *Cambridge Journal of Economics,* vol. 1 (1977).

Sked, Alan and Cook, Chris, *Post-War Britain: A Political History* (1979).

Skidelsky, Robert, *Oswald Mosley* (1975).

Skidelsky, Robert, *Politicians and the Slump: The Labour Government, 1929–31* (Pelican edn. Harmondsworth, 1970).

Skidelsky, Robert, 'Retreat from leadership: the evolution of British foreign economic policy 1870–1939', in Benjamin J. Rowland, (ed.), *Balance of Power or Hegemony: The Interwar Monetary System* (New York, 1976).

Skidelsky, Robert (ed.), *The End of the Keynesian Era* (1977).

Skidelsky, Robert, 'The political meaning of the Keynesian revolution', in Robert Skidelsky (ed.), *The End of the Keynesian Era* (1977).

Skidelsky, Robert, 'Verdicts on Versailles', *The Times Literary Supplement* (15 September 1978).

Slaven, A., 'A shipyard in depression: John Browns of Clydebank, 1919–1938', *Business History,* vol. 19 (1977).

Smith, Trevor, *The Politics of the Corporate Economy* (1979).

Smout, T. C. (ed.), *The Search for Wealth and Stability: Essays in Economic and Social History Presented to M. W. Flinn* (1979).

Solow, Robert M. and Temin, Peter, 'Introduction: the inputs for growth', in *Cambridge Economic History of Europe*, Vol. 7, pt 1, ed. Peter Mathias and M. M. Postan.

Stewart, Michael, *The Jekyll and Hyde Years: Politics and Economic Policy since 1964* (1977).

Stout, D. K., *International Price Competitiveness, Non-price Factors and Export Performance* (1977).

Stout, D. K., 'De-industrialisation and industry policy', in Frank Blackaby (ed.), *De-industrialisation* (1979).

Strange, Susan, *Sterling and British Policy: A Political Study of an International Currency in Decline* (Oxford, 1971).

Strauss, William L., *Joseph Chamberlain and the Theory of Imperialism* (New York, 1971).

Sullivan, Edward, 'Isolated free trade', *Nineteenth Century,* vol. 10 (1881).

Supple, Barry, 'A framework for British business history', in Barry Supple (ed.), *Essays in British Business History* (Oxford, 1977).

Supple, Barry (ed.), *Essays in British Business History* (Oxford, 1977).

Svennilson, Ingvar, *Growth and Stagnation in the European Economy* (Geneva, 1954).

Taylor, A. J., 'Labour productivity and technological innovation in the British coal industry, 1850–1914', *Economic History Review,* 2nd series vol. 14 (1961).

Taylor, A. J., 'The coal industry', in D. H. Aldcroft (ed.), *The Development of British Industry and Foreign Competition 1875–1914* (1968).

Taylor, Robert, 'Scapegoats for national decline: the trade unions since 1945', in Chris Cook and John Ramsden (eds), *Trends in British Politics since 1945* (1978).

Thatcher, A. R., 'Labour supply and employment trends', in Frank Blackaby (ed.), *De-industrialisation,* (1979).

Thirlwall, A. P. (ed.), *Keynes and International Monetary Relations: The Second Keynes Seminar Held at the University of Kent at Canterbury, 1974* (1976).

Thirlwall, A. P., 'The U.K.'s economic problem: a balance of payments constraint?', *National Westminster Bank Quarterly Review* (February 1978).

Thomson, A. W. J. and Engleman, S. R., *The Industrial Relations Act: A Review and Analysis* (1975).

Thornton, A. P., *The Imperial Idea and Its Enemies* (1959).

Trebilcock, Clive, *The Vickers Brothers: Armaments and Enterprise, 1854–1914* (1977).

Triffin, Robert, *Our International Monetary System: Yesterday, Today and Tomorrow* (New York, 1968).

Turner, Graham, *Business in Britain* (1971).

Tyson, R. E., 'The cotton industry', in D. H. Aldcroft, (ed.), *The Development of British Industry and Foreign Competition, 1875–1914* (1968).

Tyszinski, H., 'World trade in manufactured commodities 1899–1950', *The Manchester School,* vol. 19 (1951).

Van Dormael, Armand, *Bretton Woods: Birth of a Monetary System* (1978).

Verdoorn, P. J., 'Fattori che regolano lo sviluppo della produttività del lavoro', *L'Industria* (1949).

Ward, D., 'The public schools and industry in Britain after 1870', *Journal of Contemporary History,* vol. 2 (1967).

Weekes, Brian, Mellish, Michael, Dickens, Linda and Lloyd, John, *Industrial Relations and the Limits of the Law* (Oxford, 1975).

Whittlesey, C. R. and Wilson, J. S. S. (eds), *Essays in Money and Banking in Honour of R. S. Sayers* (1968).

Wigham, Eric, *What's Wrong with the Unions?* (1961).

Williams, D., 'London and the 1931 financial crisis', *Economic History Review,* 2nd series, vol. 15 (1962–3).

Williams, D., 'Montagu Norman and banking policy in the 1920s', *Yorkshire Bulletin of Economic and Social Research*, vol. 11 (1959).

Williams, D., 'The 1931 financial crisis', *Yorkshire Bulletin of Economic and Social Research,* vol. 15 (1963).

Williams, D. J., 'The evolution of the sterling system', in C. R. Whittlesey and J. S. S. Wilson (eds), *Essays in Money and Banking in Honour of R. S. Sayers* (1968).

Williams, Ernest, *Made in Germany* (1896).

Williams, Francis, *Ernest Bevin,* (1952).

Williams, L. J., *Britain and the World Economy 1919–1970* (1971).

Wilson, Harold, *The Labour Government 1964–70: A Personal Record* (Pelican edn Harmondsworth, 1974).

Wilson, T., 'Instability and economic growth: an international comparison 1950–65', in D. H., Aldcroft and Peter Fearon (eds), *Economic Growth in Twentieth Century Britain* (1969).

Winch, Donald, *Economics and Policy: A Historical Study* (Fontana edn of 1972).

Worswick, G. D. N., 'The end of demand management?', *Lloyds Bank Review* (January 1977).

Worswick, G. D. N., 'Trade and payments', in Sir Alec Cairncross (ed.), *Britain's Economic Prospects Reconsidered* (1971).

Worswick, G. D. N. and Ady, P. H. (eds), *The British Economy, 1945–50* (Oxford, 1952).

Wright, J. F., *Britain in the Age of Economic Management: An Economic History since 1939* (Oxford, 1979).

Young, S., 'Industrial policy in Britain, 1972–77', in Jack Hayward and Olga Narkiewicz (eds), *Planning in Europe* (1978).

Young, S. and Lowe, A. V., *Intervention in the Mixed Economy: The Evolution of British Industrial Policy 1964–72* (1974).

Youngson, A. J., *Britain's Economic Growth, 1920–1966* (1967).

Zinkin, M. and T., *Britain and India* (1964).

Zuckerman, Sir Solly, *Scientists at War* (1966).

Government Publications (in oder of publication)

Report of the Departmental Committee Appointed by the Board of Trade To Consider the Position of the Shipping and Shipbuilding Industry after the War, Cd 9062 (1918).

Committee on Currency and Foreign Exchanges after the War, *First Interim Report,* Cd 9182 (1918); *Final Report,* Cmd 464 (1919).

Report of the Royal Commission on the Coal Industry (1925), Vol. 1, Cmd 2600 (1926).

Committee on Industry and Trade, *Factors in Industrial and Commercial Efficiency* (1927).

Committee on Industry and Trade, *Survey of Textile Industries* (1928).

Committee on Industry and Trade, *Survey of Metal Industries* (1928).

Committee on Industry and Trade, *Final Report*, Cmd 3282 (1929)

Memoranda on Certain Proposals Relating to Unemployment, Cmd 3331 (1929).

Economic Advisory Council, *Cotton Industry Report*, Cmd 3615 (1929–30).

Report of the Committee on Finance and Industry, Cmd 3897 (1931).

Report of the Committee on National Expenditure, Cmd 3920 (1931).

Agreement on the Principles of Mutual Aid, Cmd 6341 (1942).

Employment Policy after the War, Cmd 6527 (1944).

The National Plan, Cmnd 2764 (1965).

In Place of Strife, Cmnd 3888 (1969).

The United Kingdom and the European Communities, Cmnd 4715 (1971).

The Regeneration of British Industry, Cmnd 5710 (1974).

An Approach to Industrial Strategy, Cmnd 6315 (1975).

INDEX

Howson, Susan 39, 52–3
Hull, Cordell 70, 87
Hungary 38, 39

ICI 43
Imperial Preference 21, 65–6, 70, 75, 87, 91–2, 94, 96, 102, 133
Import Duties Act 65, 112
Import Duties Advisory Committee 66
Incomes policy 108, 114
India 17, 20, 21, 26, 27, 41, 66, 86, 92
Industrial Reorganisation Corporation 124, 127, 130
Industrial Revolution 7
Industrial Training Act 124
Industrial Transference Board 50
Industry production pre-1914, 2; post-1918, 29 productivity, pre-1914, 2; post-1918, 29, 32; post-1929, 74; post-1950, 105; structure, 7–8, 34–5, 45–6, 52–3, 74, 76, 79, 102, 112, 126–8
Inflation 107, 113–15, 129–30, 134–5
Institute of Bankers 22
International economy pre-1914, 4, 17–20; post-1918, 54–6, 59
International Monetary Fund (IMF) 90–1, 95, 98, 116
Investment industrial, 5; domestic pre-1914, 14–16; post-1918, 52; post-1929, 73; post-1950, 105 overseas; pre-1914, 2, 14–19; post-1918, 47, 55–6, 69, 82; post-1945, 104
Invisible trade balance pre-1914, 2; post-1918, 28, 41, 58; post-1931, 70
Iron and steel 3, 4–5, 30, 33, 34, 58, 66, 74–5
Italy 113

Janeway, W. H. 65
Japan 17, 20, 21, 26–7, 69, 83, 84, 102, 103, 106, 109, 116, 119, 127
Jarrow 80

Kahn, Richard 70
Kaldor, Lord 5, 112
Kay, J. A. 128
Kennedy, John F. 131
Keynes, J. M. on the international economy, 19; on Versailles treaty, 24–6; on gold standard, 42; on relief works, 50–1, 78; and *General Theory*, 70; and US loan, 83, 96–7; on multilateralism, 84; and Bretton

Woods, 83–93 *passim;* Clearing Union scheme, 89–90; on postwar commercial policy, 95; *see also* Keynesianism
Keynesianism 113–14, 124
Korean War 102

Labour force distribution pre-1914, 4; *see also* De-industrialisation
Labour governments 1929–31, 58–65, 72; 1945–51, 84, 95–6, 100–2; 1964–70, 124, 136; 1974–9, 108, 130
Labour Party 101, 125, 128, 130
Labour productivity 2–3, 5
Labour relations pre-1914, 8; post-1918, 42–3
Lancashire 80
Latin America 27, 55
Law, Richard 93
League of Nations 25
Leisching, Sir Percival 93
Lend-lease 82–8 *passim,* 100–2
Liberal Party 50, 59
Lloyd George, David 11, 33, 36, 50
London Passenger Transport Board 78

Machine tool industry 9, 16, 31, 33
MacDonald, Ramsay 58, 61, 63
McKenna, Reginald 41
Mackinder, H. J. 21–2
Macmillan Committee 62
'Macmillan gap' 52
Macmillan, Harold 120, 124, 131–2
Malaya 17
Management *see* Entrepreneurs
Marshall Aid
Marwick, Arthur 67
Matthews, R. C. O. 133
May Committee *see* Committee on National Expenditure
May, Sir George 59
Meade, James 93
Mechanical engineering 9, 30, 33
Melchett, Lord *see* Mond, Sir Alfred
Middle East 84, 86
Migration 14
Mining Association 31
Ministry of Health 78–9
Ministry of Munitions 31
Ministry of Supply 102
Ministry of Transport 172
Moggridge, D. E. 39, 47, 53, 54, 96
Monckton, Sir Walter 120
Monetarism 114–15, 128–9